THAT ART OF DIFFERENCE

'Documentary-Collage' and English-Canadian Writing

Documentary has increasingly been appropriated by fiction, drama, and poetry writers. In *That Art of Difference* Manina Jones defines the kind of writing that emerges as 'documentary-collage,' writing that self-consciously takes non-fiction documents, including photographs, advertisements, newspapers, and historical manuscripts, into the literary text. Jones considers as examples the found poem, Robert Kroetsch's *The Ledger*, Michael Ondaatje's *The Collected Works of Billy the Kid*, James Reaney's *Sticks and Stones*, Lionel Kearns's *Convergences*, Joy Kogawa's *Obasan*, and Daphne Marlatt's *Ana Historic*. These texts use citation for the purposes of questioning the historical record and foregrounding its role in the textual construction of reality. In these works the *already said*, or the cited, is re-cited with a critical difference. It is the space of that difference that Jones explores.

The documentary impulse in Canadian fiction, drama, and poetry of the past twenty-five years is given a rereading in this book, informed by a poststructuralist critique of history and by a reader-oriented dialogic aesthetics. Jones combines theoretical explication and critical readings of the individual works; offers a theoretical vocabulary and critical strategy that can be used in the discussion of others' works; engages in a post-realist reading of a form traditionally read within realist conventions; and uses an interdisciplinary approach in order to take into account works that undermine conventional distinctions between literature and history, verbal and visual representation, high and low culture, and aesthetic and political writing.

MANINA JONES is Assistant Professor, Department of English, University of Waterloo.

THEORY / CULTURE

General editors: Linda Hutcheon and Paul Perron

THAT ART OF DIFFERENCE: 'Documentary-Collage' and English-Canadian Writing

Manina Jones

UNIVERSITY OF TORONTO PRESS

Toronto Buffalo London

© University of Toronto Press Incorporated 1993
Toronto Buffalo London
Printed in Canada

ISBN 0-8020-2871-3 (cloth)
ISBN 0-8020-7370-0 (paper)

Printed on acid-free paper

Canadian Cataloguing in Publication Data

Jones, Manina
That art of difference : 'documentary-collage'
and English-Canadian writing

(Theory/culture)
Includes index.
ISBN 0-8020-2871-3 (bound) ISBN 0-8020-7370-0 (pbk.)

1. Canadian literature (English) – 20th century –
History and criticism.* I. Title. II. Series.

PS8071.J65 1993   C810.9'0054   C93-093563-2
PR9189.6.J65 1993

This book has been published with the help of a grant
from the Canadian Federation for the Humanities,
using funds provided by the Social Sciences and
Humanities Research Council of Canada.

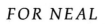

FOR NEAL

Contents

Acknowledgments

For their generosity, insight, and encouragement in assorted forms and at various moments, I would like to thank the following people: Frank Davey, Linda Hutcheon, Eli Mandel, Stan Dragland, Tim Whiten, Marie-Christine Leps, Terry Goldie, Bill Whitla, Percy Walton, Brenda Carr, Marty Kreiswirth, and Susan Rudy Dorscht. I would also like to thank Gerry Hallowell, editor, Jim Hartling, who proofread parts of the manuscript, and John St James, who copy-edited it.

Parts of this book have appeared in print before, although in most cases previously published material has been substantially revised. Portions of chapter 1 appear in *Canadian Poetry* 25 (1990) and *Double Talking: Essays on Verbal and Visual Ironies in Contemporary Canadian Art and Literature* (ed. Linda Hutcheon). An earlier version of chapter 3 appeared in *Canadian Literature* 122–3 (1989). Earlier versions of chapters 4, 5 and 6 were published in *Canadian Drama* 16.1 (1990), *Beyond Tish: New Writing, Interviews, Critical Essays* (ed. Douglas Barbour), and *Theory between the Disciplines: Authority/Vision/Politics* (ed. Mark Cheetham and Martin Kreiswirth).

I would like to thank Carleton University, the Social Sciences and Humanities Research Council, and the Canadian Federation of the Humanities for their financial contributions to the research, writing, and publication of this work.

Most of all, I would like to thank my husband, Neal Ferris, for his humour, patience, support, and partnership in all things. Robert Kroetsch says that the archaeologist is 'the finding man'; in this case, he is himself a find of inestimable value.

THAT ART OF DIFFERENCE

God help us we are a people raised not on love letters or lyric poems or even cries of rebellion or ecstasy or pain or regret, but rather old hoards of field notes.

Robert Kroetsch

'This is (not) a documentary': Dialogues on Canadian 'Documentary' Writing

This is not a documentary of the *Clallam*'s
sinking. There are documents
but no objective witnesses
of the *Clallam*'s sinking. The survivors
were not objective. I
am not objective. Only
the objects we survive in.
All the stinking white corpses.

Frank Davey, *The Clallam*

It has become a critical commonplace to say that the documentary is the quintessential Canadian form of representation, perhaps partly because the term itself was first added to the vocabulary of film analysis in 1926 by John Grierson, a producer and critic whose association with the National Film Board of Canada during and after the Second World War instigated that institution's long and illustrious history of expository non-fiction filmmaking ('Flaherty's Poetic *Moana*' 25). Grierson's review of Robert Flaherty's *Moana* called it 'a poetic record of Polynesian tribal life,' praising the film for its 'documentary value' (25). Grierson later wrote that the documentary 'has given itself the job of making poetry where no poet has gone before it' ('First Principles of Documentary' 84). His use of the term makes the link between aesthetic ('a *poetic* record') and factual representation ('a poetic *record*'). It also establishes an implicit analogy between film and the written account: it presents the non-fiction cinema as a kind of visual inscription, a celluloid document of historical events.

In her 1969 article 'The Documentary Poem: A Canadian Genre,' Dorothy Livesay shifts the term's reference back to writing. In particular, she uses it to identify an impulse that she sees as the impetus for a genre of Canadian literature that is analogous to documentary film and radio: she alludes specifically to the influence of the Grierson legacy of Canadian non-fiction film as well as the radio documentaries of the Canadian Broadcasting Corporation (267). Livesay's paper announces the existence of a class of Canadian 'documentary' poetry that is marked by its use of particularized historical and geographical data, as well as its basis in research. This poetry, Livesay argues, presents a theme or precept in a dramatic, didactic fashion, employing a representative protagonist rather than an individualized hero (280). 'What interests me in these developments,' Livesay writes, 'is the evidence they present of a conscious attempt to create a dialectic between the objective facts and the subjective feelings of the poet' (267).

Livesay's article is important less because it makes a definitive statement on documentary writing in Canada than because it makes a provocative one – provocative in the sense that it calls forth other voices in response to it. Much of the writing around the notion of the documentary in Canada has been self-consciously framed as a reaction to Livesay's paper. Robert Kroetsch's poetic essay 'For Play and Entrance: The Contemporary Canadian Long Poem,' for instance, an article that is in many ways about the problems and pleasures of initiating the poetic and critical process of writing, calls Livesay's article 'a place to begin' (93).

'The Documentary Poem: A Canadian Genre' locates the idea of the documentary within the ongoing construction of the Canadian literary canon and the establishing of 'traditions' within it. This is a process in which Livesay's writing on the documentary clearly participates. In a paper delivered in 1984 that constitutes a kind of postscript to her earlier essay, Livesay advocates the expanded dissemination of documentary poetry via CBC radio ('The Canadian Documentary: An Overview' 128). She concluded her oral presentation of the paper with a reading from two documentary poems, Jon Whyte's *Homage, Henry Kelsey* and Donna E. Smyth's 'We Have Been Here Before' (130). Stephen Scobie suggests that Livesay's critical identification of the documentary in her 1969 paper may well have moved (or 'provoked') poets to contribute to the tradition and thus extend and redefine its sense: 'Once a form is *named*,' he observes, 'its possibilities are opened up, liberated, made widely available. The poet may assume the reader's familiarity with certain conventions. The works within a tradition build upon and refer to each other' ('Amelia' 270).

So too do the works within a critical tradition engage in dialogue with one another, and Livesay's argument places the documentary within a critical debate on the historical-referential and literary character of Canadian writing, a discussion that continues to focus around the interpretation of her remarks. In this introduction, I would like to participate in the critical conversation, first by rereading Livesay's article and the writings of some of those critics who renegotiate her terms, in the light of my own interest in the distinctly textual energies of documentary writing – and the theorizing of the documentary – in Canada. Second, I would like to focus on a more specific definition of the documentary form that has these energies as a central concern. I want to read 'documentary' not simply as a term of reference that may be used unequivocally to categorize and label literary works, but as itself situated at the intersection of the various voices/texts that have been drawn into a discussion on the very issue of reference and the usefulness of literary categories.

Livesay's description of the documentary tradition may itself be seen, for example, as a response to Northrop Frye's writing on the 'literariness' of Canadian letters. While Livesay aligns her discussion with Frye's early article 'The Narrative Tradition in English Canadian Poetry' (1946), which traces a narrative tradition that begins in the nineteenth century and culminates in E.J. Pratt's *Brébeuf and His Brethren* (Frye 154), she laments the fact that Frye later seems to abandon his interest in this tradition, dismissing it as mere 'versified rhetoric, and versified rhetoric has a moral but not an imaginative significance: its place is on the social periphery of poetry, not in its articulate centre' ('Preface to an Uncollected Anthology' 176). Livesay's objection to Frye's statement, clearly, lies in her belief that writing concerned with (and 'rhetorically' embedded in) social relations and issues *is* central, and not peripheral, to the literary: 'What Frye means, presumably, is that ... 'social poetry' can be dismissed as 'cold-blooded carpentry' (to use Professor Whalley's term). This is precisely the point on which I mean to take issue. For in my view the long storytelling poem with a theme may indeed be the most interesting *poetically*, as well as being deeply representative of the Canadian character' ('The Documentary Poem' 268–9). Livesay is extending the sense of social responsibility that Grierson saw as central to realist documentary film.

In doing so she is clearing a space in the Canadian canon for historical, issue-oriented poems like her 'Call My People Home,' Anne Mar-
riot's 'The Wind Our Enemy,' or Earle Birney's 'Trial of a City' ('The
Documentary Poem' 269).[1]

Her reading of the Canadian literary documentary as more than
simply narrative engages with what Barbara Godard calls 'the famous
double bind of Frygian theory, that an aesthetic object cannot be both
Canadian and generic' ('Epi(pro)logue' 302). Frye's well-known statement in the 'Conclusion to a *Literary History of Canada*' that 'the conception of what is literary has to be greatly broadened for such a
literature' may, in fact, be seen as an extension to Canadian 'literature'
in general of his comments on 'rhetorical' poetry in particular (214).
'The literary, in Canada,' he continues, 'is often only an incidental
quality of writings which, like those of many of the early explorers,
are as innocent of literary intention as a mating loon. Even when it is
literature in its orthodox genres of poetry and fiction, it is more significantly studied as part of Canadian life than as part of an autonomous
world of literature' (214).[2] A number of contemporary documentary
poems, incidentally, have implicitly challenged Frye's statement by
pointedly using the language of explorer journals as poetry: Whyte's
Homage, Henry Kelsey (1981), Lionel Kearns's *Convergences* (1984),
George Bowering's *George, Vancouver* (1970), Birk Sproxton's *Headframe:*
(1985), Marion Smith's *Koo-Koo-Sint: David Thompson in Western Canada*
(1976), John Ferns's *Henry Hudson or Discovery* (1975), Gerald St Maur's
Odyssey Northwest (1983), and Don Gutteridge's *The Quest for North:*
Coppermine (1973), for example, all include citations of explorer jour-
nals in a self-consciously poetic arrangement and context.

Livesay's central assertion that there is a dialectical relationship
between 'objective facts and the subjective feelings of the poet' in
documentary writing allows her implicitly to contradict Frye's statement too, by attributing to this writing not 'innocence,' but self-consciousness and irony about its subject: 'The effect is often ironic' ('The
Documentary Poem' 267). In other words, an aesthetic distance or
displacement from the historical record marks its translation to the
documentary poem. The documentary poet, in Livesay's terms, is a
reader of the historical record who inserts into that genre the 'subjective' perspective of the lyric poet.

In a crucial violation of Frye's 'autonomous world of literature,'
Livesay also links 'the use of documentary material as the basis for
poetry' with 'the employment of the actual data itself, rearranged for
eye and ear' ('The Documentary Poem' 267). Particularly significant for

my own definition of a form I would like to call the 'documentary-collage' is the fact that Livesay's first – and, for my purposes, proto-typical – examples of documentary poetry are John Robert Colombo's *The Mackenzie Poems*, which 'used the speeches of William Lyon Mackenzie as the basis for a printed poem,' and F.R. Scott's *Trouvailles*, which 'set down lines from native Indian historical documents with ironic intent' ('The Documentary Poem' 267). These are both instances of 'found poetry,' a genre whose central gesture is the representation (Livesay calls it 'rearrangement') of prosaic, non-fiction texts in poetic form, and whose documentary status is the subject of the first chapter of this study.

Ironic or interpretive displacement is a key to Livesay's estimation of the *aesthetic* impact of poetry that appropriates the 'non-literary.' The 'documentary,' then, as I interpret Livesay's argument, may be situated in a dialectic not simply between two forms of writing (factual and poetic), but between two conventions of reading: the 'objective' or 'literal' reading of the document and its 'subjective' interpretation *as poetry*. This evaluation of Livesay's argument suggests an ironic reassessment of Frye's statement quoted above, in which the found poem (and, potentially, the documentary in general) *radically* expands the category of the literary to the point that the very distinction between the supposedly 'autonomous' realms of 'social/historical' writing and 'literature' is undermined. Livesay's shifting of critical ground is, significantly, associated with the literary strategy that reassesses or, to use a term Colombo applies to found poetry, 're-deems' (*Mackenzie Poems* 17) conventionally non-literary prose. Her critical move also makes poetic meaning a function of reception, an 'incidental' social act rather than strictly the product of the 'original' writer's 'literary intention.'

Fifteen years after Livesay's presentation of her paper to a meeting of the Association of Canadian University Teachers of English, at York University, Stephen Scobie's survey of numerous examples of docu-mentary poetry, 'Amelia, or: Who Do You Think You Are? Documentary and Identity in Canadian Literature,' demonstrated the prophetic (or at least influential) nature of her observations. Scobie's article reinterprets Livesay's discussion in the light of contemporary develop-ments in Canadian poetry and literary theory. He later substantially revised the article and included it as a chapter in his book on the relations between poststructuralist literary theory and Canadian litera-ture, *Signature Event Cantext*. While he agrees with Livesay that the documentary draws on a sense of 'the authoritativeness of fact,' Scobie interrogates the basis of the objective–subjective polarity when he notes that the very category of 'objective fact' or 'historical reality' is currently being rethought by poststructuralist theorists who have demonstrated the basis of 'fact' itself in textual constructions, and have shown it to be subject to the same contextual and interpretive contingencies often associated exclusively with fiction: 'The documentary invokes the authority of fact only to consign it to a systematic blurring of limits' (*Signature* 122).

Like Livesay, Scobie sees 'the actual data itself' as an active component of documentary poetry: 'The idea of the "document" remains within the poems, as a source of historical fact, and as an element of intertextuality' ('Amelia' 269). The idea of the document within the 'documentary,' then, may be seen both as evidence of its basis in research and as a manifestation of the more general linguistic condition of intertextuality, in which, as Julia Kristeva defines it, a given text functions, not as a univocal utterance complete unto itself and attributable to a single authorial/authoritative voice, but as the intersection of numerous utterances, from other texts ('The Bounded Text' 36).

The 'documentary,' therefore, paradoxically reminds readers both of the 'factuality' of history and of the construction of that factuality through the collection and interpretation of textual or materially 'documentary' evidence. This is evidence whose 'sources' cannot be objective; they are, inevitably, positioned subjects whose particular positioning needs to be taken into (the historical) account. This is not a subjectivity that can be simply opposed to an unimpeachable non-relative 'objective' perspective, but an undermining of the very opposition between subjectivity and objectivity. The 'documentary,' in this formulation, might be similar to what Philippe Carrard calls 'the voice of the new history,' which 'does not want to go on pretending: pretending that documents are objective givens and that the historical text ... can unfold itself, "naturally," without someone doing the unfolding' (27). The historical text, Carrard contends, is thus 'no longer the mode of reporting "reality" in a way that would be transparent and non-problematic. It is thought of as a construct, and presented as such' (27). The foregrounding of the idea of the document or the incorporation of the document itself as a material of construction in the documentary is one way of resisting such transparency. Indeed, a (critical *or* creative) work that self-consciously examined the processes of *constructing* 'the authoritativeness of fact' through documents would be, as Scobie calls Leonard Cohen's novel *Beautiful Losers*, a 'meta-documentary' ('Amelia' 272). Such a work would transgress generic bound-aries between history, literature, and criticism, since it would place the document in question, not simply for the facts it might yield, but for how and why those facts are rhetorically produced in and through language.

Among the documentary works Scobie cites in his article is George Bowering's long poem *George, Vancouver*. That work's subtitle, 'a discovery poem,' he observes, 'describes not only the immediate subject of George Vancouver exploring the West Coast but also the whole experience of the documentary poet discovering (as opposed to the fiction writer inventing) what is already there, in the factual material and also in his or her self' ('Amelia' 278). Susan Rudy Dorscht's reading of Eli Mandel's poetic/critical/historical work 'The Long Poem: Journal and Origin' questions the basis of this distinction between 'discovery' and 'invention' in claiming that, fundamentally, 'there are no poems that are not documentary,' since *all* poems 'are constructed out of what Livesay called "the actual data itself"' (253).[3] Rudy Dorscht does recognize, however, that the self-conscious incor-poration of multiple texts within a poem might be termed literally 'documentary,' and, further, that this strategy can work to foreground 'the act of writing as a particular way of reading documents' (253).

Both Robert Kroetsch's poem *The Ledger* and Daphne Marlatt's novel *Ana Historic* demonstrate Rudy Dorscht's proposition in a particularly apt way: each poem uses dictionary entries as 'found' documents that gesture towards the linguistic pre-texts that underwrite our notions of just how 'the actual data itself' is always linguistically defined and interpreted. In his criticism and poetry, Kroetsch uses the word 'find-ing' rather than Bowering's 'discovery,' a word associated with the found poem, but one also that allows him to draw on the metaphorical structures evoked by the archaeological 'find,' structures themselves self-consciously borrowed from the work of philosopher Michel Foucault. Kroetsch's criticism evinces an interest in writing that he considers 'an archaeology' because it 'challenges the authenticity of history by saying there can be no joined story, only abrupt guesswork, juxtaposition, flashes of insight' ('For Play' 93).

Kroetsch's own fragmentary, juxtapositional method of composition in poems like *The Ledger* or *Seed Catalogue* (or, indeed, in 'critical' works like 'For Play and Entrance: The Contemporary Canadian Long Poem' and *Labyrinths of Voice*), in which portions of found documents participate in a collage effect, encourages a sense of the writer as an archaeological finder and provisional interpreter of fragmentary evidence, rather than the creative originator (or 'author') of a literary work, or the recuperative, totalizing agent Foucault labels the 'historian.'

Chapter 2 of this study focuses on *The Ledger*, and its incitement of a rereading of historical materials, a rereading that takes intertextual processes into (its) account (book) through the strategy of citation. *The Ledger*, I want to argue, reframes the idea of a 'local history.' For Kroetsch, as for other poets like Daphne Marlatt in *Steveston*, Don Gutteridge in *A True History of Lambton County*, and Don McKay in *LePendu*, the local history becomes a kind of archaeological project that is both geographically local – particularized geography, we might recall, was one of Livesay's documentary criteria – and *graphically* or textually local to a particularized reading of the documentary 'finds' that define the region.

This specifically geo-graphical 'grounding' is also shared by several of the works I will examine in more detail: James Reaney's Donnelly plays, Lionel Kearns's *Convergences*, and Marlatt's *Ana Historic*, all of which address what Frye calls the typically Canadian question, Where is here? ('Conclusion' 220), as what E.D. Blodgett designates 'a problem in discourse' ('After Pierre Berton What?' 62). These works are interested in the local place, yes, but they are also interested in how that space is 'mapped' textually, and in the ways the individual speaker is discursively as well as geographically and historically positioned. Some works, like the 1975 edition of *The Ledger*, Reaney's play *Sticks and Stones*, Kim Morrissey's long poem *Batoche*, McKay's *LePendu*, Marlatt's long poems *How Hug a Stone* and *Steveston*, make the metaphor literal by incorporating maps into the text.

One way of rephrasing the concerns raised by Frye and Blodgett into yet another question important to the consideration of the documentary might be taken from the title of Rudy Wiebe's short fiction, 'Where Is the Voice Coming From?' The production and reception of voice in the 'documentary' is of interest both to Livesay and Scobie. In fact, Scobie replaces Livesay's insistence on a broadly representative hero ('The Documentary Poem' 269) with the proposition that the documentary may be a biographically structured 'persona poem' that adopts the individualized speaking voice of historical characters, who 'are frequently artists (writers or painters), or else keep journals, draw maps, or in some other way produce 'collected works' which the poem may either quote directly or else refer to' ('Amelia' 269). Scobie identifies dramatic irony, produced from the interplay between 'the voice of the poem and the implied stance of the author,' as 'the major form taken by the documentary dialectic' (268).

In *Signature Event Cantext*, he complicates this scenario with the more textually based notion of the 'forged signature': 'documentary material forms a continuous weave of intertextuality: the "presence" of the "original" texts, continually staged under the seal of the forged signature' (123). In chapter 1, I want to focus on the equivocation of the signature as it occurs in the found poem. Chapter 3 reads a poem Scobie obviously has in mind in his discussion of dramatic irony, Michael Ondaatje's *The Collected Works of Billy the Kid*. That poem, I argue, thematizes the very problematic of the historical persona and the persona's location in the dramatic interplay between and within *multiple* 'outside' texts, an interplay that cannot be contained within the dualistic, stable subject positions required by dramatic irony. As Barbara Godard observes, 'Through its incorporation of other texts, other perspectives, other voices, the documentary long poem moves to drown out the singular represented subject in a chorus of voices. Moving rapidly between the speaking subject(s) and narration, the documentary poem offers a relative position for the subject' ('Epi-(pro)logue' 315). The 'experimental method' employed by *The Collected Works of Billy the Kid* involves the collection of documentary evidence that, instead of conclusively proving the existence of a historical figure, explores how that figure has been produced (or linguistically figured) in various and often contradictory ways *through* historical writings. In the legal terms suggested by Billy the Kid's legendary criminal career, the poem's 'experimental method' puts its/the subject on trial, while at the same time persistently questioning the possibility of reaching a final verdict (or 'true saying'). The image of the trial is raised in a number of documentary writings, including perhaps most notably Wiebe's novel *The Temptations of Big Bear*. This recurrence, I believe, has to do with the way these works often question the nature of the evidence that contributes to both legal and historical verdicts, as well as the institutional processes by which the 'true story' is determined. In Wiebe's novel, for example, the author implicitly becomes a kind of advocate for the condemned Cree leader, after the (historical) fact, exposing the prejudices of the historical record, presenting alternative forms of evidence. The dramatic models used by both Wiebe and Ondaatje offer multiple forms of testimony, as does Don Gutteridge's poetic 're-staging' of the Louis Riel trial in *Riel: A Poem for Voices*.

This strategy constitutes a virtual exposé of what we might call the 'truth-telling' approaches to the documentary outlined by Frank Davey in his essay 'Recontextualization in the Long Poem.' The first approach Davey describes consists of an appeal to pre-existent truths based on the evidence of 'external authority,' whether it be the written word, divine inspiration, personal authority, or research ('Recontextualization' 123). Davey suggests, second, that the documentary poem may attempt to represent a 'higher' level of poetic or metaphorical truth that transcends historical sources and details (123–4). Finally, and most generally, he identifies the roots of the twentieth-century documentary long poem in 'the modernist envy of the scientist's access to "self-evident" testimony and precise measurement' (125). As Barbara Godard indicates, these approaches frame Davey's analysis within versions of the documentary that demonstrate 'a general preoccupation with absolute truth, with presence, with the transcendental ego' ('Epi-(pro)logue' 319).

Different in kind from these three schemes, however, is a documentary mode Davey describes as founded on the impulse to question the possibility of absolute truth, which argues, 'truth's variability, or as bp Nichol in *The True Eventual Story of Billy the Kid*, its "eventualness" – i.e. its being in a contingent relationship to the needs of the present moment' ('Recontextualization' 124). It is this latter formulation that, as Godard points out, seems to inform Davey's examination of most of the examples he discusses. It is, further, a formulation that expands on Livesay's subjective–objective dialectic by allowing that the writer who works 'out of a ground of inherited written material' brings to it the possibility of further meaning in the '*interaction* of past with present, of earlier writer with later writer' (131).

Ultimately, this approach displaces the dialectic to intertextual relationships that do not privilege a pre-textual objective (or 'historical') ground over a derived, subjective (or 'poetic') figure, as Livesay implicitly does. 'A dialectic occurs here,' Davey writes, 'but not so much between the "objective facts" (presuming that there can be "objective facts") and the subjective feelings of the poet as between the original texts and the new one' ('Recontextualization' 133). This approach to the issue of truth in the documentary bears some resemblance to Mikhail Bakhtin's characterization of the Socratic dialogue as a 'truth testing' apparatus (*Problems* 111), in which a 'dialogic' means of seeking truth is set against '*official* monologism, which pretends to *possess a ready-made truth*' (110). In this interpretation, truth is not a priori objective fact, but is produced from the dialogic, linguistic interaction between people (ibid.). Such a 'dialogic' project Davey terms 'recontextual,' and opposes to documentary ('Recontextualiza-tion' 135), thereby aligning it with the sense of rereading discussed earlier in relation to Kroetsch's work.

Barbara Godard points to the difference between Davey's first three categories and the last as a clash in the very meaning of the term 'documentary,'[4] in which the notion of 'absolute truth' contrasts with an alternate definition of the documentary as 'appropriation, recontext-ualization, textual subversion, in short the countertextuality of the title' ('Epi(pro)logue' 319).[5] The doubleness that Godard identifies as a 'strange loop' in Davey's argument (319), I would contend, is a linguis-tic paradox that (as I hope we have seen) structures the very theory of the 'documentary.' It reinforces my earlier suggestion that the term itself exists *in dialogue* and must be viewed as the intersection point of contradictory impulses. As Scobie remarks, 'Doubling is the funda-mental gesture of the documentary poem' (*Signature* 128).

Although I want to focus on and refine what Davey defines as 'recontextual,' I maintain the term 'documentary' here because it, appropriately, conveys the ambivalence I see as central to the general idea of documentary writing: the word both retains the conventional meaning of a 'factual' report and sustains the potentially subversive trace of a material sense of the *document*ary as writing or even text-uality, and, as I will discuss shortly, also takes in the concept of citation. The two meanings inevitably exist in a tense relation to one another since, as Dominick LaCapra observes, the 'fact' of the past is accessible only 'in the form of texts and textualized remainders – memories, reports, published writings, archives, monuments, and so forth' (*History & Criticism* 128). Linda Hutcheon portrays this tension somewhat more violently as the 'head on' collision in contemporary Canadian fiction of 'the documentary impulse of realism' and 'the problematizing of reference begun by self-reflexive modernism' ('The Politics of Representation' 24). She sees the contradiction as worked through (although certainly not resolved) in postmodern literature's thematizing of the 'process of turning events into facts by means of interpreting documents – the material traces of events – thereby creat-ing historical representations' (22).

This study concentrates on a group of writings that engage in just such a project. These works both formalize and thematize the very docu-mentary juncture I have been discussing. I argue that a common formal strategy of a body of contemporary Canadian works is a 'col-lage' technique that self-consciously transcribes documents into the literary text, registering them as 'outside' writings that readers recognize both as taken from a spatial or temporal 'elsewhere' and as participating in a historical-referential discourse of 'non-fiction.' The works both invoke and undermine the oppositions between categories such as textual/referential, intratextual/extratextual, literary/non-literary, or fiction/non-fiction, and thus stage a kind of documentary dialogue.[6] The document (or Livesay's 'actual data itself') is foregrounded as a strategic site/cite of contending readings.

I have chosen (for lack of a better term) to call this approach the 'documentary-*collage*,' since its central gesture is citation, and the term 'collage' draws from the visual arts the sense of fragmentation and radical recontextualization I want to indicate in that activity. 'Collage' also tends to overturn the conventional distinction between a framing 'master-text' and a cited text that exists in supplementary relation to it, a relation imaged in Herman Meyer's culinary question, 'Are quotations anything more than simply the raisins in the cake?' (4). As Mary Ann Caws has observed of what she calls literary 'intertextual collage': 'Like one of the figure/ground plays in contemporary optical art, the frame can be considered on either side, as the effect seems to move in and out' (71). In fact, the visual arts 'collage' usually complicates the matter further by soliciting materials from multiple – and often remarkably disparate – sources. E.D. Blodgett and Antoine Compagnon both describe the effect of such a project in the literary realm as 'interdiscursive,' one that depends on spatial relationships in which texts comment on each other (Blodgett, 'The Book, Its Discourse, the Lyric' 202; Compagnon 50).

The central citational project of the documentary-collage affiliates it with a group of writings Mikhail Bakhtin refers to as the 'seriocomical genres,' which bring a multiplicity of disparate styles and voices into a single contextual space. 'Seriocomical' works often mix prosaic and comic concerns (*Problems* 108). They make extensive use of what Bakhtin calls 'inserted genres,' such as letters, found manuscripts, parodies of high genres, and parodically reinterpreted citations (ibid.). The formal strategy of 'insertion' puts into play doublings that might be seen in relation to the doubleness of citation in the documentary-collage. Bakhtin comments, for example, that the inserted genres place 'the representing word' alongside 'the *represented* word' (ibid.). That is, the insertion of 'outside' writings draws attention to a duality between the word as factual report and the word as textual remainder.

Bakhtin reinforces the latter category elsewhere when he observes that heteroglossia (the incorporation of multiple discourses into a text) elicits a feeling for 'the materiality of language' (*Dialogic Imagination* 323–4). Martha Rosler goes further when she asserts that 'quotation has mediation as its essence, if not its primary concern' (80). In the documentary-collage the feeling of mediation or materiality is strengthened by a diacritical marking of cited texts as *substantially* different, through, for example, inferential agents,[7] italics, quotation marks, spatial configuration, or even bibliographical notation. This marking allows a distancing of citer from citation and indicates a refusal, not just of authorship and the position of comprehensive narrator, but of objectivity and authority itself. As Antoine Compagnon puts it of quotation marks, which in this discussion may stand in for the various other markers, 'What quotation marks say, is that the word is given to an other, that the author displaces himself from the enunciation to the profit of an other: quotation marks designate a re-enunciation, or a renunciation of the right of the author. They create a subtle sharing among subjects' (40).[8] Such markers confer on what they frame a sort of foreign accent and a prolonging or attenuation of meaning. They may also be a sort of ironic 'wink,' or gesture the author gives to indicate that he is not fooled by the statement he reproduces (Compagnon 41). The author is inscribed, then, not as a truth-teller, but as a 'reader or listener, structuring his text through and across a permutation of other utterances' (Kristeva, 'The Bounded Text' 46).

As Bakhtin claims, the use of 'inserted genres' may establish a 'zone of contact' between past writings and the ongoing present, thereby violating a sense of the past as a finished and unchangeable truth (*Dialogic Imagination* 33). The corresponding act of citation in the documentary-collage thus both engages in and encourages a *critical* and potentially playful re-creative, exploratory rereading of the documentary past. Intertextual citation is, as Laurent Jenny observes, 'a mechanism of perturbation. Its function is to prevent meaning from being lethargic – to avert the triumph of a cliché by a process of transformation' (59).

In this project the documentary-collage might be distinguished from the recuperative 'mythical method' of the Eliotan version of modernism. While the primary strategies of the mythical method may be reference, citation, allusion, and quotation, it seeks to 'confirm art as "timeless" repetition of the Same, repetition as incorporation' (Riddel 346). In other words, citation is used for the maintenance of tradition and cultural continuity (Morawski 691) – as Eliot himself put it in *The Wasteland*: 'These fragments I have shored against my ruins' (79) – whereas in the documentary-collage, repetition or re-citation always foregrounds recontextualization as alterity or reassessment. Citation in the documentary-collage may, in fact, parody the reification of past writings both as artefacts within the timeless museum of Tradition and as the definitive documentary evidence that founds what Dominick LaCapra calls the 'fetish of archival research' of traditional historical inquiry (*History & Criticism* 20–1).

In contrast to a conventional historical endeavour, or the similar 'truth-telling' documentary approaches Frank Davey surveys, the documentary-collage may provoke a 'truth-testing' challenge to the authority and autonomy of the documents it cites, and consequently the belief systems and institutions they represent. This, clearly, is a reversal of the ecclesiastical tradition of quotation, in which 'the authority of the institution is ... harnessed to truth in the textual sense' (Morawski 690). The documentary-collage frames its challenge, first, by fragmenting received texts, and then by translating them from one context to another. This latter move may work to displace the cited text from a conventional, referential level of reading to a textual level of productivity or dialogue. As Bakhtin indicates, all language is 'dialogic' (*Dialogic Imagination* 279), inhabited by the aspirations and evaluations of others, by its various enunciations. To self-consciously mark a piece of writing as having been translated from one context to another could act, as Régine Robin puts it, 'to introduce a dialogical process within the heart of a formalized monosemia' (234), thereby pitting the interpretive openness of textuality against 'institutional discourse' (235). Therefore, not only does the documentary-collage encourage multi-voicedness by incorporating a number of outside texts, in so doing it may also expose the multiplicity of interpretive possibilities at play *within* apparently monologic or referential documents.

This form of literary exposé may be considered part of a 'carnivalistic' project similar to that Bakhtin examines in the writings of Rabelais and associates with the intrusion in medieval carnivals of the anarchic energy of the unofficial, popular realm into the élitist world of institutions of authority and order (*Rabelais* 154). 'Carnivalization as described by Bakhtin,' Dominick LaCapra summarizes, 'involves dismemberment or creative undoing that may be related to processes of renewal' ('Rethinking Intellectual History' 55). LaCapra concludes that 'one strategy of dismemberment is the use of montage and quotation through which the text is laced or even strewn with parts of other texts' (ibid.).

Julia Kristeva's discussion of carnival reinforces a key ambivalence also central to the documentary-collage. She argues that the scene of carnival is a *dramatic* locus in which 'prohibitions' (as in representation or monologism) and their transgression (as in dialogism) coexist ('Word, Dialogue, and Novel' 79). In chapter 3 I will argue that the functioning of *The Collected Works of Billy the Kid* as a 'docudrama' depends on an opening up of the language of the document to what Kristeva terms the drama located in language (ibid. 79). The *literal* staging of carnival as a documentary process in James Reaney's play *Sticks and Stones* is discussed in chapter 4. Reaney's drama is marked, perhaps more than any work examined here, by the folk culture that Bakhtin sees as the informing principle of carnivalesque writing. Reaney, in fact, implicitly acknowledges the popular festival as a model for an indigenous Canadian theatre when he comments ironically of the celebration of Hallowe'en: 'That festival is the one theatrical event put on in this country that doesn't seem to need directors brought in from foreign lands; it is put on by thousands who are really into their parts ... The audience for Hallowe'en numbers in the millions, understands the script thoroughly even when it concerns the most esoteric matter of light's yearly fight with darkness ...' ('A Letter' 11). In *Sticks and Stones*, narrative disordering, the multiplication of historical voices, and the use of a wide variety of generic conventions create a carnivalistic 'riot' in the discourse of history, allowing the play to resist offering the Donnelly story to its audience as a finished, consumable historical product. The remarkable 'enacting' of documents on stage in *Sticks and Stones* gestures towards a performative value; their meaning is tied up in the context of enunciation and reception. Therefore, the play engages the audience in a continuing historical research project typical of the documentary-collage, in which spectators must participate in the (re)construction of story.

As Stephen Scobie suggests, an open form that presents itself as incomplete encourages the reader 'to repeat the poet's research and engagement with the facts' ('Amelia' 275). The documentary-collage, indeed, depends on a foregrounding of the reader's position as a sense-*maker* or interpreter of documentary evidence, implicating him or her in an active process of reading as rewriting. The incorporation of 'raw' textual materials, therefore, allows for responses within the documentary-collage at the same time as it provokes them from without. As Magdalene Redekop notes, 'The more deliberately intrusive the documents are, the more they serve to distance the story and to make us self-conscious about our participation in the construction of the story' (48).

We may also become aware of the extent to which *we* are constructed *by stories*. If the documentary-collage relativizes the historical
subject, it may also relativize the 'present' reader/speaker *as* historical
subject, inscribed within the texts of history. Scobie hints at this process when he notes that the documentary poem directs readers 'back
to their own subjectivity, to their definitions of themselves' ('Amelia'
275). This observation draws attention to the status of the documentary-collage as an *'interrogative* text' that calls into question the reader's
conventional, unified (and 'invisible') position, as well as his or her
role in the production of the text, thereby inviting the reader 'to
produce answers to the questions it implicitly or explicitly raises'
(Belsey 91). Lionel Kearns's poem *Convergences*, examined in chapter
5, uses a recurrent 'genetic' metaphor that thematizes the constitution
of subjectivity via the inheritance and reading of various historical
'codes,' a metaphor that also plays a key role in Marlatt's *Ana Historic*.
In *Convergences*, subject position, geographical location, and historical
situation are all revealed as mutually intricated in textual processes.
In Kearns's poem the authoritative position of the contemporary white
speaker of Anglo-European origins is implicated in the events of the
imperialist past. The poem attempts to undermine its own speaker's
position of authority. In Marlatt's poem, by contrast, the feminine
speaker searches for a form of address, a position from which it is
possible to speak, since she has inherited a gendered code of silence.

The formal strategy of recontextualized citation of historical 'codes'
or documents in the documentary-collage unsettles or dis-places
established positions, thereby allowing for the possibility of 'mediat-
ing' (in all three senses of connection, intervention, and indirect transmission) the 'given' historical past. *Convergences*, in fact, is structured
by a model of discursive exchange that engages in a conversation with
the documents it cites. It makes the interpellation of the reader into
that conversation explicit, something other works of documentary-
collage do implicitly. Narrator and reader engage in an exploration of
historical records of exploration – the journals of James Cook and his
crew describing their encounter with the Mooachaht Indians – revealing those records as embedded in a cultural perspective whose assumption of authority and 'objectivity' continues to silence and
marginalize voices outside it.

As passive 'inheritors' of historical records, reader and narrator are
necessarily implicated in their project, but as *subversive* rereaders they
may undermine their own and other positions of exclusivity and

authority, opening a gap in authoritative speech for the circulation of alternative discourses. Such active rereading – put into play by formal repetition, with a *difference* – constitutes what Susan Rudy Dorscht describes as a negotiation with 'the "actual data" within which we find ourselves spoken' in order to 'say it differently by saying it again and again and again from many positions' (253).

David Carroll casts Rudy Dorscht's statement in narrative terms when he writes that 'the point is then that one is always-already situated within narrative, within various and conflicting philosophical, political, historical, biographical, etc., narratives and that one *acts* by countering and responding to these narratives and by occupying different places within different narratives' (74). The central character of Joy Kogawa's novel *Obasan*, through her reading of historical documents, literally 'finds' herself located at the intersection of contradictory philosophical, political, historical, and biographical narratives that designate her both 'Canadian' and 'Japanese.' Chapter 5 deals with *Obasan*, a novel whose treatment of the oppression and internment of Japanese-Canadians during the Second World War explores the process and problems involved in narrative as a form of signification that conditions both individual and collective history and subjectivity. It uses documentary citation to undermine what narrative theory defines as the *histoire*/story, or 'narrative content' (Genette 27), as divorced from contextually embedded textual transmission as *discourse*. It thus refuses the authority both of a particular history that 'produced' Japanese-Canadians as threatening 'others,' and then effaced them from the record, and of a mode of historical telling that enforces monologic – and therefore exclusive – truth.

Marlatt's *Ana Historic: a novel* opens up similar concerns with relation to differences of gender and the historical record. As Frank Davey comments, women writers as a group may particularly distrust the inherited documentary past, 'coming as it does from a presumptively authoritative and patriarchal tradition' ('Recontextualization' 136). Marlatt's novel incorporates that tradition through the transcription of the historical writings that its central female character encounters during the process of conducting historical research. It also en-counters those writings by situating them in the midst of other, non-institutional discourses, thereby multiplying what constitutes the 'historical voice' and attenuating the significance of particular historical writings. Barbara Godard identifies such dialogic techniques with Marlatt's feminist poetics, in which 'truth is not singular, logocentric, but multiple, polyphonic. There is no single speaking voice, but many voices, many languages at play in her work. Without *an* author, the texts are unauthorized, subversive' ('"Body I"' 481).

Ana Historic investigates the processes by which supposedly neutral monologic historical language constructs 'woman's place' in history as 'unreadable' or 'unrecognizable.' In citing historical texts, Marlatt re-enacts the traditional position of woman as secondary copyist who silently serves the historical institution. She also, however, strategically exceeds and undermines that position by allowing those texts to incite a strong, gendered rereading. *Ana Historic*, like *Obasan* and *Conver-gences*, uses a central character in the process of conducting historical research to discuss the intrication of history and subjectivity, and to gesture towards reading as a political act with the potential to reinter-pret history.

Antoine Compagnon introduces his study of citation with the state-ment that 'this book does not have a final object, but it does have a point of departure, it asks a principle question: how does one disen-tangle oneself from the tangles of the *already said*?' (9). As Compagnon insists, citation sol*icit(e)s* a reaction (23). The variety of the works of documentary-collage examined here share a formal strategy, and through it, they propose a provocative response to Compagnon's principal question: they engage the *already said* in dialogue by re-citing it, with a critical difference. It is the space of that difference that this study explores.

This is not an exhaustive survey of Canadian works that employ the strategies of documentary-collage. I would like, instead, to examine in detail a number of what I consider to be important examples of these strategies in order to establish a vocabulary and theoretical framework for dealing with the issues they raise. I have chosen works that might conventionally be considered under the generic headings 'lyric,' 'long poem,' 'drama,' 'novel,' and 'prose poem,' less to demonstrate that the documentary-collage can inhabit different generic spaces, or to indicate that the documentary-collage constitutes a genre of its own, than to suggest that its strategies tend to place clear-cut generic categories in question. Certainly one effect of incorporating conventionally prosaic, non-fiction writings into a supposedly fictional, literary work is to draw attention to the role of convention in reading, and to the role of reading in determining the very identity of a text.

Finally, it may be worth noting that the structure of this study does not develop a unilinear argument that progresses according to a strict logic from chapter to chapter. Bakhtin asserts that the scholarly article may be 'one instance of a dialogic interrelationship among directly signifying discourses within the limits of a single context' (*Problems* 188). I hope to have lived up to this definition, and also to have encouraged another level of interaction in the larger context of the book as a whole, in which each chapter is interrelated dialogically with the others.

CHAPTER ONE

Finding(:)
A Reading of the Document
as Found Poem

Some texts are born literary,
some achieve literariness,
and some have literariness thrust upon them.

Terry Eagleton, *Literary Theory: An Introduction*

In the opening of his article 'How to Recognize a Poem When You See
One,' Stanley Fish describes the now-famous experiment he once
conducted with one of his classes. He takes a list of names written
vertically on the blackboard – the reading assignment from a previous
seminar – draws a frame around them, writes 'page 43' at the top, and
tells the unsuspecting (though, as the exercise demonstrates, far from
innocent) students it is a poem to be interpreted. What was a reading
assignment to the previous class becomes an assignment in *reading* to
the class that follows. Skilled in 'detecting' poetic imagery, Fish's
students develop an ingenious series of interpretations of the passage,
interpretations produced, Fish infers, not because his students know
poetry when they see it, but rather because they see poetry when they
know it. The text as poem does not exist a priori, he submits; their
shared repertory of interpretive conventions generates it (322–7).
    The series of literally and contextually framing acts Fish performs
in 'setting the snare' for his students (acts that, as Peter Nesselroth
points out, Fish's account virtually ignores ['Literary Identity' 41]) are
analogous, if not identical, to the gestures that 'create' 'found poetry,'
the genre defined by Franz Stanzel as 'poetry not written by a poet but

found, that is to say, taken from a nonliterary context and printed in the traditional format of poetry' (91). Fish's exercise is, first of all, based on the fact that the 'text case' is not of his invention, but found, more-or-less arbitrarily chosen. It is central to his argument that its 'poetic' qualities not be due to the conscious artifice of its writer, or even to his own perspicacity as selector, but to the interpretive capacity of its student readers.

Second, Fish's selection is (intentionally or not) strategically divided into vertical lines. The found poem too is often typographically (re)arranged in a manner associated with poetic convention. John Robert Colombo, in fact, defines it simply as 'a passage of prose presented as a poem,' whose transformation 'usually involves rearranging the lines on the page' ('Found Introduction' 308). The formal (re)arrangement into lines, however, is just one sign of a larger contextual transformation. Like Fish's list of names, the found text undergoes a conceptual shift from a 'purely' referential to an 'aesthetic' context, that is, a context in which a particular set of interpretive procedures is put into play. Tom Hansen's definition of the found poem points to this movement from practical to aesthetic contexts of reading, and highlights certain of the reader's interpretive capabilities that enable the transition: 'Most found poems begin their lives as passages of expository prose. Their intended purpose is to feed easily digestible information to the reader. Nothing could be less poetic. But suddenly poetry is discovered imbedded within the prose. The discoverer is someone alert to the possibilities of irony, absurdity, and other incongruities' (271). The sense of one genre 'imbedded' in another is crucial. The found poem always bears the traces of contextual shifts. To his students, for example, Fish's passage is 'only' a poem. To readers of Fish's article, it is a found poem, since in that context it operates as a kind of pun; it cannot be read without consciousness of its plural contexts and a perception of its doubled voice. In this doubling the found poem is also affined with the operation of irony, which, as Allan Rodway points out, is based on an irresolvable duality that 'is not merely a matter of seeing a "true" meaning beneath a "false," but of seeing a double exposure ... on one plate' (cited in Muecke 45).

Found poetry, then, in Hansen's terms, is 'easily digestible' utilitarian or monologic prose made, somehow, 'indigestible.' A readily identifiable or familiar piece of prose can no longer passively be consumed because it is now perceived as (at least) two things at once: prose and poetry, obvious and devious, ordinary and literary. The process of reading the found poem creates a double exposure: not only is a specific alternative meaning 'exposed' on the reader's plate, but expository prose in general is 'exposed' as encoding something other than simple monologic reference. The apparent closure of the cited passage is disrupted. Hansen's digestive metaphor suggests a Barthesian approach in which the reading of the found passage transforms it from a readerly work whose 'message' may be easily consumed, to a productive, writerly text, whose 'felicitous' elements (like those that are formally interesting, or those that involve conflict and indeterminacy) are foregrounded (see Barthes 'From Work to Text').

Both Fish's classroom example and the found poem are formally shifted and socially repositioned. Fish directs attention to the list of names as a specifically *written* form and associates it with the larger formal context of the book by literally placing a frame around it: he draws and numbers a page. Fish also exploits his own position of dominance as Professor Fish in what can only be termed a *class*-room, by overtly stating an interpretive challenge to a class full of literature students trained in literary interpretation. The found poem, similarly, is framed by formal elements that denote a book of poetry, literary magazine, or some such similar context, which authorize the found text's status as literary, and which also imply both a community of readers and a particular kind of challenge to interpretation.

Fish's own definition of what creates the category of the literary invokes the image of framing as a structure of interpretation. He contends that literature 'is language around which we have drawn a frame, a frame that indicates a decision to regard with a particular self-consciousness the resources language has always possessed' ('How Ordinary Is Ordinary Language?' 108–9). Fish points out that 'formal signals trigger the "framing process" in the reader,' adding that these signals are themselves 'evaluative criteria' (ibid. 109). Franz Stanzel's discussion of the found poem suggests several such contextual signals, among them the 'frame provided by place and format of publication,' and left-justified printing and typographical spacing of stanzas and lines (95). George Dickie further notes that a title (even the title *Untitled*) acts as an aesthetic 'badge of status' (39). These are literally contextual (con-textual) cues, since they condition the reader to read the passage at hand with a certain set of (literary, poetic) texts and conventions in mind. Such contexts are balanced in the found poem by alternative 'non-poetic' associations triggered by, for example, a specific title, a preface, the name of a historical writer, a date, a footnote, or the reader's recognition of a familiar document.

Finally, it is worth noting that Fish makes no verbal changes to the list on the blackboard. To do so would somehow constitute 'cheating' at his newly invented game. Stanzel, Colombo, and F.R. Scott are all similarly punctilious. Each insists, with Stanzel, that the 'found poem proper' involves the 'authentic reproduction' of the found text, although 'with a rearrangement of the lines according to the typographical format of traditional poetry' (Stanzel 93). Colombo distinguishes between the 'pure' found poem that reproduces the original source verbatim and the 'impure' form that re-words or 'assists' the found text ('Found Introduction' 308), and Scott notes that, while there are various ways of presenting a found poem, 'in the strict manner no words should be added or subtracted; the original should be reprinted with only a change from the prose to a free verse form' (*Trouvailles* 5).

The discussions of Colombo, Hansen, Scott, and Stanzel provide the basis of a working definition of the found poem: it is a text (1) not written by the poet, but appropriated from elsewhere, (2) quoted verbatim, but formally rearranged, (3) displaced from a practical to an aesthetic context, and (4) read as poetry. This definition, however, is deceptively categorical; the found poem itself demonstrates the problematic nature of so-called definitive statements. Fish's exercise demonstrates the general difficulty of attempting to identify a text objectively in terms of its 'inherent qualities,' and the central gesture of the found poem involves the *violation* of (assumed) identity in which the 'same' text becomes somehow 'other.'

At least three writers have supplemented their definitions of the found poem by referring to a historical relationship between the contemporary found poem and the Dadaist 'ready-made' or *objet trouvé* of the visual arts from the years following the First World War practised most notably by Marcel Duchamp (Stanzel 91; Colombo 'Found Introduction' 308, 'A Note' 124; Nesselroth 'Lautréamont's Plagiarisms' 185). The analogy between the two projects is based on a significant similarity of operation. Arturo Schwartz, for example, defines the visual-arts ready-made as 'any *common*, *elaborated* entity, real or ideal, concrete or abstract, existing in everyday life, which, solely by reason of having been chosen by the Author, without undergoing *any* modification, is consecrated a work of art' (24). Schwartz even sets out a subcategory he calls the 'printed readymade,' in which the extract of a printed text is 'grafted' onto the larger poetic composition (28–9). This subcategory is similar to what I am calling the documentary-collage.

The Dadaist 'ready-made' presents everyday, practical found objects like a coat rack (Duchamp's *Trébuchet*), urinal (Duchamp's *Fountain*), or stove-pipe (Picasso's *La Vénus de Gaz*) in an aesthetic context (such as the art museum, the private gallery, or the art exposition), thereby placing in question not just the meaning of the specific object displayed and the observer's relation to it, but the very definition of the art object and the institutional processes that define it. Bruce Barber observes that the ready-made's procedure of aesthetic appropriation 'allowed the primary interrogatives: "What is the status of this object if not by my hand, if not unique, if an object originally of functional use value? and how is it that this can come up for the count of art?"' (218).

Such questions, clearly, are pertinent both to the production of the literary *objet trouvé* and its elaboration in the documentary-collage. The fact that the visual-arts ready-made has been subject to such a wide variety of interpretations – from Hegelian, to formalist, to realist, to institutional (see Fowkes, Hofmann, Dickie, Foster) – draws attention to the fact that, because it poses such problems of definition, it must, like the found poem, be *self-consciously* read. Indeed, Jack Burnham sees the ready-made as an object that by definition is in surplus of any closed, monologic reading: 'the ready-made suffers from excessive meaning (its functional use) and a lack of articulation by the artist (its rawness so to speak)' (61). The same might well be said of the found poem.

Duchamp himself notes a connection between the ready-made and the act of reading appropriate to literature: 'Dada was an extreme protest against the physical side of painting. It was a metaphysical attitude. It was intimately and consciously involved with "literature"' (125). The found poem is not, then, a minor subcategory of the visual-arts ready-made. Rather, the perception of both a multivalent language *of* the visual arts, and the particular use of language *in* visual art was an integral element of the ready-made from the time of its inception. For example, in Duchamp's work, the irony or visual punning implicit in the aesthetic display of an ordinary object is accentuated – and complicated – by complex, often self-reflexive linguistic punning in titles and inscriptions (see, for example, P.N. Humble's discussion of *Trébuchet*, 60; or Bert M.-P. Leefmans's discussion of Duchamp's *Why Not Sneeze Rose Sélavy?*, 207). For Duchamp, as for the 'writers' of found poetry, language itself is seen as a found object that produces multiple 'ready-made' interpretations.

The resurgence of interest in Dada and the revival of Dadaesque techniques in artistic endeavours like pop art and collage in the 1950s and 1960s were coincident with the popularizing of the found poem.

In the introduction to his 1966 volume of found poetry, *The Mackenzie Poems*, John Robert Colombo writes of the found poem: '[It] seems stylish in the 1960's. It seems part-and-parcel of our informal relationship with the past, in the same way that pop art, camp, environments, happenings, events, son-et-lumière productions, the non-fiction novel and town houses are part of a contemporary approach to the world of the past' (25). The 'salvaging' of the 'refuse' of the past was also consonant with the environmental movement of the same period. Colombo whimsically notes that 'found art is the most conservation-minded of the arts, for it recycles the waste of the past and reuses it in a surprisingly different way, thereby giving the original a new lease on life' ('Found Introduction' 309). In his book of poetry in dialogue with collages by Dada/Merz artist Kurt Schwitters, *The Merzbook: Kurt Schwitters Poems*, Colin Morton describes the collage artist's creative process in a poem called 'Garbage Picking on Kaiserstrasse' (18).

Canada had particular reason to reassess its relationship with the past at this time: the date of Colombo's comments is the year preceding the nation's centennial celebrations. Nineteen sixty-seven saw the publication of F.R. Scott's volume of found poetry *Trouvailles: poems from prose*, much of which transformed historical documents into contemporary found poems. Colombo produced five volumes of found poetry between 1966 and 1974, two of which focused on writings by figures from Canadian history: *John Toronto* and *The Mackenzie Poems*. In 1975 the appropriately titled 'Towards a New Past' project of the Government of Saskatchewan's Department of Culture and Youth released its *Found Poems of the Métis People*, a revisionist account of the history of Native participation in the two world wars, achieved through the presentation of 'poems [that] should be read as documents in poetic form, rather than as contrived poems in the classical European literary tradition' (iv). This volume used quotations to elevate a generally unknown, devalued aspect of history, enacting what Martha Rosler designates 'a revolutionary break in the supposed stream of history, intended to destroy the credibility of the reigning historical accounts in favour of the point of view of history's designated losers' (81). Rather than incorporating already written documents, this project countered the given historical record by creating a voice transcript of the recollections of Métis participants in historic events. The poetic presentation of this transcript (accompanied by a photographic record), far from aesthetically neutralizing the political importance of the elders' testimony, works to reinforce its value: 'Characterized by modesty or restraint,' the writer of the Introduction observes, the poems that result 'are sometimes eloquent. It is the eloquence that is closest to silence, the silence of painful experience, the silence of truth' (*Found Poems of the Métis People* iv). The Métis venture shared a similar historical/poetic 'salvage project' with the roughly coincident 'Aural History' enterprise of the Provincial Archives of British Columbia, which resulted in the 'documentary' volume *Steveston Recollected* and, ultimately, Daphne Marlatt's long poem *Steveston*, which mixes poetry, transcribed interviews, and photographs.

In his 'Found Introduction,' which precedes the found poetry section of *Open Poetry: Four Anthologies of Expanded Poems*, Colombo begins a 'Background. Literature' discussion with more historically distant analogues of the found poem including 'stichometry,' the practice of arranging rhetorical texts into meaningful lines, and nineteenth-century 'whimseys,' poems shaped from popular prose texts (432). He notes such obvious modernist 'finders' as Joyce, Eliot, and Pound. Colombo, however, calls W.B. Yeats 'perhaps the first poet in the English language to practise the literary alchemy of turning the base metals of prose into the rare metrics of poetry,' since, when he edited the 1936 *Oxford Book of Modern Verse*, Yeats included as its first entry a versified passage from Walter Pater's prose essay on Leonardo da Vinci from *Studies in the History of the Renaissance* (*Mackenzie Poems* 21). Yeats's comments on his selection in the introduction to the volume explain, in effect, that he has found in Pater an unrecognized modernist poet whose role in the movement can only be revealed by printing the essay selection in *vers libre* (viii). Colombo adds to his list of historical predecessors such writers as Blaise Cendrars, Marianne Moore, and José Garcia Villa ('Found Introduction' 306–7).

Colombo writes of his volume of found poems taken from the writings of Upper Canadian rebel William Lyon Mackenzie: 'The poems might or might not be the most revolutionary writing being done in Canada today, just as the prose was certainly the most revolutionary writing being done in the Canadas of more than a century ago' (25). The ironic observation that these historical writings are 'being done in Canada today' as poetry points to a temporal and generic doubling, as well as an element of active reprocessing at the heart of the found poem. Colombo's statement further distinguishes between the prosaic historical and poetic contemporary status of the collected documents, and their separate 'revolutionary' functions. Read as historical documents, their simply referential 'content' relates a rebellious political platform; as contemporary poetic documents, I would argue, they – and other found poems and cited documents in the documentary-collage – have a *linguistically* rebellious status: their 'revolutionary' character rests on the multivalent or deobjectified conception of the 'document' they make necessary, and on their consequent resistance to conventional – one might say conservative – frames of reference provided by traditional notions of the literary work.

In a sense, the found poem is the most straightforward form of the documentary-collage, because it 'simply' presents a textual extract. That presentation, however, involves less-than-simple issues fundamental to the documentary-collage, since it requires an appropriative rereading that interrogates the status of the non-fiction document as simultaneously present-ed and absent-ed within the literary text. In the found poem, 'outside' non-fiction documents *are* the poetic text, whose self-consciously displaced language is subject to reinterpretation along lines that exceed conventional readings of the non-fiction text. The attempt to come to terms with the found poem, then, is fundamental to the consideration of the documentary-collage. While this chapter examines selections from the collections of Canada's best-known found-poetry practitioners, John Robert Colombo and F.R. Scott, it is primarily a reading of the reading of the found poem. That is, it focuses on issues of interpretation, using individual selections as case studies of key points and delineating the strategies that make the found poem possible and problematic.

In his article 'The Death of Literature,' Jacques Ehrmann considers a number of found documents (a mathematical statement, a mouthwash-bottle label, an advertising slogan) that lead him to the central question of authorship: 'Who *made* these texts?' (236). He then turns his attention to the implications of the very question he poses: 'We must put to the test the very meaning of this question while attempting at the same time to answer it. In other words: What does it mean to "compose" a text? Who composes a "text"? How is a "text" composed? Or, to formulate the question in yet another manner, "Of what and by whom is a text composed?"' (Ehrmann 236). Ehrmann's complex interrogation of his own seemingly simple question has obvious consequences for the similarly 'simple' definition of the found poem as one that is not written by the poet but appropriated from elsewhere. The central gesture of the found poem is somehow 'inappropriate' to traditional standards of authorship, based as it so obviously is in appropriation. The found poem, then, raises questions about literary 'originality'; both the notion of the poet as 'originator' of the poem's language, and the corresponding Romantic notion of the poem as something new and unprecedented are challenged.

John Robert Colombo's reviewers have often called him to account for both a lack of 'originality' and behaviour 'inappropriate' to a poet. Alan Pearson's comments on Colombo's collection *ABRACADABRA* are typical of his detractors when, for example, while allowing that the results of found poetry may be 'amusing' (as opposed, presumably, to the high seriousness of 'real' art), he remarks: 'But surely this kind of activity is the last resort of the creatively impotent. Taken to its logical conclusion, one could write volume after volume of "poetry" of which not a line is one's own ... The result of all this is a learning that Colombo is culturally sophisticated. But the *real* Mr. Colombo has not stepped forward. And that's what comes of living parasitically off the blood and guts of someone else's paintings or prose' (283). It is no surprise that Pearson's desire to read the volume in question as expressive realism has been frustrated. The attempt to see work like Colombo's in terms of Wordsworth's definition of poetry as 'the spontaneous overflow of powerful feelings,' or of the poet as the 'overflowing' individual 'possessed of more than usual organic sensibility' (Wordsworth 126) is almost perverse, but Pearson's language suggests just such a conception. In Pearson's terms, the author must be a 'creatively potent' agency (with all the gendered reproductive connotations the term conveys) whose writing unambiguously expresses his *true* character ('the *real* Mr. Colombo has not stepped forward'), in language that he may therefore claim as property (the prose writer's work presumably plays unwilling – or unwitting – 'host' to Colombo's 'parasite'), and that represents an organic ('blood and guts') whole that, like a body, can be violated.

The found poem is flagrant – and often facetious – in flouting this view of art and authorship. In so doing, it represents what Henri Béhar calls 'an essential idea of modernity: one can be a poet without ever having written a single line' ('Le Collage' 67).[1] *Leonardo's Lists*, a small volume Colombo produced in 1972, provides one example. The book consists of selections from the (translated) notebooks of Leonardo da Vinci. Da Vinci, surely, is the great Renaissance artist-as-inventor par excellence. Colombo's book, however, places its readers on an informal (first-name) basis with a significantly *non*-canonical da Vinci – not the 'great' painter or designer, but the scribbler and preserver of notes who, as a gloss at the end of the volume informs us, compulsively took inventory of the world around him (20).

This last information about da Vinci makes him, ironically, very much like his contemporary 'co-author' Colombo, whose career, as Douglas Barbour points out, has been 'founded' on his reputation as a 'pack rat' of historical-cultural materials ('John Robert Colombo' 139). Entries in *Leonardo's Lists* vary from a 'List of Household Utensils' (10) to a recipe ('Untitled List' 11), to anatomical and historical sketches (for instance, 'Vital Functions of the Body' 19, and 'Events in Milan in 1500' 15). Leonardo's journalistic act of 'inventory' becomes in Colombo's hands (or at least in his implied reading) an act of poetic 'invention' that reinvents the lists. The root of both 'invent' and 'inventory' comes from a word meaning to find or come across.

The notion of a 'previous' authorial intention, or at least the notion of a conventionally acceptable reading, is both necessary to the effect of the poem and undermined by the poet-reader's (mis)appropriation of the found document. The found poem requires that its readers wilfully – and radically – 'misinterpret' or 'overinterpret' texts whose meaning is, superficially at least, obvious. In a chapter from *On the Margins of Discourse* entitled 'Licensing the Unspeakable,' Barbara Herrnstein Smith proposes that a context perceived as literary allows the extension of a kind of poetic licence to the audience as well as to the poet. This licensing 'involves not merely formal or even thematic features of the utterance, but quite fundamental aspects of the linguistic transaction itself' (111).

The legal trope evoked by Smith's use of the term 'licence' is quite proper to the found poem, since the shift in context from practical to poetic changes the rules of reading and, as Smith points out, the very nature of the linguistic transaction. The poem 'Ticket,' from Colombo's *Translations from the English*, might be read as an example of the way a contextual shift can change the nature of the linguistic transaction, introducing questions about the identity and meaning of the given document. The found document of the poem is obviously identifiable by its title and footnote as a luggage claim check. The ticket, in its practical context, has to do with the transaction involving the referential labelling or exchange of things with words. Like a lawyer looking for a loophole, the found poet focuses on the 'fine print' of the tag. It is what seems to be an expendable supplement that merely clarifies the meaning of the ticket, but the poem's citing and implicit re-evaluation of its 'clarifying' language allows an ironic reading in which the fine print complicates the simple process of identification, and may be seen as fundamental to the nature of the (linguistic) transaction the ticket allows:

THIS IS NOT
THE LUGGAGE TICKET
(BAGGAGE CHECK)
DESCRIBED BY ARTICLE 4
OF THE WARSAW CONVENTION
OR THE WARSAW CONVENTION
AS AMENDED BY
THE HAGUE PROTOCOL 1955

(*Translations* 10)

Removed from, as Smith puts it, 'the economics of the linguistic marketplace' (111), a reading of the poem might accentuate not just the function of signs as tags or labels, but of signification as a process of interpretation based on a system of differences. For example, the importance of 'convention' as 'legitimate' procedure within a system of exchange might be emphasized, as well as convention's roots in consensus. 'Ticket' also suggests the changeable nature of convention and its determination by relation to and difference from other texts: the ticket is defined by its divergence from 'The Warsaw Convention,' which itself may be an 'outside' document that in turn differs from another text, an alternative version of itself, distanced in space and time: 'THE WARSAW CONVENTION / AS AMENDED BY / THE HAGUE PROTOCOL 1955.' The poem itself both is and is not a ticket, both is and is not 'itself.' Because readers of poetry are usually interested in the way language works, in reading the poem, one kind of interpretive 'baggage,' which would ignore or suppress the intricacies of fine print, is provisionally 'checked,' while another comes into play. A baggage ticket, after all, is simply an authoritative certificate of identification. In *Translations from the English*, however, a different kind of linguistic 'claim' is staked.

A poetic reading of this document might even see it in intertextual relation with René Magritte's famous painting entitled/inscribed '*ceci n'est pas un pipe*,' a work whose title, like the first lines of 'Ticket,' undermines the illusion of reference at the same time as it alludes to it. Anna Whiteside comments of the painting that because the inscription is within the work's frame, it ironically refers to the pipe's 're-presentational but *non-referential* status and, perhaps equally ironically, to perceptual and interpretive conventions: particularly that of equating the signifier (the painting here) with its referent (an actual pipe, an existent)' (26). The aesthetic framing of both painting and poem establishes an ironic, ambivalent 'frame of reference' for their reading.

In her tribute to Colombo, 'Documentary Poet as Visionary,' Jean Mallinson comments on the blithely transgressory nature of his work: 'He is in public and by profession the poet as supreme opportunist, and joyfully exploits instead of lamenting his position as epigone or, to use Harold Bloom's term, "belated poet"' (67). Bloom's sense of the creative process as an agonizing Oedipal struggle with strong poetic forebears of the 'great tradition' (see *The Anxiety of Influence*) is replaced in the found poem by a *release* from the necessity – or possibility – of originality, a displacement to the margins of the literary canon, and an opening up of the possibility of re-creative textual *play*, not with strong poets, but with writers and writing in general.

Father figures such as those highlighted by Bloom are difficult to avoid when discussing authorship and authority in writing. It is, however, precisely by seeing the father-author as a *rhetorical* figure that structuralist and poststructuralist criticisms have sought to 'empty out' (a-void) and recast the issue of authorship. In his essay 'The Death of the Author,' Roland Barthes contends that 'it is language which speaks, not the author; to write is, through a prerequisite impersonality ... to reach that point where only language acts, "performs," and not me' (143).

Though I want to provisionalize 'the death of the author' (who says 'death' is absolute?) in several ways, this idea is suggestive of the way language can continue to perform in the absence of, and sometimes in conflict with, its 'original speaker' (the latter term is obviously problematic). Elaborating on a point similar to Barthes's, Michel Foucault notes that while writing was once considered something to ward off death by somehow prolonging the presence of its writer in his physical absence, freed of its strictly expressive dimension it 'possesses the right to kill, to be its author's murderer' ('What Is an Author?' 142). Colombo's found poem 'Memory Gardens Association Limited' might be read as figuring the scene of this metaphoric crime. It appears in *Translations from the English*, a volume of which the title assigns Colombo the role, not of author but of translator or interpreter. The poem transcribes a 'circular letter' advertising a funeral parlour. The reading of a correspondence between the letter's language and the gestures defining the found poem itself, and indeed the circulation of language in general, may be traced to the overriding awareness in the reading of the found poem of shifts in context and meaning.

Much of the language in the circular combines the 'terminal' languages of death and finance: it concerns 'the purchase of a final resting place / for our loved ones,' for the sake of 'FINANCIAL PROTECTION and PEACE OF MIND,' and offers help recording information for 'your estate settlement' (15). In colloquial terms, the message is to tie up those loose ends before the inevitable happens. The 'limited' in the company's name is therefore appropriate both to its legal status as a business and to the aim of its business, which is to close off unforseen possibilities, making the future – even the future beyond death – secure; one might even say carved in stone.

A parenthetical postscript attempts to limit yet another form of 'liability,' this time liability for the language of the circular itself:

> ... (This letter
> is in general distribution. Should
> it reach any home in which there is illness,
> it is completely unintentional).

(*Translations* 15).

This postscript, like the cited portion of the claim check in 'Ticket,' involves an attempt to limit or control meaning. It might, therefore, be seen as a kind of memorial to the letter's absent scriptors, testifying to their intentions, but irrevocably marking their inability to enforce them. Because the letter (and this applies to the condition of letters in general) is 'in general distribution,' its context – and therefore its reading – constantly differs, and is therefore necessarily beyond the control of its authors. A reading of the letter by a member of a household in which there was illness would change the letter's frame of reference in such a way as to violate its otherwise 'decorous' character(s). The inclusion of the letter in Colombo's volume of poetry is a version of 'translation,' another route in the inevitable circulation of the letter beyond its appointed rounds.

Jacques Derrida's article 'Signature Event Context' argues that the possibility of just such translation or recirculation is the very condition of writing, based as it is on a lack of 'filial ties' and the ability to remain readable despite the absence of its author:

> To write is to produce a mark that will constitute a sort of
> machine which is productive in turn, and which my future
> disappearance will not, in principle, hinder in its functioning,
> offering things and itself to be read and to be rewritten ...
> The situation of the writer and of the underwriter [*du sous-
> cripteur*: the signatory, trans.] is, concerning the written text,

> basically the same as that of the reader. This essential drift
> [*dérivé*] bearing on writing as an iterative structure, cut off
> from all absolute responsibility, from *consciousness* as the
> ultimate authority, orphaned and separated at birth from the
> assistance of its father, is precisely what Plato condemns in
> the *Phaedrus*. (180–1)

Colombo's 'The Type Riots,' the final poem from *The Mackenzie Poems*, both describes and puts into play writing's 'essential drift,' and asks its readers self-consciously to 'adopt' the provisional role of author. It is a 'post-script' (it begins with 'P.S.'), both to the prose letter it originally followed and to the volume of poetry in which it currently appears, which is itself a collection of typographical letters. The poem might be seen as a retrospective comment on the strategy of the volume as a whole. 'Post-script' is a significant term for this analysis, since it denotes what comes after the fact, after writing. Finding is literally post-scripting: both after writing and writing, after.

The poem's title alludes to a historical incident, described in the volume's introduction, in which William Lyon Mackenzie's newspaper, *The Colonial Advocate*, a polemic journal founded in 1824 and known for its violent verbal attacks on the ruling clique, was itself literally 'verbally' attacked: 'After two years of mounting invective, the newspaper was on the verge of bankruptcy. Mackenzie's unwitting creditors came in the form of fifteen young gentlemen who broke into his printing office on Front Street, smashed the printing press and proceeded to distribute the type into Lake Ontario' (9). The title 'The Type Riots' may simply denote a historical event. But it may also be read as an allegory of the textual event it enacts, that of language 'overflowing' the author-enforced boundaries placed on it. As Duncan Smith puts it, concentration on the language text itself 'evokes somehow a discontinuity between apparent intention and possible or potential subjective response. It unlocks a chaos within what appears an almost "prim" order' (109). In/citing, (the type) riots.

The incident described in this case, as in 'Memory Gardens Limited,' involves the placing of language in 'general distribution,' the circulation of letters or, literally, the scattering of type. Language, here, is literally out of the controlling hands of its compositor. In a historical/legal context this means that the vandals are guilty of trespass and the destruction of property: 'I will surely get justice of the government people / for destroying my property' (94). In the poetic context of *The Mackenzie Poems*, the same charges may be pressed: the reader/writer's act of finding the passage as poem 'trespasses on' its original context, breaking down the rules of authorship and literary property in effect since the seventeenth century (Compagnon 361). When the historical figure writes that his journal 'is dead and drowned and ended,' he marks the conclusion of a journalistic career. When we read those words in Colombo's *The Mackenzie Poems*, we are rewriting that journalistic career as a poetic one. *The Colonial Advocate* is no longer in material production as a newspaper, but its reproduction in *The Mackenzie Poems* affords a recirculation of its language, inviting a re-creative reading that paradoxically both counteracts the vandal's attempt at censorship by circulating Mackenzie's writing and allowing him his byline *and* re-creates the act of the vandals, not as an act of censorship but rather as one of verbal de(con)struction; the type is both de- and re-composed.

The reading of the found poem does not *abandon* the type to its 'essential drift,' nor does it abolish the author, although it does violence to the latter's absolute authoritative status. It rather salvages the text for other readings, readings that are otherwise sanctioned or author-ized. Barbara Herrnstein Smith notes that in uses of quotation like book titles, epigraphs, and found poems, where language is candidly appropriated from one purpose to another, the language is 'reauthored' (150). Barthes advocates a similar 'relativization of the *scriptor*'s, the reader's, and the observer's (the critic's) relationships' ('From Work to Text' 74) in what he calls the irreducibly plural, infinitely productive 'text,' which is 'read without the father's signature' (78). He opposes the 'text' to the bounded, coherent nature of the more traditionally 'familiar' 'work,' which is 'caught up in a process of filiation ... The author is regarded as the father and the owner of his work' (ibid.). The found poem, in effect, allows its readers to glimpse the textual potential within all works by drawing attention to the possibility of alternative routes through apparently 'closed' passages.

In the documentary-collage, however, the found poem and the cited document are not read *without* the author's signature, because their effect is contingent on the recognition of a conflict between a set of conventional 'intended' meanings and the 'additional' or 'excessive' meanings readers might legitimately attribute to them. The theoretically infinite productivity that Barthes and Derrida recognize in the text is always limited in and by the act of reading. The (at least) dual attribution of the found poem to both an 'original' writer or writers and a 'quoter' whose role is recognized as 'poetic' contributes to a reading that takes into account the conventional ways the figure of the author always works to limit meaning, while at the same time demon-strating how the text can always exceed that limitation. Language may be an orphan, but the ways it is continually adopted and readopted – perhaps it would be better to mix the metaphor and say *con-script-ed* – into different roles, different relationships, different grounds of legitimacy should not be ignored. Any interpretation involves an inhibition of meaning, and the author, as Foucault makes explicit, is one device erected in order to reduce the multiplicity of possible interpretations to a particular limited range of readings: 'He is a certain functional principle by which, in our culture, one limits, excludes, and chooses; in short, by which one impedes the free circula-tion, the free manipulation, the free composition, decomposition, and recomposition of fiction' ('What Is an Author?' 159).

A key element of the found poem, then, is its undermining of the distinction between the author or poet whose traditional function is seen as the production of language, and the roles of the anthologist, the collector, the editor, the translator, and especially the *reader*, who put it into circulation. Found poetry, or, as Colombo aptly terms it, 'redeemed prose' (*Mackenzie Poems* 17), is precisely a *re*circulation of the linguistic coin with an implicit reappraisal of its value. 'Redeem-ing' is perhaps a better word here than 'redeemed,' since it implies an ongoing process of redefinition and reconsideration (re-deem-ing), as well as a reciprocal relationship between reader and text. The economy of found poetry suggests that language is *never* 'produced' in any strictly creative sense, but rather that it is always borrowed, and with a varying rate of interest.

Many works of documentary-collage, including Kearns's *Conver-gences*, Kogawa's *Obasan*, Marlatt's *Ana Historic*, and several found poems I would like to examine shortly, point to the dangers of a linguistic economy in which the production of meaning is regulated by unacknowledged and unexamined sources of authority, to the deficit of oppressed 'others.' Antoine Compagnon indicates that trans-gressory uses of citation may create an 'economic perversion,' or perturbation of the system of exchange that he terms 'antiauthori-tarian' (367). Citation, in other words, can operate as a challenge to the ideological assumptions of the received text. Marlatt, in particular, indicates the patriarchal nature of this economy: her citational style disrupts the patriarchal monopoly on the meaning of (the texts of) history, implicitly developing an alternative 'line' of feminized reading and writing.

Jacques Ehrmann notes that the found poet uses quotation marks both as an indication of a borrowing and as a sign of the refusal to accept the borrowed passage at face value. 'Being a "writer" or a "poet,"' he asserts, 'no longer corresponds to any particular identity, but to a particular *situation*, accessible however to everyone' (243). For Ehrmann, the act of appropriation or *finding* displaces the privileged act of creation: 'To write would be first of all to quote. The "writer" would not be the one who 'listens to a voice from within,' but rather the one who quotes, who puts language in quotes; who both sets it off and calls it to himself, who, in a word, *designates* it as language' (242–3). In a footnote to his poem 'Some Artifacts of the Twentieth Century,' Colombo quotes a similar statement by Marshall McLuhan: 'The poet dislocates language into meaning' (*Translations* 65). To be a writer in this sense is to be a critical 'interpreter,' a reader for whom the very act of quotation is an act of self-conscious translation.

The found poet becomes not just a reader and translator, but an explicit signatory or co-signer of the represented document, though 'co-signing' clearly does not necessarily qualify as endorsement. The found document carries a doubled signature. The term 'signatory,' in addition to being Weber and Mehlman's translation of Derrida's '*souscripteur*,' is a variation on Michel Foucault's use of 'signature,' of which he writes, 'more than an indication, a gesture, a finger pointed at someone, it is the equivalent of a description' ('What Is an Author' 146). 'Signatory' combines the inevitable effect of the personal – intentional fallacy and all – with the explicitly written, and also defines the reading of the text as a kind of (negotiable) contract. In the case of the documentary, the 'initial' contract is suggested and implicitly broken. As Stephen Scobie writes of the documentary poem, it self-consciously 'forges' the signature of the document's initial inscription: 'The documentary material forms a continuous weave of intertextuality: the "presence" of the "original" texts, continually staged under the seal of the forged signature' (*Signature* 123). The word 'forge' itself hints at the inevitable correlation of making and copying, inscribing and transcribing.

Colombo's work is often quite explicit in its use of doubled or multiple signatories in order to redirect the reading of the found text and thereby suggest its multivalence. *The Mackenzie Poems*, for example, is credited not to a single, but to a collaborative author: 'William Lyon Mackenzie & John Robert Colombo' (iii), and the Introduction grounds this volume in a self-conscious contradiction involving authorship: 'To begin with a paradox: the poems in this book were written by William Lyon Mackenzie, but they were not written by him as poems ... *The Mackenzie Poems*, then, is the product of a creative collaboration spanning a hundred years between the long-dead Mackenzie and another writer living in Toronto today' (7). This is one way of literally 'equivocating' on the issue of authorial voice. That is, the title proposes two, equally weighted voices within the work. Colombo's 1969 volume, composed of excerpts from the letters of Bishop John Strachan, offers a similar example. It is titled *John Toronto: New Poems by Dr. Strachan Found by John Robert Colombo*. The word 'new' plays ironically on the contemporary reader's historical distance from prose selections 'originally' written almost a century before this publication, but re-present-ed to us in an a*pproximate* fashion (close, but not quite the same).

The 'John Toronto' of the title, then, is neither simply John Colombo nor simply John Strachan, but the textual meeting place of both, a kind of double-voiced entity formed by the (re)writing of the passage. Indeed, it might be recalled that the commonly accepted meaning of the word 'Toronto' is 'meeting place.' The 'fortuitous' correspondence of proper nouns becomes a textual locus where two historically disparate writers 'cross paths.' It is also worth noting that the correspondence is one of 'given' names: even the supposedly personal or individual is not original; it is always marked by given or found associations.[2]

Multiple signatories also evoke a general point about the interactive, social process of creating meaning. Martha Rosler asserts that quotation points 'to the existence of a received system of meaning, a defining practice' and 'can reveal the thoroughly social nature of our lives' (80). When Colombo and F.R. Scott 'sign' 'their' texts, they are identifying their roles as both receivers (one 'signs for' a letter) in an ongoing series of discursive transactions in which subsequent readers take part. This is one place where I want to diverge from Barthes's remarks in 'The Death of the Author.' Barthes personifies language when he says that it 'performs' (143), but I would argue instead that language *is performed* by its different enunciations through time and space and that it bears the traces of its constitution within this social and historical field.

F.R. Scott's poem 'One Cure for Loneliness' might be read in this context as an ironic comment affirming language's social status. Taken from the *Montreal Star*, 15 July 1965, it notes 'the recent letters / from people who are lonely' and recommends an inexpensive hobby:

> News events
> or stories and articles
> from the press and magazines
> can be clipped and pasted
> in a scrapbook. (38)

One cure for loneliness is 'social' interaction with texts; the linguistic act is a social one even if it is not interpersonal. 'One Cure for Loneliness' is also social interaction with texts: it does the very thing it describes by excerpting, rearranging, implicitly reassessing the newspaper passage, and passing it on.[3]

A number of found poems point to the irredeemably social nature of meaning by quoting 'sources' that simply cannot be attributed to individuals. 'Love in Quotes,' for example, from Colombo's *Variable Cloudiness*, is selected from the index of *Colombo's Canadian Quotations*:

> a golden hook
> a great dream
> comes after marriage
> doesn't last long
> have conspired against
> joined in together
> laughs at locks
> leads the Eskimo
> make way for
> making in a canoe
> of humanity
> power huzza
> revolutionary does not
> single night of
> where the nights are long
> with a dimple
> with Canada
> without climax
> your first be your last. (30)

Colombo's Canadian Quotations takes utterances from specific contexts and offers them for other uses, as what Barbara Herrnstein Smith would call 'prefabricated utterances' to be applied to a wide range of possible situations (59). As Herrnstein Smith comments, 'When we appropriate someone else's words, we confer on them our own context of meanings, often quite remote from that of the original' (66), but the quotation retains traces of its 'source(s)' elsewhere. When Colombo comments that 'all quoting is "out of context,"' he says at least two things at once: that all quoting derives its meaning *in* context, and that all quoting is *displaced* from its 'original' context, or its previous uses (*Mackenzie Poems* 19). This sense of movement is implicit in the etymology of the verb 'to cite': *citare*, in Latin, means to place in motion.

The citation by 'Love in Quotes' of the index raises quotation itself as an unavoidable issue involving intertextual relations, since the poem is a quotation of a series of quotations that 'refer' back to (or index) quotations in *Colombo's Canadian Quotations*. The poem also reveals something about the intertextual 'prefabrication' of meaning. Love, it might be inferred, is not something that exists essentially and univocally as an absolute Platonic ideal. It is, rather, located provisionally as a function of its various already-determined readings, each of which may be located in terms of what Martha Rosler would call its differing defining practice. In other words, there is never a simple one-to-one correspondence between concept and word: it is never simply Love, but always 'love,' in quotes. The poem, therefore, locates 'love' not just textually by alluding to a particular source, but intertextually. 'Love' becomes the point of intersection of the potentially contradictory, fragmentary discourses that both compose the poem and decompose it by pointing beyond it to other texts.

F.R. Scott's 'Dew Lines' is another poem that overtly points beyond itself. It takes an excerpt from the index of *The Oxford Dictionary of Quotations* under the heading 'Dew,' and presents it in poetic form. Dew is a substance in the process of condensing or evaporating; it is always becoming something else. Similarly, these poetic 'dew lines,' rather than circumscribing the concept or marking a boundary (like the northern 'tree line'), are incomplete and lead outward to other citations and redefinitions. Inserted in capitals at the end of each stanza is yet another version of dew: 'DISTANT EARLY WARNING' (43). 'D.E.W.' is also an abbreviation: its very graphic components, when broken down, 'stand for' other words, are involved in their own intertextual relations, and even those other words herald, as do all the dew lines, an event or meaning never-yet-present: they are a distant early warning. These 'index poems' and others, like Colombo's 'On Tiptoe' (*Translations* 87) and 'Light' (*Translations* 1), ironically undermine the straightforwardly indexical function of the sign, that is, its ability simply to refer or point to 'its' referent.

The act of quotation is by definition a repetition after the fact. Even a seemingly 'original' enunciation is already a kind of quoting, since it draws from an already-written system of significations a kind of cultural dictionary. As Herrnstein Smith puts it, 'any utterance consists wholly of what are, in truth, prefabricated verbal structures – not merely idiomatic phrases and conventional formulas but individual words themselves, which we need not buy or borrow because they are freely donated to us for our immediate use by the linguistic community' (62). Colombo's work often makes use of standard lexical dictionaries, specialized dictionaries of clichés, dictionaries of rhyming words, and collections of proverbs, all of which stress both the 'found-ness' of language itself and its determination by communal use.[4] Any use of language is, then, always already after the fact. Jacques Derrida would contend that this is the inevitable consequence of the fact that writing's defining characteristic is its iterability (we might also say 'quotability') in the absence of either sender or receiver: 'Such iterability – (*iter*, again, probably comes from *itara*, *other* in Sanskrit, and everything that follows can be read as the working out of the logic that ties repetition to alterity) structures the mark of writing itself, no matter what particular type of writing is involved (whether pictographical, hieroglyphic, ideographic, phonetic, alphabetic, to cite the old categories)' ('Signature' 180). The found poem's emphasis on its status as repetition or quotation foregrounds such characteristics of language at the same time as it stresses the element of past and present layerings of contextual determination. The Acknowledgments to *Translations from the English*, for example, credit in the conventional manner places where its poems have been previously published. They conclude, however, with an unconventional note on the book's lack of originality, acknowledging both the iteration or quotation of already-written prose works, and also the 'alternate' contextual presentation inextricable from their repetition: 'All of the poems in *Translations from the English* have appeared in print before, as prose' (ii). Imagine my own chagrin when I felt (legally) compelled to contact Colombo for permission to use citations of his found poetry in the present volume: how does copyright apply here?

The title of F.R. Scott's volume *Trouvailles* sets a precedent for the book as a whole, since it can be read as a found poem composed of but a single word. It conforms to all aspects of the working definition. Not written by the poet, it, like all language, is appropriated from the lexis. Quoted verbatim, it is, however, formally rearranged on the title page of the volume in approximately this form:

TROUF.R.SCOTT
VAILLES

It is displaced from its conventional use to an aesthetic context (the cover of a volume of poetry), and read (here at least) as poetry.

The literal foreignness of the word is one reason it seems to attract attention; unfamiliar to English-speaking readers of a volume otherwise in English, it seems to require an interpreter. The literal translation of 'trouvaille' is, appropriately enough, a windfall or lucky find. This may refer to the found contents of the volume, but it may also be read self-reflexively: the word itself is a 'find.' The arrangement into lines literally opens it up, exposing a hole or gap (un trou), a break in the simple correspondence of reading within the unexamined communicative circuit. The signature of the poet here literally interposes itself into the gap, breaking up even the apparent coherence of the word as physical object. As a result, that word can undergo a shift in value, and, in fact, 'value' here is literally shifted: 'vaille' is a form of the French verb valoire, to be worth.

Reading the found poem is potentially a way of tracing value judgments to 'received' systems of meaning, and of marking potential shifts from the latter: this is a reading that concentrates less on the free play of meaning than on the ways interpretation invariably constitutes a power play. As Douglas Barbour puts it in his discussion of Eli Mandel's found poem 'First Political Speech': 'The particular aesthetic and ethical frame of the concept "poem" can ... focus attention on the problems raised by those forms of discourse that surround and seek to manipulate us' ('Transformations' 32). 'First Political Speech,' included in Crusoe: Poems Selected and New, cites a list of transitional words and phrases from a writing handbook (4). As a style guide, the passage operates as a compendium of conventions, but as a poem/'political speech' it can be read ironically, since it is all convention and no content. As Barbour puts it, the poem 'furiously and wittily calls political and poetic discourse into question, opposing form and content' (ibid. 33). The cited passage as poem is not just a guide to stylistic conventions, then, but to stylistic conventions as the rhetorical terms that persuasively 'frame' positions of power; it is a guide to political speech.

Louis Dudek refers to the found poem as 'really a piece of realistic literature,' referring, presumably, to its strategy of merely excerpting writing that really exists in the world (2). If we are to accept his view, however, 'reality' itself must be read as a found text, a space of intersecting discourses, open to the possibility of (re)interpretation. Duncan Smith writes that one function of poetry is 'to recognize the ambiguity in reality so that experimental analysis of reality may take place' (102). He acknowledges found poetry's special claim to this demystifying procedure (108). A reading of Colombo's poem 'The Electronic "Everything" Doll' might be offered as an example of just such a demystifying procedure. It cites a 'real' advertisement from a 1975 issue of *Elite: The Magazine for Today's Man* (*Variable Cloudiness* 32). The advertisement is for a female doll intended to function as an erotic toy. In its context in the magazine, the advertisement acts as a message marketing a specific product to a specific group of readers/consumers. In order to be effective, the latter must be both unselfconscious consumers of the ad's 'message' and potential consumers of its product. This, apparently, is the role of 'today's man.' The advertisement is both 'faithfully' reproduced by the poem, and is itself intent on describing the 'realistic' qualities of its product; it is about the representation of a woman. The doll, we are told, is 'full of life,' and the ad insists 'She is as REAL as she can possibly BE.' It also returns obsessively to the 'completeness' of the doll, which is, it turns out, a euphemism for the duplication of the female genitals.

Placing the advertisement in the context of poetry allows at least for the potential for reassigning power to woman as a critical rereader of a text to which she would normally be denied access (*Elite* is *the magazine for today's man*), and who is represented but does not speak in the advertisement. The citation of the advertisement allows it to be read seriocomically: its initial impact for the feminist reader may be laughter – it is patently ridiculous. This is, however, serious business indeed, for the advertisement has a (financial) stake in *establishing* just what constitutes the real, while at the same time appearing only to *represent* it. The implied reader of the magazine advertisement is not only male, but in a position of dominance ('*Elite*') over an objectified/commodified 'feminine' body whose integrity is determined only by its sexual organs and their use value. What is for sale here is not simply a product, but the process of inscribing (and consuming) the positions of gendered subjects and objects in particular ways. This reading is made especially viable in the light of two other poems in the same volume: 'Prescription for a Woman,' which quotes a book enumerating courtly conventions defining feminine beauty (33–5), and 'Roget's Girl,' which reproduces the thesaurus's list of linguistic 'equivalences' for 'Woman,' but is, as the title indicates, also involved in marking proprietary – and political – boundaries (37). All three poems are 'pre-scriptions' for Woman that displace the conventions of lyric love poetry, demonstrating the way gender and/as value is implicated in and determined by 'found' or already written texts.

Martha Rosler stresses that it is through irony that the act of quotation can be critically forceful: 'One speaks with two voices, establishing a kind of triangulation – (the source of) the quotation is placed *here*, the quoter over *there*, the hearer/spectator *there* – and, by inflection, one saps the authority of the quote' (196). F.R. Scott's poem, 'Treaty,' from *Trouvailles*, examines another set of prescripted values involving Native peoples: it transcribes an 1854 agreement for the transfer of the Newash or Owen Sound Indian Reserve to the Governor-General. A footnote identifies it as taken 'From a Treaty displayed at Indians of Canada Pavilion, Expo 1967' (10). The title of the poem highlights the document's status as contract, or agreement. Superficially, this is simply a land transaction among parties who agree, presumably, on a 'literal' reading of the document that implies not just ownership of the land, but also a certain proprietary sense of words: in a legal contract, one means what one says.

The date of both Scott's and the Expo quotation is, significantly, 1967, Canada's centennial year, a time of revival and celebration of the nation's history. However, the Expo 67 presentation of the document puts that history in question, inviting an ironic reading, since the centennial celebration itself marks the emergence of a nationhood that erodes, both legally and psychologically, the 'other' first nations apparently 'within' but actually marginalized by 'Canada.' Expo's 'Indians of Canada Pavilion,' in one sense, is a pat symbolic gesture that simplifies the complex historical dilemma of Native peoples, much of which involves treaty negotiations, by constructing a stable space for them as mere tokens in the celebrated Canadian multicultural mosaic without really taking them or their aboriginal status seriously. 'Indians *of Canada*' makes Indians both subordinate and possessed by the Canadian nation.

The ironic quoting of the historical document is one way of resisting that dismissive gesture without abandoning the forum it makes possible. The contemporary enunciation of the document breaks a verbal contract because it puts words to uses for which they were not 'originally' intended. In doing so, the citation foregrounds the element of betrayal in the contract itself, exposing both its supposedly 'dated' terms (both the terms of agreement and the language in which they are framed) and the extent to which the subsequent treatment of Native groups in Canadian history in fact continues to fulfil those terms. The very trope of the 'familiar' relation of parent and child ('our kind Father the Governor General') is, in its contemporary context, de-familiarized and read ironically as paternalistic in a negative sense. The manifestly written context of the quotation draws attention to related verbal incongruities, exposing com*promis*ing positions. The contradiction between 'Having the fullest confidence' and 'surrender,' or the ironic contrast between 'We have after mature consideration ...' and 'Indian children' are significant examples.

We might also note that the signatures of the Natives Ningaram and Wabuminguam are absent, substituted for by symbols and explained in brackets as '(HIS MARK)' (10). Ningaram and Wabuminguam literally do not participate in the contract because they do not participate literally, that is, in its written language, a language imported by Europeans and framed within their culture. The 'We' of the opening line (emphasized by Scott's line break), then, is ironic, since Indians do not speak in the historical treaty. This irony is emphasized by the poem that follows 'Treaty' in *Trouvailles*, 'Pavilion Misrepresents Outlook.' This poem is a transcription of a letter to the *Montreal Gazette*, 11 July 1967, in which a Catholic missionary claims to speak for 'the majority of Canadian Indians,' concluding that: 'Most Indians aren't so bitter – / They're happy with what is being done for them / By the Government and by the missionaries' (11). The Expo citation of the 1854 treaty allows its readers to 'listen' for the exclusion of Native voices and consider its significance to both the historical contract and the ongoing contracts that structure current beliefs. At the same time, the document itself functions, ironically, as an enunciation by contemporary Native peoples who can engage subversively with its language, and as such it constitutes a transgressive seizure of European language.

Scott's insertion as signatory also contributes to the reading of the document in significant ways. In a sense, the poetic reading of 'Treaty' is a verbal contract F.R. Scott frames, especially since our biographical knowledge of Scott as law professor, social philosopher, political activist, and poet-satirist seems to encourage a combined consideration of the social and literary. Scott's phrasal line breaks may attempt to 'restore' a Native voice to the original written contract (although they may also function less positively as an allusion to the legendary 'native eloquence' that has so often been used to relegate the political to the realm of the 'merely' – that is, marginally – aesthetic).

Since Scott is co-signer of the treaty, his own position is an ambivalent, compromised one quite similar to the role of the highly ambivalent speaker of Lionel Kearns's poem *Convergences*. Scott may be seen as in a position of complicity with the framers of the document, who were, like him, white, affluent, English-speaking and -writing males of Anglo-European descent. Scott's position of authority, particularly as professor of law, depends on the very discourse he cites. His quotation of the treaty and acknowledgment of its Expo re-citation, however, also points to an attempt at alignment both with the historical Natives whose geographical/discursive 'place in history' is determined by the treaty, and with the contemporary Natives who seek to dislocate its terms, putting geographical *and* discursive place at issue. Like Kearns's quotations of Cook's exploration journals in *Convergences*, Scott's quotation of the treaty, without presuming to speak *for* 'the Indians of Canada,' opens up gaps in the dominant discourse that defines them as such, a disruptive gesture that may also tend to unsettle Scott's own positions as 'expressive' poet, as professor of law, and most generally as figure(r) of authority.

Lenore Keeshig-Tobias's '(a found poem)' is a text that virtually demands to be read in tandem with 'Treaty.' Its context and signature – and therefore the effect of its 'voice(s)' – differ from those of Scott's poem in that '(a found poem)' appears in a collection of work by Native writers and is 'signed' by Keeshig-Tobias, an Ojibwa poet/storyteller from the very community designated by the document Scott cites. Keeshig-Tobias's poem quotes another legal text, 'An Act Respecting Indians':

> Section 11. Subject to section 12,
>   a person is entitled to
>   to be registered, if that
>   that person (c) is a male who
>   who is a direct descendant in
>   in the male line of a male
>   male person described in
>   in paragraph (a) or (b);

> Section 11. Subject to section 12,
>   a person is entitled to
>   to be registered, if that
>   that person (f) is the wife or
>   or widow of a person who is
>   is registered by virtue of paragraph
>   paragraph (a), (b), (c), (d), or (e);

Section 12 (1) (b)
> The following persons are not
> not allowed to be registered
> registered namely, (b) a woman who married
> married a person who is not an Indian,
> Indian, unless that woman is subsequently
> subsequently the wife or widow of a person
> person described in section 11. (123)

Wendy Waring observes that 'the irony in this poem hinges on the doubling meaning of single words such as "respecting" and "person," and is actualized through the recontextualization of a piece of legislation into the body of this found poem' (148). The Act involves the definition in terms of institutional, legal discourse of what it means to be an Indian, who is 'en-titled' (in the legal sense) to and who is excluded from that status. Keeshig-Tobias both subversively appropriates the language of (the) record, and replies to 'her master's voice' of legal authority, appending the following passage as a form of 'talking back' to the document:

> AN ACT RESPECTING INDIANS
> (subsequently and
> without reservation)
>
> Fathers brothers uncles
> chiefs warriors politicians
> Where are the Women
>
> 'out there' you point
> 'somewhere'
>
> we reach out into the mist
> to women you refuse to see
> to strength you cannot give
> and will not give to emotion
> you cannot feel to the other
> half of our beginnings
>
> we have ourselves and our daughters
> and you my fathers have
> sons and sons and sons

and section 12(1)(b)
in the Act Respecting Indians. (123–4)

The second half of the poem, like the first half, is headed 'AN ACT
RESPECTING INDIANS.' The second half, however, is not a legal document, but a self-conscious gesture of difference and response: it is an
act, respecting Indians. With the addition of this counter-text (which
is the point where the found poem becomes a documentary-collage),
the reader of the cited document is identified as a Native woman, but,
ironically, this identification is one the document itself suggests is
contradictory. The Native woman's enunciation interrupts the male
line enforced by the legal document. In so doing, it also makes the
word 'respecting' doubly ironic, since, as Waring perceives, it now
alludes to the lack of respect for Native culture associated with white
conquest and its repercussions, but also refers to the legal exclusion of
Native women from their own culture, indeed their own race (149).
The last paragraph of the cited document, in particular section 12
(1)(b), is a kind of exclusion clause that defines Indian women's status
in terms of their relationship to men.

Ironically, the latter half of the poem offers its reservations about the
document 'subsequently and / without reservation,' appropriating
legal terminology and punning on the word 'reservation,' which
denotes both doubt and the land that was 'reserved' for Natives to
inhabit when their own land was taken over and occupied by European incursions. The pun also points to a kind of semiotic 'occupation'
of the word 'Indian' and what might be called the space of 'Indian-
ness' ('reservation') by men, to the exclusion of women. Indian
woman's place is displaced, 'without reservation'; it is the un-
cited/sited place of/in the 'mist'/missed. The voice of the poem
gestures towards relocating this position: 'we reach out into the mist
/ to women you refuse to see' (124).

The poem literally interrogates the document from a position 'subject to' but subversive of its provisions: 'Where are the Women' (124).
In contrast to the language of the supposedly neutral/neutre document, the responsive passages take the situation personally. They
adopt a form of direct address, speaking to the document's enunciator
– and, potentially, the reader of the present text: 'Where are the
Women / "out there" you point / "somewhere"' (124). The poem
questions the definition of Indian identity offered by the document,
asking, in effect, as Waring observes, 'Who is "we"?' (38). The speaker
speaks both as a Native and as a woman, allowing for the opening up

of the exclusiveness and certainty of the document's language. The responsive section, significantly, uses equivocal pronouns that allow for a subjectivity informed by difference. When it refers, for example, to 'the other / half of our beginings,' 'our' may refer to Native culture and more inclusively to humanity. Similarly, when she addresses 'you my fathers,' those fathers may be both the fathers of white patriarchy who framed the Act Respecting Indians, and the patriarchal figures of Native culture, both of whom are implicated in the exclusions of 'section 12 (1)(b) / in the Act Respecting Indians.' As Waring puts it, the poem creates an irony 'which comments on both the sexual oppression produced by a white European state and the complicity of male Indian band chiefs who condoned and policed this state's intervention in reservation sexual politics' (37). The 'you' of the poem also, potentially, implicates the reader as a member of this patriarchal body.

Keeshig-Tobias and Scott speak from different positions and achieve different effects. While 'Treaty' works to undermine Scott's own position of authority as a white Anglo-European academic speaker, Keeshig-Tobias's poem interpellates a speaking position for the marginalized Native woman (perhaps that is why it is important that her poem includes a response to the document); both texts work to rupture the given discourse of dominance. As in several of the found poems examined here, the gesture of citation may draw the reader's attention to places where she or he habitually and strategically forecloses on signification, where meaning seems 'obvious' or 'natural' or 'innocent'; in so gesturing the found poem may provoke the reader to look – and think – again.

In a footnote to the poem 'Dear Ann: I'm Afraid,' Colombo quotes Ronald Gross: 'Found poetry turns the continuous verbal undertone of mass culture up full volume for a moment, offering a chance to see and hear it with a shock of recognition' (*Translations* 69). That 'shock' of recognition is perhaps best explained by the dislocation Colombo describes in *ABRACADABRA*: 'these days the aesthetic distance between an *objet trouvé* and an *objet d'art* is a short one indeed – a short circuit, some might say' (124). The shock of recognition, and the short-circuiting of conventional strategies of reading may also involve the exposure and interruption of power lines. Redeeming prose involves a blurring of the conventional distinctions between 'ordinary' and 'poetic,' 'work' and 'text,' 'reader' and 'writer' that reveals *all* language as a highly charged social text.

CHAPTER TWO

Kroetsch's Balancing Act:
The Ledger as Local History

> We all begin our literary careers with scissors, pastepot and scrap
> book in hand, cutting out images and words from the Eaton's cata-
> logue – that child in emerald green leggings, that jovial Santa Claus,
> Jane or Barbara or Bill – gluing them painstaking into 'our book.'
> The thick floury paste on our hands spreads to the scissors, the
> cover of the catalogue, the cover of the book. Soon a trail of white
> sticks the tools of excision and inscription to the texts of our imagin-
> ation, the scene of writing layered in one sprawling, incandescent
> (w)hole. Pleased with the book of received ideas, the young collage
> maker moves on to other action.
>
> Barbara Godard, '*The Diviners* as Supplement'

In a statement included in *The Long Poem Anthology*, Robert Kroetsch
notes his interest, as a prairie writer, in 'the dream of origins' (Statement by the Poet 311). 'Obviously in the prairies,' he writes, 'the small
town and the farm are not merely places, they are remembered places'
(ibid.). Kroetsch then turns to another question of origins, speculating
on both history *in* and the history *of* his own 'life-long poem,' *Field
Notes*: 'I don't know when I began my continuing poem. It was years
ago that my Aunt Mary O'Connor, one afternoon at her house in
Edmonton, handed me the ledger that had been kept by her father, my
grandfather, at a watermill in Bruce County, Ontario. Up until then I'd
had no idea that my grandfather and Aunt Mary and I were in complicity. I finished the poem, their poem of the ledger, and called it *The*

Ledger' (ibid.). A casual turn in Kroetsch's discussion points to the radical displacement of poetic origin *The Ledger* has in common with found poetry. Kroetsch's comments significantly shift from the notion of beginning the poem to that of *finding* a hand-me-down 'pretext' for it, the ledger. Finding, for Kroetsch, as for the writer of the found poem, is both a beginning and an always-already-having-begun. Kroetsch's emphasis moves, therefore, from his own role in giving genesis to the poem ('I don't know when *I* began *my* continuing poem') to the idea of a 'complicitous' poetic writing dependent on the participation of others: it is not just 'my continuing poem,' but 'their poem of the ledger.'

The Ledger's formal structure is based on the double columns of the financial ledger. It imports into this structure passages from the inherited ledger, maps, and fragments from a historical atlas, the dictionary, a newspaper, census records, letters, and tombstone inscriptions. Shirley Neuman refers to the effect of this discursive borrowing using Kroetsch's term 'intertext' ('Allow self' 115). 'The "intertext,"' she explains, 'is the space shared by, the relations between, different poetic texts in the frame of a larger "Collected Poem." The "poem" exists in the lacunae and intersections between the different texts it holds in its space' (ibid.). *The Ledger*, like Kroetsch's *Seed Catalogue*, is both part of the collected poem *Field Notes* and is itself a 'collected poem,' since its constituent elements are collected from elsewhere.

The poem's citation and spatial rearrangement of various discourses allows a dramatic conversation among them, in which they 'become commentaries for each other' (Blodgett, 'The Book, Its Discourse, and the Lyric' 202). In his speculations about the visual-arts collage, Max Ernst identifies the notion of collaboration, or 'the systematic fusion of the thoughts of two or more authors in a single work' as 'a relative of collage' (266). The idea of collage itself makes collaboration a relative gesture (in Kroetsch's case, literally so), since, as Kroetsch's comments make clear, the 'complicity' among those who contribute to a work like *The Ledger* is not always deliberate, and all parties are not necessarily coterminous. It is more appropriate, perhaps, to talk about a dialogic relationship between various utterances and languages as Décio Pignatari does when he discusses the effects of the 'semantic montage, or collage' (43–4).

Like found art and poetry, the collage appropriates and displaces given texts. It is distinguished, however, by its central principles of fragmentation and, especially, juxtaposition – or 'cut and paste' – in which excerpts from texts not explicitly connected are placed in relation – literally *made relative* – to one another (Leefmans 186). *The Ledger* uses a literary form of 'collage composition'[1] that draws fragments of the nineteenth-century ledger and other documents into complicity with each other and with poetic 'annotation,' subjecting them to what Jean-Jacques Thomas would call 'a new graphic economy' (79), an economy that builds dialogically on the found poem's revaluing of the 'coined' phrase. Barbara Herrnstein Smith's comments elaborate on this financial metaphor: 'Any verbal structure ... has the potentiality to fulfil multiple functions: just as the metal disc that once served Roman citizens as a coin of the realm may now be exhibited in a museum case as an archaeological 'find' or, duly set by a jeweller, be displayed as a body ornament, so a text that once was (and still could be) linguistic currency may serve other functions and thereby acquire a different sort of value' (116).

To a large extent my own appraisal of the found poem in the last chapter was governed by the economic trope: just as the meaning of a given text is governed by the particular readerly economy in which it is situated, so ethical issues are subject to re-evaluation in 'redeeming prose.' Both *The Ledger*'s specific formal strategies, and a more general re-verse-ible metonymic displacement in which the ledger 'stands in for' the poem and the poem substitutes for the ledger, suggest the importance of economic concerns, or issues of value, to its functioning: the poem re-creates the double-columned debit-credit system of the traditional account book, and duplicates the windowed ledger cover, facsimiles of ledger pages, and passages from a historical ledger, thereby formalizing the theme of value.[2]

This 'enfolding [of] the outside' (document) (Blodgett, 'After Pierre Berton What?' 76) suggests a parallel, doubled economy of *reading* that Henri Béhar asserts is symptomatic of collage. The collage, he observes, implies a 'double production of sense,' at the habitual level of literal reading, and at the specific level of material reading, in which the work is situated intertextually, in its relation with the larger body of writing ('Le Collage' 68). Béhar suggests the hermit crab as an emblem for the practice of the literary collage: like the 'double named' crab (in French the hermit crab is called *pagure* and *bernard-l'ermite*), collage appropriates a form and a substance, feeds off it, and creates from the remains a new thing, of which the collage is both a carrier and a life-giving element (ibid. 43).

The documents that compose *The Ledger*, as Kroetsch's comments indicate, are not simply found: they are *inherited*. *The Ledger*, then, is not just a collected poem; it is also, notably, a *re*collected poem, since the documentary materials it takes in are the textual substance of personal, family, and communal memory. In effect, the poem pieces together an individual and folk pattern of heredity. The first inscription inside the poem's cover is a date nearly one hundred years distant from the poem's publication: '1887' is written at the top of a reproduced manuscript ledger page. Frank Davey states that documentary 'writers who work out of a ground of inherited written material attempt to bring that old material ... to the possibility of further meaning,' allowing an interaction between past and present ('Recontextualization' 131). The ledger is language that both records history and *has* a history, and the poem's incorporation of / displacement by the ledger announces its own engagement with both the language of the past and the past of language as the local ground from which the present poem/poet is generated. This engagement is 'genealogical' in the Foucauldian sense that it operates on the 'genetic' codes of the past without presenting them either as original or continuous ('Nietzsche' 77): 'Genealogy,' Foucault writes, 'is gray, meticulous, and patiently documentary' (ibid. 76). As Smaro Kamboureli asserts, in Kroetsch's writing, 'the dream [of origin] is occasioned by the writing process that recasts origins in the field of language' (106).

Like Béhar's hermit crab, whose very home is borrowed, the poet and/as reader of *The Ledger* inhabits a 'home base' that is also a 'foreign' space, constituted as it is by inherited discourses. Indeed, at one point the poem includes language that is literally both foreign and familiar: the German inscription on the tombstone of the poet's great-grandfather. The goods that appear in the sawmill's ledger include 'construction materials' suitable for homebuilding. The documents included in *The Ledger*, analogously, are part of a construction project defining a historical space that 'houses' the writer's present position. Like the crab's house, this is a discursive 'mobile home' that may be shifted into different positions of significance. Its cited materials are part of a historical account (book) whose meaning is obviously 'predicted' or already said, but whose fragmented re-citation or reconstruction as part of the collage of discourse that composes the poem offers a responsive 'post-dicting,' a colloquial (as both communal and informal) form of poetic-historical 'back-talk.'

In his article 'Strange Loops,' Eli Mandel associates postmodern writing with regionalism, asking, 'If postmodernism is ... deconstruction, demystification, failure, beginning, a text of language, in what way can we say it is regional?' (22). He answers this question by arguing that regionalism 'can be thought of primarily in linguistic terms, as language, and as a version of discontinuity or process in poetry' (20). The postmodern 'regional' poem, in Mandel's terms, combines a sense of regionalist particularism, and itself is seen as a region of discourse, 'a self-referring' structure (22) ... or, as Kroetsch would have it, a 'field' of 'notes.'

Peter Baltensperger, by contrast, views the regional poem as a much more literally conservative entity that reinforces continuity and stasis. He labels 'regional historical poetry' poetry that 'compresses the past ... of a specific region or community into compact capsules of images and symbols in order to record and preserve the history of its locality ... [and] it provides its region with a poetic and symbolic framework within which to establish a historical perspective of its past, and a clearly defined picture of its various roots' (50). Such poetry's use of reproduced historical texts, Baltensperger adds, 'fixate[s] the past and focus[es] on the underlying meaning of local history' (52). *The Ledger*'s inclusion of historical materials may be seen in part as a conservative device, a way of preserving the given past of a region by reiterating its documentary remains and affirming the value of local folk culture. It also, however, in keeping with Mandel's comments, *un*-fixes that past by re-citing it, focusing in a subversive manner on the underlying meaning of 'local history' by reviewing (and undermining) the inscription of both region and history in particular documents and contextualized enunciations of them.

One of the documents cited in *The Ledger* is a traditional volume of local history, *The Illustrated Atlas of the County of Bruce*, first published in 1880. In a section the atlas calls a 'Historical Sketch of the County of Bruce' (*Illustrated Atlas* n.p.) the author describes his project:

> With no effort or pretension to literary merit, the object will be rather to present a plain statement of facts of general interest which bear upon the past growth and development of this wonderfully prosperous section of the Province, in such manner as to render future comparisons more easy, and offer to the rising generation an incentive to emulation in the examples of the pioneers, whose self-reliant industry and progressive enterprise have conquered the primeval forests, and left in their stead, as a heritage to posterity, a country teeming with substantial comforts and material wealth, and reflecting in its every feature the indomitable spirit and true manliness of a noble race, whose lives and deeds will shine

> while the communities they have founded shall continue to
> exist.

One of the ironies of this passage is that it is duplicated in the poem
precisely with effort and pretension to literary merit. Quoted 'out of
context,' the rhetorical exuberance of the description stands in stark
contrast with its stated claim to objectivity: it brims over with the
language of value, and in fact links economic with ethical worth.

As Don McKay observes, the passage 'presents the solemn voice of
rational forms and civilized values poised on that brink where it
teeters over into a parody of its own rhetoric' (148). The citation's
placement in the poem reveals it as a historically embedded *reading* of
local history on which the region's communities are founded. It might
also be seen as a minor example of the sort of totalizing 'monumental'
history that erects a monolithic (Bakhtin would say monologic) discourse at the site of a loss, both venerating the past and making it
remote. 'Monumental history,' Foucault writes, 'is itself a parody'
('Nietzsche' 94). The poem both disrupts and repeats that history
through fragmentation and citation, thereby inciting a parodic reading.

Foucault's opposition of monumental history with genealogy draws
on the Bakhtinian notion of 'carnival' that, as I argued in the Introduction, is an element of the documentary-collage: 'Genealogy is history
in the form of a concerted carnival' ('Nietzsche' 94). Kroetsch himself
is fond of an archaeological analogy, also borrowed from Foucault, to
describe what I am calling his 'local history' project. For my own
purposes (which diverge somewhat here from Foucault's), each term
highlights a different aspect of the same project: while genealogy raises
the specific historical inscription of the subject and a dispersal of its
origin, archaeology suggests the fragmentation of traditional history
and the investigation of local space. In the essay 'Beyond Nationalism:
A Prologue,' for example, Kroetsch writes that 'document *opens up*
the site,' rather than compressing the past: 'it is the archaeological act
that resists the over-arching generalization of history' (87, emphasis
added).

Eli Mandel observes of Kroetsch and novelist Rudy Wiebe that 'their
place is as much language as geography' ('Strange Loops' 23). Indeed,
the region of *The Ledger* is literally 'charted' by the poem. This gesture
blurs the border between geographical and discursive space, and
suggests that *The Ledger* might function as a kind of revisionist
response to the *Illustrated Atlas of the County of Bruce*. The poem is
'framed' by maps of Culross and Carrick townships and a detail from

a map of Upper Canada; these are also texts *within* the poem's collage. The documents the poem includes are both geographically local, and *graphically* localized. That is, like an archaeological find, they must be read in situ (site/cite).

In the 1975 edition of *The Ledger*, the location of the sawmill on the map of Carrick Township is circled (thus *en*-circled by the inscription of the poem), and an apparently 'handwritten' note in the margin, signed 'RK,' adds, 'Yes, that's the *place*.' The poet literally signs the appropriated document, drawing attention to his re-authoring of it, after the fact, and self-consciously situating the conventionally abstracted lyric voice: the note literally puts Kroetsch on the map. The gesture also directs the reader to focus on local space. Similarly, a detailed geographical situating of the poet's ancestor in one column of *The Ledger* is formally paralleled with a notation regarding his graphic or textual remains, in the other:

my grandfather, Henry (dead)	the ledger itself (surviving)
in his watermill (gone)	purchased in the Bruce County
on the Teeswater River,	Drug and Book Store (Price:
on the road between Formosa and	$1.00 PAID), the leather cover
Belmore, needing a new ledger:	brown. In gold: *THE LEDGER*:

The textual placing of the ledger in the poem, is, in a sense, a replacing of that 'remembered place,' the sawmill, since Henry and his mill are lost, and the (found) written text survives. In the incident described in the right-hand column, Henry needs 'a new ledger' in order to continue his accounts. The poem's re-citation of the document fulfils a parallel need to continue the historical account book with a 'new' accounting, the 'continuing poem' that replaces at the same time as it subsumes or re-places the old.

In his essay 'On Being an Alberta Writer,' Kroetsch again associates historical documentation with the archaeological act:

> It is a kind of archaeology that makes *this place*, with all its implications, available to us for literary purposes ... I am aware that it is the great French historian, Michel Foucault, who has formalized our understanding of the appropriateness of the archaeological method. But the prairie writer understands that appropriateness in terms of the particulars

> of place: newspaper files, place names, shoe boxes full of old
> photographs, tall tales, diaries, journals, tipi rings, weather
> reports, business ledgers, voting records – even the wrong-
> headed histories written by eastern historians become, rather
> than narratives of the past, archaeological deposits.' (76)

Locality is defined here as an intertextual locus: the site is a 'cite' of
reading, and 'the particulars of place' include the materials of everyday life. If this passage is considered in relation to *The Ledger*, we can
see how the archaeological trope is infiltrated by economic language,
since *The Ledger*'s account is a repository of both financial and literary
'deposits.' It registers the historically given quality of inherited language, but its give-and-take structure also implies that that language's
reader/heir must contribute to the (interpretation of the) historical
record, participating in a discursive *exchange* with past writing. Hence,
perhaps, the speaker's obsession with debt: 'What do I owe you?' he
asks over and over, dwelling on past accounts receivable. Barbara
Godard makes this observation about *Labyrinths of Voice*, but it might
equally be applied to *The Ledger*, since, like *Labyrinths*, the poem
functions as a '*process* of collage, opening up infinite other discourses
and possibilities of discursiveness. Here speech is event, a dynamic
process of exchange between sender-message-receiver offering a
processual hermeneutics' ('Other Fictions' 14, emphasis added).

   The Ledger is both a record and a medium of such exchange. These
lines, for example, follow a cited fragment of the 1893 financial
account:

> the poet: by accident
> finding in the torn ledger
> (IT DOESN'T BALANCE)

  .the green poem:

In archaeological terms, the poet both finds the document (that is,
locates it) and, in re-locating it in the space of the poem, makes it a
'find.' When the reader fortuitously comes across and re-reads the
fragmented ledger, he becomes a poet 'by accident.' His finding in the
old ledger of the renewed 'green poem' is also 'accidental' in the sense
that it is unintentional; it exceeds the apparent 'intentions' of the text
as given.

   The technique of excerpting 'the torn ledger' 'deconcatenates' an
established 'verbal chain,' allowing the formation of 'new networks of
significance' in the resultant verbal collage (Thomas 80). The reading

of the account book, therefore, is not a simple exchange of meaning. It contributes to the value of the text: 'IT DOESN'T BALANCE.' Both the inscription and the reading of citation reveal that meaning is not a matter of an individual's 'sole ownership,' but belongs in the social domain. The poem's use of documents therefore creates what we might think of as a historical collective poem, as well as a collected poem, since it both allows interaction among its constituent documents and draws out within each the traces of voices disparate in space and time. Or, to put it another way, the poem both cites/sites its documentary materials and re-cites/re-situates them.

The Ledger contains a quoted anecdote that simultaneously describes and enacts just such a layering of voices. The 'source' of this passage is a scrap of paper inserted into the 1861 census record, a document that accounts for the lives and deaths of people within a particular region at a particular time. The note describes an incident in the history of the census's composition: 'The enumerator "got his feet frozen and another had to finish the work. / Both made oath to their respective sheets and these are numbered and designated separately."' The paragraph, because of its quoted context within the poem, potentially refers to *the poem's* history of composition, the collection of material by the poet-speaker of *The Ledger*, who takes over the work of 'enumeration' or naming from other writers and, like the census-takers whose sheets are 'numbered and designated separately,' demarcates the various discourses within the poem by using quotation and the spatial configurations of collage. Nevertheless, because the quoted passage simultaneously tells *both* historically disparate stories, these formally marked distinctions are theoretically blurred, and the quotation is opened up to a double contextual reading.

The title page of *The Ledger* formally manifests the doubleness described in the census passage: the reproduction of a page from the 1887 account book and the poetry book's title and publication information are superimposed on one another. While it is technically the third page of the poem, the title (or 'enumeration') page is 'numbered and designated separately' as page '95' (of the ledger). 'Brick' also resonates doubly here as the name both of the 'entrant' in the 1887 account (Mr Peter Brick) and the poem's publisher, Brick Books, a participant in the production of the 1979 volume. As Le Roy C. Breunig suggests, such a use of names allows them to function as a 'collant' in the collage of the poem, since they constitute 'an external element affixed to a text so as to alter its overall effect' (105).[3] Naming (or 'enumeration'), then, in a general sense, is not just something the poet spontaneously does. It is something that has already been done.

'Brick' is both a pre-existent 'external element,' and one of the constituent (re)construction materials that compose 'the / book / of /
columns' – both architectural and verbal.

'Brick' also appears as a literal construction material in *The Ledger*
when John O. Miller's account is settled 'by Brick 2500 / at 50¢ 12.50.'
The doubled 'brick/Brick' account is reopened later in the poem when
we read that

> Mr. Peter Brick, on the road
> from Belmore to Formosa,
> intending to stay ('Beer
> also was also plentiful and cheap.')
> bought new furniture for his
> new brick house ...

Mr Brick constructs a lasting architectural structure that, like Henry's
linguistic structure (the ledger), outlives its author's intentions: the
account cited above appears in the left-hand column, balanced in the
right by a reference to death: 'ledger: a resident. / Pushing up daisies.
/ *Obsolete*.' Mr Brick is both lost and found; he dies, but stays (as he
intended) 'a resident,' and his physical remains nourish a crop of
flowers at his grave site, just as Henry's textual remainder (the ledger)
becomes a productive textual site/cite despite its (and his) functional
obsolescence. This situation suggests a fundamental irony in *The
Ledger*, since, contrary to the last, cited, words of the poem, the
account is not 'Settled By death.' It, rather, continues to be written and
read as the 'continuing poem.'

A passage from the *Illustrated Atlas of the County of Bruce*, quoted on
the same page of *The Ledger* as the census anecdote offers what
amounts to another historical account that doubly describes and enacts
an instance of the recycling of architectural/linguistic materials by
appropriation. The quotation reports on the homesteading experiences
of the Clements, settlers who 'were rather roughly used by a wander-
ing band [of Indians] on one occasion, who forcibly took possession of
the whole roof of their shanty (which was composed chiefly of birch-
bark) for the purpose of canoe-making.' The (birchbark/paper) 'sheets'
of one party's 'construction' (the shanty / the quotation) both literally
and figuratively become the 'vehicle' of another's (the Indians' / the
poet's) intentions. In the census example a problem of stasis – the case
of frozen feet – was solved by the second enumerator's aid, just as the
poet's quotation supplemented the 'preserved' meaning of the histori-

cal passage. In this instance, similarly, an apparently 'settled' site/ citation is reoccupied in the spirit of the carnivalesque.

The doubling of voices seen in these examples is one symptom of an ambivalence central to *The Ledger*'s formulation of the documentary problem. Kroetsch's work is both historical and historically subversive, serious and playful, representational and antirepresentational, or, to use Dominick La Capra's terms, 'documentary' and 'worklike.' La Capra, significantly, sees these two dimensions as operative in and held in tension by *both* 'historical' and 'creative' writing. The 'documentary' tendency, he submits, situates the text in terms of its literal dimensions involving reference to empirical reality, while 'the worklike is critical and transformative, for it deconstructs and reconstructs the given, in a sense repeating it but also bringing into the world something that did not exist before in that significant variation, alteration, or transformation' (*Rethinking Intellectual History* 30). *The Ledger*'s collage composition literally repeats the documentary given by quoting it, but alters its context and/or form, relativizing without completely discrediting the 'documentary' dimension, both engaging in and inviting a 'worklike' reading as well.

Bakhtin locates a related ambivalence at the level of the sign itself, an ambivalence that results when the writer gives new meaning to another's word, while maintaining its 'old' meaning too. 'This ambivalent word,' as Julia Kristeva explains it, 'is therefore the result of a joining of two sign systems' ('Word, Dialogue, and Novel' 73). In *The Ledger*, the 'other's' word is apparently functional, representational prose, the 'primary material' of the historical record. The poem's speaker/citer is engaged in an attempt to 'balance the books,' split between two projects, one that has him act as a 'bookkeeper' who preserves and revalues the monologic, functional, referential unity of the historical account, and the other that has him act as a playful interpreter of the multivoiced 'worklike' linguistic potential of the document.

The tension between these two impulses is clearly at work in the pattern of including dictionary definitions of the signifier 'ledger' throughout the volume. 'Ledger' (the word) becomes an epitome of the larger processes that the document as signifier undergoes in the context of the poem. If we want to settle the matter of what the ledger means, the dictionary seems a natural place to turn, but as Don McKay observes, this is an unsettling operation indeed, since the definitions 'both close and disclose' (150), in a process Susan Wood would describe as 'reinventing the word' (28). The desire for (one) meaning is dispersed into multiple interpretations that 'open up the word "ledger," enabling the poet to mine its possibilities and undermine its fixities with puns and implicit meanings' (D. McKay 150). Underlying all the dictionary definitions is an implicit (false) etymological connection between 'ledger' and the Latin *leger*, meaning to read. *The Ledger*'s writing inscribes a process of reading the document and/as sign.

'Ledger' is here not simply an object, then, but a sign whose complexity is multiplied in the poem; the apparently objective, 'denotative' word (Kristeva, 'Word, Dialogue, and Novel' 72) is itself dis-integrated into a network of citations, just as the historical document is 'torn,' re-cited, and re-defined by the poem. The dictionary definitions reveal the potential of the apparently representational word to be what Kristeva following Bakhtin calls a 'literary word': 'an *intersection of textual surfaces* rather than a *point* (a fixed meaning) ... [It is] a dialogue among several writings' (ibid. 65).

As 'inserted genres,' the dictionary definitions also allow, as Bakhtin suggests, the represent*ing* word and the represent*ed* word to appear alongside one another (*Problems* 108). Like the poem's other citations, they further present the possibility that the representing and represented word may be different aspects of the same ambivalent text. Early in the poem, for example, the word 'FINDING' appears in both a formally central and contextually ambivalent position on the page, *between* the double columns:

FINDING

everything you write
my wife, my daughters, said   *the book of final entry*
is a search for the dead   *in which a record is kept*

One reading of the right-hand entry might conclude that the poet simply finds the ledger itself, which is, after all, the book of final entry in which a record is kept. The italics used in the lines cited above, however, remind the reader that these are not just represent*ing* words, but represent*ed* words: they function as material found *objects*. '*the book of final entry / in which a record is kept*' is a quotation of a quotation; it repeats a fragment of the dictionary definition from the previous page. The passage refers, then, not just to the ledger itself, but to the dictionary definition of the ledger, which the poet also 'finds' and excerpts in 'poetic' form.

Terry Eagleton remarks that consulting a dictionary in search of the signified only turns up 'more signifiers, whose signifieds you can in turn look up, and so on' (128). The dictionary, in other words, *is* other words; it is itself a found document that can be 'mined and undermined.' Dictionary definitions in *The Ledger* thus both define and put definition at issue, since they present multiple 'readings' of the word, and are themselves 'textualized,' opened to (re)citation and (re)interpretation. For example, definition 'f.,' '"a book that lies permanently in some place,"' is radically re-defined when it is re-produced 'poetically,' that is, with a line break that brings out a pun on the word 'lies': 'The book that lies / permanently.' An added line redirects the referent of the 'new' definition to the poetic text itself, a form of writing known for its persistent deviation from literal 'truth': 'The book that lies / permanently. / *e.g.*, the poem.' In *The Ledger*, however, the 'poetic' text and the 'documentary' text are verbally identical; the documentary text is read as 'lies' or fiction when it appears 'in some place': the intertextual space of the 'collected poem.' Just as the 'truth' of its definition can be reinterpreted, so the meaning/identity of the ledger as document differs from itself. The ledger therefore both 'lies permanently,' that is, remains verbally the same, and 'lies / permanently' because its meaning undergoes a transformative process that takes place over time, and whose variants may 'intersect' in the present moment.

The dictionary citations develop this operation in epitome by literally bringing historical usage to bear on the present context. In this way, the diachronic intrudes on the synchronic, suggesting that the word, like the document, is a record, not just of past events, but of its past enunciations too. For example, definition 'c.' describes 'ledger' as '"one who is permanently or constantly in a place; a resident. *Obs.*,"' both confirming the historical 'outdatedness' of the meaning and negating it by bringing the 'obsolete' definition into effect. Paradoxically, though, the definition 'one who is permanently or constantly in a place' *must* be made obsolete in order to make possible the movement of form and meaning put into effect by the poem's citation of the ledger.

'Obsolescence' is balanced in the debit-credit structure of *The Ledger* by 'survival.' The opening lines of the poem, for instance, describe the ledger as paradoxically outliving its own obsolescence:

the	the ledger survived
ledger	
	because it was neither
itself	human nor useful

The ledger is a 'dated' document: it both bears the traces of its 'lost' historical uses and is open to 'gain' differing interpretations. In a sense, the ledger survives itself.

The ledger, in 'bookkeeping,' is defined as a volume 'in which a record ... is kept.' *The Ledger* is a volume that preserves historical records. In its re-citative or 'book-keeping' project of documentary-collage it also becomes both the record and the locus of historical linguistic transactions. The account book, as we have seen, is literally an inheritance from the poet/speaker's grandfather. It 'outlives' Henry's limited functional intentions for it, and in so doing preserves an 'unintentional' trace of his presence: 'my grandfather Henry (dead),' an entry in the left-hand 'debit' column of the poem, is 'balanced' in the right-hand 'credit' column by 'the ledger itself (surviving).' The poem *The Ledger* is a kind of compensatory response to a death/debt in the family.

It implicitly inquires after other family connections too. For example, it takes in an excerpt of a letter to 'Bob' (ambiguously, either the poet in the poem or the poet of the poem, or both) from 'Aunt Mary O'C' in response to inquiries about his great-grandmother Theresia Tschirhart. Theresia's name as of her last marriage, Theresia 'Hauck,' significantly evokes an expression of debt: the poet as her descendent, one might say, is 'in hock' to Theresia. In incorporating the letter into the poem Kroetsch responds to a family obligation, and in so doing he participates in the dialogic, genealogical project of inquiring into and responding to the codes of his personal past.

Theresia was, the letter states, a 'well read' individual. This is a quality she obviously passes on to her poet/great-grandson, by whom she is well read after her death. Kroetsch playfully invokes the notion of reading as an extension of (the) life (of the text) when he invents a sign for a graveyard-less Alberta town where Theresia is buried that reads: 'DEATH PROHIBITED / ON THESE PREMISES.' Obsolescence itself is made obsolete (by the sign) 'on these premises,' both 'at this site,' and on the basis of previous 'statements' (or premises): 'some people go to heaven / Some people write poems.' In a definition placed next to the letter from Aunt Mary, we learn that 'ledger' can also function as both a sign and a tombstone: 'e. "a large flat stone, esp. one laid over a tomb"'; the poem both includes and counters this 'monumental' approach by offering alternative interpretations.

The document is more than just a personal legacy. It is also the 'statement' of a community's sociolinguistic transactions: the ledger is signed and re-signed by various inhabitants of the region, a list of whom appears in the poem's 'final reckoning.' In an even broader sense, the document inscribes an inherited world view, for, as Russell Brown points out, 'To use a pre-existing document is to engage in a recovery of the past, of course, but ... from the apparently innocent, "documentary," past we may inherit imported meaning and ways of seeing' (158). Citing, in other words, also involves a historical 'sighting,' but one the poem places in question: 'I can't believe my eyes,' the poet says. As Smaro Kamboureli puts it in her discussion of the preface to Eli Mandel's long poem *Out of Place*, the poet's temporal, spatial, and discursive displacement 'exposes the illusions of factuality that have shaped our notions of self and place, a displacement that reveals fiction as the way to discovery' (124).

The township maps that preface *The Ledger*, for example, imply a geographical 'siting' in citation and sighting. While they seem simply to represent the region, the maps are involved in a 'fictional' construction of it in the image of the ledger, *re*constructing the rational, commodity-oriented vision of settlers and map-makers: the maps' vertical lot lines parallel the columnar markings of the ledger reproduction on the page that immediately precedes them. The 1975 edition of the poem actually labels the maps 'The Ledger,' since they appear on its title page. The map may be seen, then, 'not so much as a representation of space but as a space of representation' (see Boelhower 479). Map and ledger represent one another as much as they reflect an 'outside' reality.

This 'ledgered' construction of the landscape is confirmed in a quotation from the *Canada Gazette*, 17 August 1854. Kroetsch comments in *Labyrinths of Voice* that 'we expect a newspaper to honour a basic meaning of a word, and we expect a writer to be slightly askew on that word, which is making it *become* again' (Neuman and Wilson 149). Here, the newspaper itself is 'skewed' by its citation in the poem. The word 'gazette,' for instance, is used by the newspaper in the basic sense of an expository news-sheet, but its history and etymology also align it with the economic realm of the ledger: a gazette is traditionally a compendium of financial notices, and the word 'gazette' comes from the Italian *gazeta*, a kind of coin (OED). The newspaper, then, both represents financial transactions, and is itself a medium of exchange, a linguistic coin 'entered' in the columns of the poem. The passage from the *Canada Gazette*, appropriately, indicates that in order for Canadian land to be 'settled' in the pioneering sense, it must *already* have been financially/discursively 'settled': 'Notice is hereby given that the undermentioned lands ... in the County of Bruce, U.C., will be open for sale to actual settlers ... The price to be Ten shillings per acre ... Actual occupation to be immediate and continuous.' *The Ledger* supplements this advertisement by cataloguing the extinction of multiple other occupations of the landscape that are disrupted both literally and by the rhetorical/financial 'figures' of the settlement described in the announcement:

	To raise a barn;
cut down a forest.	
	To raise oats and hay;
burn the soil.	
	To raise cattle and hogs;
kill the bear	
kill the mink	
kill the marten	
kill the lynx	
kill the fisher	
kill the beaver	
kill the moose	

The extent to which these columns are perceived as balanced clearly depends on the value one places on pioneer (agri)culture. As this example makes clear, the columns of *The Ledger* are not, strictly speaking, structures of equivalence, but ambivalence. They indicate a doubling of dissonant economies of value. The superficially ordered system of the ledger is shown to suppress imbalances of a fundamental sort, but the poem's dis-ordered quotation of it suggests the differences of value that the rational balancing of the columns is erected to conceal:

you must see	under the turning wheel
the confusion again	the ripened wheat, the
the chaos again	razed forest, the wrung
the original forest	man: the nether stone

The account book is, like the census, involved in a balancing of construction and destruction as life-and-death issues. 'Ledger' is described in definition 'b' as 'a horizontal piece of timber secured to the uprights supporting the putlogs in a scaffolding, or the like.' The ledger is both a literal structure and a verbal one, and the literal structure, like the verbal one, is an ambivalent undertaking: scaffolding may be part of a construction project, or an instrument of destruction in its use as a platform for hanging.

An entry placed between the two columns describes the settling process as an equivocal combination of potentially literal or verbal activities: 'Shaping the trees / into ledgers / Raising the barn.' This shaping might be the literal cutting of wood for a homestead as in the documentary prose passage that describes the cutting and preparation of elm, maple, pine, and cedar for construction by the settlers. 'Shaping the trees / into ledgers' might also be the corresponding 'entry' of trees into the account book as goods of exchange, as in the ledger excerpt that begins 'to sawing Butternut ...' The trees are described as shaped into 'logs' – the ledger is both a daily account or 'log book' and a book of words, or in Greek, *logos*, that shape the 'outside' world.

Kroetsch indicates that the lesson of the document is always that 'a reading of the world is at best a misreading of the world' ('Beyond Nationalism' 87). This is, perhaps, why Robert Lecker comments that while *The Ledger* is Kroetsch's 'inward journey to the record of his past ... he never finds that past, only the act of "FINDING" it' (135). Rather than a record, he finds records; instead of a definitive account, he finds an account book; in lieu of a history of settlement, he reads and writes an unsettling history. The 'remembered places' of the past are not a fixed ground. They are, rather, caught up in the collage process of reading as re-collection, a process that balances a historical 'dream of origin' with what E.D. Blodgett calls 'the textualization of origin' ('The Book, Its Discourse, and the Lyric' 200).

CHAPTER THREE

The Collected Works of
Billy the Kid:
Scripting the Docudrama

> 7. FABLE, EDMUND, JR. *The True Life of Billy the Kid*. Denver: Denver Publishing Co. This title was recorded with the Copyright Office of the Library of Congress on September 7, 1881, but there is no record that the copyright deposit copies were received by the Library. Was this item ever printed? If so, is there a copy extant?
>
> J.C. Dykes, *Billy the Kid: The Bibliography of a Legend*

In 'What Is in the Pot,' the essay that introduces *The Long Poem Anthology*, Michael Ondaatje comments: 'In a country with an absurd history of film, real film goes underground. And it comes up often in strange clothes – sometimes as theatre, sometimes as poetry' (15). Ondaatje does not specify just what he means by 'an absurd history of film,' but he does go on to discuss documentary poetry, so it seems reasonable to make the connection between the 'absurd history' he mentions, and the tradition of journalistic cinema often traced to documentarist John Grierson's tenure as Canadian film commissioner (1939–45), the tradition to which Dorothy Livesay alludes in 'The Documentary Poem: A Canadian Genre' (267). Livesay seeks a continuity between this realist documentary tradition and Canadian 'documentary' poetry, defining the documentary poem in a manner similar to Grierson's view of the documentary film: as a realist form important for its didactic potential, for its sociological value (Grierson, 'The Course of Realism' 140; Livesay 280).[1]

Ondaatje's poetic theory and practice provide a subversive response to this approach: the documentary 'goes underground' in the literary text. In 'What Is in the Pot,' Ondaatje comments on Livesay's require- ment that the documentary poem be didactic, disclosing the extent to which he and his contemporaries were deliberately rethinking her view of the form: 'What is needed now is perhaps a new look at the documentary poem in Canada – how it has changed in intent, how it has become (in Susan Sontag's term) "infradidactic." For in spite of the poems being *long*, there is little evidence of a didactic formal voice' (15). Ondaatje, significantly, associates didacticism with a controlling 'formal voice' that might be related to the authoritative voice-over narration of documentary film, a device that guides – indeed literally dictates – both the film's narrative and the viewer's interpretation of its images. His comments suggest that the contemporary practice of the documentary poem replaces the literally ab/surd history (it speaks *out of deafness* to other voices) that this monologic voice offers with an 'infradidactic' poetic 'lecturing' as self-*reading* that corresponds to the multivoiced 'interdiscursive' aspect of the documentary-collage I discussed in relation to *The Ledger*. *Infra* is, after all, a way of referring to a citation within (but further on in) a given text.

Smaro Kamboureli affirms this idea when she writes of *The Collected Works of Billy the Kid* that 'Ondaatje denies himself the authority of the author; instead, he foregrounds his role as reader, a reader of found narratives, a reader who becomes a writer' (186). *The Collected Works*, like Kroetsch's *The Ledger*, is a fragmentary 'collected poem' whose historical memory depends on a re-collection and rereading of docu- ments within the documentary-collage. *The Collected Works*, further, is an assembled group of writings in which Livesay's 'dialectic between the objective facts and the subjective feelings of the poet' is displaced into an intertextual dialogue that in*cites* responses from its present reader. As Barbara Godard sees it, the poem is a form of 'modular fiction,' 'which posits an active co-creator in the reader who is invited to make her own modulations' ('Stretching the Story' 32).

Rather than functioning as evidence of objective, verifiable events, then, these writings themselves compose a series of self-consciously textual events put into play by the reader. The reader may participate in a process that explores the dialogic composition of historical 'fact.' *The Collected Works* counters the notion of a monologic 'formal voice' both by offering a multiplicity of alternative discourses, and by draw- ing out alternate readings of official texts. This move constitutes a kind of strategic misreading of Livesay's related requirements that the documentary poem use a dramatic technique and a representative protagonist ('The Documentary Poem' 267, 269): *The Collected Works* may be seen as a revisionary or experimental 'docudrama' that presents language itself as spectacle – George Elliott Clarke calls it a 'theatre of literature' (4).[2] It is indeed a drama of documents, or 'play' of texts. Although the film docudrama traditionally 'seeks to achieve an effect of authenticity and credibility' in its dramatization of historical events (Kronigsberg 88), the documentary-collage places such impressions in question by focusing on the documents that produce what Roland Barthes would call 'the reality effect,' in which '"reality" is always an unformulated meaning sheltering behind the apparent omnipotence of the referent' ('Historical Discourse' 154).

Julia Kristeva sees Bakhtinian 'carnival' in dramatic terms that reinforce the kind of *textual* processes *The Collected Works* puts into play. The carnivalistic activity, she argues, dismantles the very subjective–objective polarities implicit in the theatrical distinction between stage and life, game and dream, discourse and spectacle. Carnival, then, is the place where 'language escapes linearity (law) to live as drama in three dimensions. At a deeper level, this also signifies the contrary: drama becomes located in language' ('Word, Dialogue and Novel' 79). The central figure of Ondaatje's poetic drama – or perhaps more appropriately, *de*-centred figure – Billy the Kid is, in the linguistic sense Kristeva indicates, an 'outlaw.' This makes him, as Livesay requires, a 'representative hero,' a hero of representation, of the drama located in language, for these are his 'collected works' not because he composed them, but because he is composed *of* them. Françoise Gaillard remarks that in totalizing history the hero is a recognizable, stable, localizable subject, 'unambiguously situated in the key position' (143). He is 'the centre of the textual apparatus; he accumulates meanings and is in return the source of their emission. He absorbs and reflects. He totalizes his (hi)story at the same time as being re-totalized by History' (142). In *The Collected Works*, by contrast, 'Billy the Kid' is a signifier that becomes a *dramatic* locus of textual intersection. As the title implies, this locus is not totalized; it is the place where problems of documentation are enacted.

Stephen Scobie observes that *The Collected Works of Billy the Kid* was one of two books published in 1970 (the other being Atwood's *The Journals of Susanna Moodie*) whose success and prestige established the documentary in the practice of Canadian literature (*Signature* 120). Ondaatje's poem certainly set the stage for his own later uses of the documentary-collage in such works as the novel *Coming Through*

Slaughter and the biographical fiction *Running in the Family. The Collected Works*, like these later texts, deals with a figure of legend, one that is obviously already filtered through layers of story and whose 'true character' is therefore problematic. Billy's 'legendary' status places him on what Linda Hutcheon would call a 'middle ground of reference' where he both is and is not a 'real' historical figure ('The Postmodern Challenge to Boundaries' 86). Hutcheon observes that in writing of Billy the Kid in a self-consciously metafictional way, Ondaatje creates 'what we might call a "historiographic" referent. Unlike the historical (or real) referent, this one is created in and by the *text's writing* (hence historio*graphic*). The referent here is doubled; it partakes of two "realities"' (86). The root of the word legend, *legenda*, means 'what is to be read'; Billy the Kid is a legendary figure in the rhetorical sense, constructed in readings and in writings. As Barbara Godard puts it, 'Ondaatje's Billy rewrites heroic legends of his life and death, confounding the concept of original in the palimpsest' ('Stretching the Story' 27). Because of the multiple, unstable, and potentially conflicting nature of readings and writings (and readings *as* writings), then, the outlaw is subject to a kind of *de*-constructive drama that interrogates what might be called 'Western' metaphysics. He is both encoded by, and refuses to stick to, the script.

While totalizing history places its hero in a 'key position' (Gaillard 143) of plenitude, then, the heroic centre of Ondaatje's poem is displaced. Its readers are asked to search for a *lost* key. They are also compelled to become aware of their own implication in the act of 'finding.' The poem approaches the problem of beginnings by addressing the reader directly: 'Find the beginning, the slight silver key to unlock it, to dig it out. Here then is a maze to begin, be in' (*CWBK* 20). Finding a beginning involves the reader in examining his or her own discursive positioning within what Barbara Godard calls this 'web of texts' ('Stretching the Story' 27). In the passage just quoted, for example, 'here' is a spatial deictic, and 'then' a temporal deictic. Both might be read in the light of what Emile Benveniste writes of 'pronomial' forms, which 'do not refer to "reality" or to "objective" positions in space or time,' but rather to a 'reality of discourse' established by the utterances within which they are situated (218–19). The pronomial, in other words, replaces a subjective–objective dialectic with intertextual relationships. 'Billy the Kid' is, I would argue, despite technically being a 'proper' noun, the poem's central 'pronomial' form, since his character is not a simple fixed entity that exists objectively independent of its representations, but is, rather, continually placed and displaced by the reading of 'his' collected works. In the invitation 'here then is a place to begin ...' the shifting relationship between the reader's proximate position 'here' and a temporally distant 'then' becomes a function of the poem's present reading, which gives past writings a 'new beginning' in the reader's 'finding' of them as 'a maze to begin, be in.'

'Be in' is 'begin' with a gap, a letter left out. Readers of *The Collected Works* should perhaps be looking less for keys than key holes, entrance not into a teleological narrative structure that terminates in a single exit, but through and into textual/narrative uncertainties. The poem's description of the entrance to the Boot Hill cemetery, literally a place one might enter to visit those who have passed/past away, represents a symbolic structure of both entrance and indirection:

> ... There is an elaborate gate
> but the path keeps to no main route for it tangles
> like branches of a tree among the gravestones. (9)

The tangled path, which might be associated with 'a maze to begin,' leads, not directly to the dead themselves, but in a tangled, indirect route 'among the gravestones,' signs of the dead. Later, the poem uses the path metaphor again, this time to mock the kind of literalist bio-graphical 'graverobbing' that would claim to find and 'resurrect' or re-present the subject of its account. This project inevitably issues in a dead end: 'Imagine if you dug him up and brought him out. You'd see very little. There'd be the buck teeth. Perhaps Garrett's bullet no longer in thick wet flesh would roll in the skull like a marble. From the head there'd be a *trail* of vertebrae like a row of pearl buttons' (97, emphasis added). The passage emphasizes both the hollowness of Billy's material remains and its in-coherence: the trail of vertebrae is obviously an intermittent one. 'What Is in the Pot' quotes a comment on documentary cinema by avant-garde film-maker Jean-Luc Godard. His statement develops the figure of the tangled path and, typically for Godard, reverses conventional wisdom on realist film ... in a manner entirely appropriate to Ondaatje's re-versing of prosaic documentary material and methods. The documentary, Godard observes, is 'a road leading to fiction, but it's still not a road, it's bushes and trees' (cited in 'What Is in the Pot' 16). Godard's statement hints at the constructed-ness of the documentary narrative, the blurring of boundaries between what is inside and outside that narrative, and the illusory nature of totalized, unilinear telling that makes such distinctions.

Ondaatje's poem's recurrent use of poetic images of photographic images points not only to a non-linear layering of documentary evidence in keeping with Godard's comments, but also to the process of producing and interpreting such evidence. To imply that the world is seen, in one form or another, 'photographically' indicates mediation at the first level of perception. To convey that 'photographic' reception in writing suggests a continuing process of 'reading' or reinterpretation that transgresses the boundaries between media. Photographic and cinematic patterns in *The Collected Works* have been thoroughly traced elsewhere.[3] In contrast to the numerous discussions of poetic images of photography in the poem, there has been a significant lack of commentary on the photographs themselves (*CWBK* 13, 23, 31, 45, 59, 91, 98, 107). Considering their resistance to interpretation as conventional 'illustrations' of the text, this fact is not surprising. The photographs do not, as one might expect, simply 'translate' written material into images or refer unambiguously to readily identifiable historical subjects.

Roland Barthes calls the photograph a 'pure deictic language,' 'the absolute Particular, the sovereign Contingency, matte and somehow stupid, the *This* ... the Photograph is never anything but an antiphon of "Look," "See," "Here it is" ...' (*Camera Lucida* 4–5). The 'this' to which 'this' refers is never made present; it is perpetually subject to the differential play/delay of discourse. When Allan Sekula asserts that the status of photographic meaning is relatively indeterminate, he uses an example appropriate to the operation of documenting the criminal career of Billy the Kid. Sekula considers the evidence offered by photographs taken by bank hold-up cameras. His reading elicits a whole system of judgment involved in their interpretation:

> Taken automatically, these pictures could be said to be unpolluted by sensibility, an extreme form of documentary. If the surveillance engineers who developed these cameras have an esthetic, it is one of raw, technological instrumentality. 'Just the facts, ma'am.' But a courtroom is a battleground of fictions ... The outcome, based on the 'true' reading of the evidence, is a function less of 'objectivity' than of political manoeuvring ... The only 'objective' truth that photographs offer is the assertion that somebody or something – in this case, an automated camera – was somewhere and took a picture. Everything else, everything beyond the imprinting of a trace, is up for grabs. (57)

The photographs included in *The Collected Works* participate in the juridical process Sekula describes, since they are 'entered' as evidence of the criminal career of Billy the Kid. *The Ledger* used the controlling metaphor of the economy of financial/interpretive value; *The Collected Works* is 'governed' by the figure of the legal trial as a 'battleground of fictions,' where evidence is presented, compared, and judged. As evidence, however, the photographs propose problems of identification that complicate that process, necessitating a self-conscious attempt to reconcile the site of documentation with a re-cited context that puts the photograph's meaning 'up for grabs.'

For example, the poem's reader cannot always definitively decide what 'this' or 'it' in the photograph is, much less decide where is 'here.' A photograph on page 23, for example, shows a structure with two windows, a woman seated and two men standing outside it on the grass. An account on the page opposite, however, contains the description 'Snow outside. Wilson, Dave Rudabaugh and me. No windows, the door open so we could see. Four horses outside' (22). The illustrative function of the photograph is both suggested and thwarted. It seems to have been quoted out of context: there has been a slippage in time and/or space. Similarly, Sallie Chisum's story about how she obtained a basset hound imported from England is accompanied by a photograph of a dog on the back of a wagon, but the dog is not a basset (59).

In the first photograph in the volume (13) it seems significant that the central figure is painting a signpost (which might help to situate the photograph), but the meaning of the sign (both within the photograph and of the photograph itself as sign) is inconclusive. The photograph portrays three unidentified men, all of whom face the borders of the picture, creating the impression of what Barthes calls a 'blind field' outside the frame beyond the access of the viewer (*Camera Lucida* 57). The orientation of figures towards such a field outside the cited text incites without fulfilling the viewer's desire for more meaning, and also suggests the extent to which the photograph selects from a given visual field.[4] This is often the effect of the citational gesture in the documentary-collage. As Jean Weisgerber perceives, citation both invokes questions of significance and sends us 'elsewhere' to investigate them: 'It is rather like a question mark, a marginal note, a signpost directing us to some unexplored ground and arousing our curiosity' (43). It evokes, in effect, a maze of textual choices.

In contrast to the formally unconventional composition of the volume's first photograph, *The Collected Works* includes another photograph that is completely conventional, but is equally reticent: it is a seated formal portrait of a man and a woman who gaze directly into the camera. The reader may associate the couple with Sally and John Chisum, since a passage in Sally's voice appears opposite the photograph, but this decision would be a provisional one based on conventions of juxtaposition, on context and not 'positive identification' (31). The photograph, with its subjects' formal address to the camera, is obviously posed; Sallie's account of Billy the Kid on the facing page, taken from Walter Noble Burns's *The Saga of Billy the Kid* (Burns 15), may similarly be seen as a formal romanticizing of the past in which Sallie adopts the conventional pose of *'a sweet faced, kindly old lady of a thousand memories of frontier days'* (CWBK 30 / Burns 11).

The acknowledgments at the end of the poem tell us that some of the photographs in the volume were taken by L.A. Huffman, a pioneering nineteenth-century Western photographer (110). These photographs are early experiments in documentation, historically valuable for both what they represent and the methods they use. The acknowledgments thus reinforce the sense that the photographs have been appropriated and reproduced from another context. Abigail Solomon Godeau identifies some reader-oriented implications of such photographic appropriation in her discussion of the work of photo-artist Sherrie Levine (88). Solomon Godeau writes that 'inasmuch as appropriation functions by putting visual quotation marks around the stolen image, its critical application lies in its ability to compel the viewer to see dialectically' (91), that is, to participate in the doubled historiographic referencing that Hutcheon described in her comments quoted earlier.

The Collected Works draws attention to the problem of representational space by beginning with an open frame. Evidence appears to have been suppressed or 'stolen': an appropriated photograph is evoked, but seems to have been removed (5). As Benjamin Buchloh comments in a discussion of Robert Rauschenberg's *Erased de Kooning Drawing*, when perceptual data are withheld or removed from the surface of display, the viewer's focus of attention is shifted 'to the appropriated historical construct on the one hand, and to the devices of framing and presentation, on the other' (169). The blank frame is suggestive of the related contextual processes of photographic, documentary, and legal 'framing' that the poem both uses and violates. While institutions of aesthetic/historical/legal authority would 'frame' the legendary outlaw within their monologic grammars, presenting evidence that would lead to an 'arrest,' or stable, unified representation, *The Collected Works* focuses on the *fictional* nature of the frame and disrupts its coherence and the appearance of plenitude via the strategies of the documentary-collage.

The blank frame also allows the formulation of a reading of the poem as a kind of documentary 'screenplay' (an expression that blends the terminology of film, drama, and writing): it opens with a blank screen, presents 'multiple exposures of prose, prose poems, poetry, dime novels, and interviews' (Tatum 145), and ends with a list of 'CREDITS' that identify documentary sources and contributors (110). The quotation that appears below the open frame is taken from one such source, the credits testify – L.A. Huffman's book *Huffman, Frontier Photographer*:

> *I send you a picture of Billy made with the Perry shutter as quick as it can be worked – Pyro and soda developer. I am making daily experiments now and find I am able to take passing horses at a lively trot square across the line of fire – bits of snow in the air – spokes well defined – some blur on top of wheel but sharp in the main – men walking are no trick – I will send you proofs sometime. I shall show you what can be done from the saddle without ground glass or tripod – please notice when you get the specimens that they were made with the lens wide open and many of the best exposed when my horse was in motion.* (5)

The very act of quotation, notes Victor Li, 'disperses meaning, first, by transgressing the protective limits of the "univocal" or autonomous text,' and then, by citing it in a different context, destroying its univocality, 'multiplying and scattering its single voice' (297). This is exactly the case for the Huffman quotation. Its ostensibly simple, referential quality is first and most clearly ruptured by the absence of the photograph in question, signalled by the open frame.

As the title of Judith Owens's paper on the poem, '"I Send You a Picture": Ondaatje's Portrait of Billy the Kid,' implies, the document's 'new' presentational context shifts it from the apparently historical and factual reference of the photograph to a fictional, poetic referent (the poem as a whole), a shift that also changes the pronominal reference of 'I' to Ondaatje as the text's 'compiler' or 'editor' if not, strictly speaking, its author. The quotation's reference is further multiplied if we decide *not* to treat the poem as a whole, but as a collection of documents – themselves neither 'univocal' nor 'autonomous' – successively 'projected' like the frames of a film onto the blank space from which Billy as photograph and referent is absent.

The diction of the Huffman passage addresses several other contexts relevant to this consideration of the poem. Its language is not just that of photography, for example, but of photography as scientific experimentation: 'I am making daily *experiments* ... I will send you *proofs* sometime ... when you get the *specimens*' (5, emphasis added). Frank Davey writes that 'much of the documentary impulse in the twentieth-century long poem begins ... in the modernist envy of the scientist's access to self evident testimony and precise measurement' ('Recontextualization' 125). The absolute authority of such 'truth-seeking' activities as legal testimony or empirical scientific evidence is challenged by Ondaatje's 'truth-testing' experimental method.

The scientific/representational language of the Huffman citation also evokes two related legal 'truth-seeking' activities: the detective's investigation of a crime (which Sekula broached when he used the phrase, 'Just the facts, ma'am,' from the television detective show *Dragnet*), and the process of legally trying a criminal, where, as E.L. Doctorow puts it, 'society arranges with all its investigative apparatus to apprehend factual reality' (227). Dominick LaCapra notes a traditional identification between the historian and 'the just judge who employs exhaustive documentation to arrive at balanced appraisals of the objects of study' (*Rethinking Intellectual History* 17). The aim of such a process is, after all, to reach a *verdict*, both a conclusive finding and, literally, a 'true saying.' As Vladimir Voloshinov notes, however, the language of positive judgment assumes a clear distinction between the verbal subjectivism of parties to a case and the objectivity of the court (123). The juxtapositional method of the documentary-collage relativizes this subjective–objective opposition. *The Collected Works* presents no single authoritative voice, and the poem's reader cannot assume a position of absolute authority since she or he acts *both* as judge and as 'conspirator' in the production of the narrative.

Parker Tyler's discussion of documentary film brings together the three 'truth-seeking' activities I have been discussing: scientific experimentation, criminal investigation, and legal trial. He writes that the experimental method of science is paralleled by the detective's endeavour, 'a tentative, and not always successful, search for the relevant, conclusive facts' (261). He later notes that, in the detective story,

> if the crimes treated are, literally or symbolically, already on
> the books, the verisimilitude tends to compass the fiction

> itself. For this simple reason: the murderer as individual is
> technically a fiction until legally convicted; even a suspect ...
> is a legal-fiction criminal only, as anxious as a certain group
> is to consider him a real one. This theoretically imbeds fiction
> in the chosen theme of fact. Crime detection is therefore
> allied to the method of scientific knowledge already men-
> tioned as a category of documentary. The whole process of
> apprehension and trial is an experiment conducted to make a
> present hypothesis secure in a past fact by connecting,
> beyond any reasonable doubt, the doer with the deed. (263–4)

The conventional documentary must present the evidence necessary
to prove its case, to demonstrate that it is the one true story – history.
Success, to extend the legal trope, is based on the strength of its
convictions. Ondaatje, however, objects to what he calls the 'CBC kind
of documentary' because it manipulates its material into a particular
point of view, and because in it the element of fiction or uncertainty
is not sustained, or indeed was never entertained in the first place.
This kind of documentary seems to have access to ready-made truth.
According to Ondaatje, it 'knows what it's going to say before the
actual filming begins' (Solecki 15). When Ondaatje comments, by
contrast, that the kind of documentary he prefers 'has no real script,'
he is referring, not to the absence of any linguistic text, but rather to
the director's lack of prescriptive control over the film's direction:
'everything is left up to the camera-man, the lighting man, the actors
and the people you are actually interviewing' (ibid.). The film, in other
words, comes from the contributions of multiple 'film-makers,' and is
also composed in the remaking of the whole film in the cut-and-paste
process of editing (ibid. 16).

   Through its 'editing' or 'collage' of documents, *The Collected Works*
ensures that Billy the Kid remains a 'legal-fiction criminal only' by, in
effect, trying the evidence without settling on a verdict. Like the
documentary described by Jean-Luc Godard, textual evidence becomes
a kind of road to fiction; the document, like the found poem, is a
'finding,' but not a conclusive finding. Billy the Kid's crimes are, quite
literally, on the books, as the bibliographical credits and J.C. Dykes's
Bibliography of a Legend indicate: they are part of the historical record.
They are also *in* the book *The Collected Works of Billy the Kid*: it contains
an itemized list of 'the killed / (By me)' (6). When, in that book, its
readers return to the (dramatic) *scenes* of the crimes, then, it should be
no surprise that they are also scenes of writing. For example, a passage

midway through the poem asks about 'A motive? some reasoning we can give to explain all this violence. Was there a source for all this? yup –' (54). Stephen Scobie suggests that 'simplistic psychological "explanations" of the source of Billy's violence' are being mocked here ('Two Authors in Search of a Character' 194). It should be added that the above-quoted passage is followed by an italicized account describing the savage murder of Tunstall. The documentary 'source' of all *this* violence is Walter Noble Burns's book *The Saga of Billy the Kid*, which the passage quotes verbatim (Burns 48).[5] The poem turns away, then, from psychologically rooted clues that require a present psyche to interpret, to intertexual ones, which send its readers 'elsewhere.' The question posed by *The Collected Works* is less, therefore, What made Billy the Kid so mean? than, What makes him *mean*? That is, How has this legendary figure acquired significance?

Paulita Maxwell represents just one of the multiple testimonies from 'character' witnesses in the fictional trial of Billy the Kid. She, like Ondaatje, exercises a right to refuse apparently conclusive information, explaining the absence of another photograph in judicial terms: '*I never liked the picture. I don't think it does Billy justice*' (*CWBK* 19 / Burns 195). Paulita Maxwell's account describes the way the excluded photograph 'constructs' Billy: '*The picture makes him rough and uncouth*' (19). Her own version of Billy is quite different, and, as an 'eyewitness account,' seems at first to supersede the photograph: '*his face was really boyish and pleasant*' (19). That testimony is itself, however, equivocal, subject to its own interpretive agenda. The phrasing of the complete quotation subtly suggests that it is not the objective, unmediated expression *on* Billy's face that was boyish and pleasant, but '*The expression of his face*,' Paulita's expression of it, perhaps, in her own description (19, emphasis added). Barthes writes: 'I am doomed by (well-meaning) Photography always to have an expression: my body never finds its zero degree' (*Camera Lucida* 12). The same might be said of Billy's textual 'expression' in the poem. The Photomat, Barthes continues, 'always turns you into a criminal type, wanted by the police' (12). That is, it functions as a kind of 'wanted poster,' affirming its own status as trace, as a sign of desire for something or someone not fully *there*. Ondaatje's use of the statement by Paulita Maxwell stresses its role as trace. Strictly speaking, this is not even 'Paulita's' testimony, since it is appropriated first by Burns and then re-cited by *The Collected Works*, which rends it into lines and renders it 'poetic.'

Another of the alternative stories *The Collected Works* presents is the tale 'Billy the Kid and the Princess,' excerpted from Carlton Comics.[6]

This extract from a 'popular' genre is here placed in paratactic rather than hierarchical relation to the poem's various other discourses, since it is equally important in contributing to the legend of Billy the Kid. In the comic book story the Princess (a 'real princess' – a real comic-book princess) tells Billy, 'I really must not go on being formal with you' (102). In a sense she states Ondaatje's mandate too, since he must avoid the marks of formal closure that denote the completion of story. The comic-book tale, for example, while it is formally set off by a page border (another story tells how Billy and Charlie Bowdre 'criss-cross' borders [20]), defies that frame by ending with an ellipsis and a conjunction: 'Before Billy the Kid can defend himself, La Princesa Marguerita has taken him in her arms and ... [sic]' (102). In a film, of course, the two would fade off into the sunset, indicating that the story continues beyond the confines of its present telling.

In *The Collected Works*, the story does indeed continue beyond the 'confines' of each of its various tellings. Interdiscursive relationships among stories violate closure by offering alternative narrative lines and alternative perspectives. Paulita Maxwell sets out to put an end to the proliferating stories about her relationship with Billy, stories that she, ironically, perpetuates by *relating* them, laying the groundwork for the comic-book legend, not to mention Burns's and Ondaatje's tellings: '*An old story that identifies me as Billy the Kid's sweetheart has been going the rounds for many years ... But I was not Billy the Kid's sweetheart ... There was a story that Billy and I had laid our plans to elope to old Mexico ... There was another tale that we proposed to elope riding double on one horse. Neither story was true ...*' (96). One place that promises to give a first-hand, and therefore genuinely *true*, story is the 'Exclusive Jail Interview' with *The Texas Star*, in which, it is stated in a bold headline, 'THE KID TELLS ALL' (81).[7] The interview, however, is more a justification of the failure of the scientific method / legal trial than a verdict in itself. In its literally dialogic method (the interview), the article is both an epitome of the poem as a whole and a parody of journalistic inquiry. When the interviewer asks Billy 'Did you have any reason for going on living, or were you just experimenting?' Billy replies that 'in the end that is all that's important – that you keep testing yourself, as you say – experimenting on how good you are, and you can't do that when you want to lose' (83). In *The Collected Works*, the experimental method is not directed towards completion, but is an ongoing activity in which Billy the Kid's character is only ever offered on a 'trial basis.'

The Kid explains: 'I could only be arrested if they had proof, definite proof, not just stories' (81). The Huffman quotation that 'opens' the volume tells readers, 'I will send you [photographic] proofs some-time' (5). The arrival of conclusive documentary 'proofs,' however, is perpetually deferred by the poem since, as Billy says in the interview, 'there is no legal proof to all this later stuff. The evidence used was unconstitutional' (83). That is, it fails to constitute him conclusively. When Judge Houston offers Billy amnesty, he refuses: 'All Houston was offering me was protection from the law, and at that time the law had no quarrels with me, so it seemed rather silly' (81). The judge proposes to give Billy the Kid what he already has; Houston offers him *parole*. In French, *parole* means (the spoken) word, or, more parti-cularly, as defined by structuralist linguistics, it means individual, situated utterances as opposed to *langue*, the system of laws that define the language as a whole (Culler 8). Linda Hutcheon observes that 'in the light of the structuralist focus on *langue* and on the arbitrary but stable relationship between signifier and signified, postmodernism might be called the "revenge of *parole*" (or at least of the relationship between the subject, as generator of *parole*, and the act or process of generation)' (*Poetics* 82). This phenomenon is part of the activity described earlier by Kristeva as language's 'dramatic' escape from linearity and law into the generative realm of the carnivalesque.

The Collected Works does violence to the principle of identity that is central to the 'legally binding' project of 'connecting, beyond any reasonable doubt, the doer with the deed' (Tyler 264). When a descrip-tion in the poem is given from two perspectives, both apparently Billy's, Dennis Cooley asks, 'How can Billy know what he doesn't know, be privileged with two visions?' ('"I am here"' 225). One answer is that Billy is not 'at one with himself'; he always has an alibi. His eye-witness/I-witness account is dubious indeed, and the coher-ence of the lyric I itself comes under suspicion. The redefinition of the 'self' as a discursive construct that is contextually framed and reframed is both enacted and thematized in *The Collected Works*. In order to avoid the law, Billy says, 'All I had to do was ride off in the opposite direction' (81). And that is exactly what 'he' (the pronoun itself becomes equivocal) does, since the documents in *The Collected Works* both conflict with each other and gesture 'outward' to other intertextual sources. Françoise Gaillard comments that opposed to the traditional logic of identity is a 'logic of juxtaposition,' which actually fosters such conflict: 'Here there is no 'right place' of meaning, simply an infinite number of positions no sooner occupied than abandoned. Every act of judgement takes on a shifting, fluctuating, unstable form.

This general indecision entails the destruction of the monadic subject' (145). Patrick Garret, it might be noted in this regard, says that Billy 'could never remain in one position more than five minutes' (44). The documents that compose him in the poem are similarly subject to the movement of texts that is citation.

In film, if all the images projected on the screen are identical, the effect is stasis, a 'freeze frame.' The juxtapositional logic of *The Collected Works* is first suggested by the volume's cover, which displays a single frame from Eadweard Muybridge's photographic motion studies, which, using a succession of still photos, each of which was taken at a slightly different moment and showed a slightly different positioning, attempted to represent the movement of animals. The differential positioning of documents in *The Collected Works* ensures that recuperation to stasis or 'arrested' movement is not possible.

Indeed, in several places the pronoun 'I,' an at least theoretical locus of identity, is, like the photographs of Billy, omitted altogether, as if in recognition that he escapes the integration it seems to signify. In one section, the poem introduces Billy in such a way as to 'burlesque' the 'confessional' form – 'confessional' both as a revealing autobiography and as a criminal's admission to his crimes:

> Up with the curtain
> down with your pants
> William Bonney
> is going to dance. (63)

The confessional form is upended: the *audience* is asked to 'expose' themselves in their roles as producers rather than passive consumers of Billy's character. Billy's address to the audience significantly skips over the pronoun that would pin him down: 'Hlo folks – 'd liketa sing my song about the lady Miss A D ...' (64). Further, when Billy's lover Angie attempts an unusual sexual position at the Chisum home, this 'indecisive' dialogue occurs: 'Come on Angie I'm drunk 'm not a trapeze artist. Yes you are. No' (68). As the exchange implies, 'Billy' moves (citationally) in the poem from position to position. Finally, the absent 'I' is equated with a dartboard, literally a field of play that again invokes 'audience participation': 'Am the dartboard / for your midnight blood' (85). In the same poem, an attempted representation elliptically/textually disintegrates before the reader's eyes: 'a pencil harnessing my face / goes stumbling into dots' (85).

Billy describes himself as 'locked inside my sensitive skin' (77), but even that boundary breaks down. Just as Billy cannot be located linguistically as a unified entity, and is formally disintegrated through the fragmentary form of his collected works, so he is physically 'opened up' to the outside. Even the human frame does not contain him. Susan MacFarlane's comment on Ondaatje's *Coming Through Slaughter* is equally true of *The Collected Works*: 'Violence is ubiquitous, permeating the book at all levels' (73). It is both a prominent structural feature and present in images and denotation (MacFarlane 73): in citing, violence / inciting violence. In *The Collected Works*, Pat Garrett's bullet enters Billy in a poem:

> leaving skin in a puff
> behind and the slow
> as if fire pours out
> red grey brain the hair slow
> startled by it all pour. (73)

This what Bakhtin would call a carnivalesque 'grotesque image' in which bodily process seems to swallow the world and be swallowed by it: a body transgresses its body (*Rabelais* 317), much as textual processes might be said to exceed the boundaries of the supposedly 'closed' document. As Nancy Glazener puts it, 'carnivalesque literary form (the grotesque rejoining of separated and transformed categories) and content (the semantic elaboration of biology) can be understood as inextricable and vital protests against the specious separation of form from content, body from meaning' (116). The effect of such a brutal carnivalesque violation in *The Collected Works* is not what one might think. The game is not up: the shooting described above is not the end of either Billy the Kid or *The Collected Works of Billy the Kid*. When Billy is asked what happens after you die, he replies, 'I guess they'll just put you in a box and you will stay there forever' (83). If that guess is right, a coffin becomes the ultimate frame-up, the final case against him, but *The Collected Works* is resistant to such conclusions. To paraphrase Robert Kroetsch, it resists endings, violently ('The Exploding Porcupine' 57).

It is no wonder then, in light of all this inconclusive evidence, that deputy John W. Poe has last-minute doubts about the man Garrett shot. *The Collected Works* quotes his version, taken from an account written by Poe in 1919, of an exchange that takes place after the shooting:

> *'It was the Kid who came in there on to me,' Garrett told Poe, 'and I think I got him.'*

'Pat,' replied Poe, 'I believe you have killed the wrong man.'
'I'm sure it was the Kid,' responded Garrett, 'for I knew his voice and
could not have been mistaken.' (103)

Using the methods of the documentary-collage, *The Collected Works*
intertextually multiplies and scatters single voice. It depends on the
apprehended Billy *always* being the 'wrong man.' In his article 'Ondaatje's Mechanical Boy: Portrait of the Artist as Photographer,' T.D.
MacLulich states that 'Billy is simply *there*, his existence a fact to be
neutrally recorded by the author' (116). I would maintain the opposite
case: that Billy is *never* simply there, that his recording in both past
and present documents is never neutral, composed as it is by both
acknowledged and unacknowledged pre-texts.

Terry Gilliam's 'science-fiction' film *Brazil* provides a suggestive
analogy for the docudramatic process of *The Collected Works*.[8] The
film's hero, Buttle, is a renegade (or 'outlaw') heating engineer who
subverts the department system by 'freelancing.' In one of *Brazil*'s
closing sequences, Buttle finally escapes the government representa-
tives who pursue him. As he walks calmly down a city street, the
wind stirs stray pieces of paper around his feet. Gradually, as the
number of papers increases, the wind picks up and blows them
against his body. He can't remove them. As more and more papers
stick he is completely covered; he becomes a paper mummy. Finally,
Buttle falls struggling to the ground. A friend rushes to help him, but
as he begins to pull the papers off he discovers only more papers.
Nothing lies beneath them. The papers disperse. There is, one might
say, no Buttle, only re-Buttle. Like Buttle, Billy the Kid is produced as
a body of texts; he becomes documentary material. Ondaatje's 'documentary history,' to its credit, leaves something to be desired: Billy the
Kid remains ... WANTED.

'The collage in motion':[1] Staging the Document in Reaney's *Sticks and Stones*

So intense was the curiosity of the time that the files of the London FREE PRESS for the crucial year of 1880 have completely disappeared, except for bits and pieces in old scrapbooks. So, apparently, had the pamphlet the FREE PRESS published some weeks after the murders; it contained unique interviews with friends of both the Donnellys and their enemies. Again, all copies seemed to have been 'read to pieces.'

James Reaney, Foreword to *The Donnelly Tragedy*

James Reaney's Donnelly plays – *Sticks and Stones*, *The St. Nicholas Hotel*, and *Handcuffs* – tell the historical story of a family who emigrated from Ireland to Canada in 1844, and who were, ultimately, murdered by a vigilante committee of their neighbours in the Township of Biddulph, Ontario, in 1880. The Donnelly trilogy is the result of the dramatist's extended research on the subject of the family and their fate. 'The microfilm as muse,' Gerald Parker wryly observes of Reaney's role as folk historian in the trilogy ('History' 154). In Reaney's own words, the story led him 'through an enormous, 8 year swamp of legal MSS, newspaper microfilm, archival vigils and the like' ('A Letter' 4). Not only is historical research an inspiration to the playwright in these plays, however, nor the role of documentation limited to background research or evidence of historical authenticity; documents are the very ground of the presentation of the Donnelly plays, and self-conscious reinterpretation of those documents is fundamental to their reception.

Sticks and Stones, in particular, establishes for the trilogy a specifically 'documentary' frame of reference. That is, the play theatrically
displays – and in doing so frequently disrupts – the documentary
'frames' that incriminate the Donnelly family; the texts that underwrite
the central characters' position in history and society become a key
element in the situation of the Donnellys in the play's theatrical discourse. *The Collected Works of Billy the Kid* foregrounds a figurative
dramatization of historical language that opens it up to multiple
voices, and emphasizes the importance of their discursive 'setting'; in
Sticks and Stones, this foregrounding becomes a literal gesture of
staging. In *The Ledger*, 'setting' was accentuated by the pre-texts of
geography and history. Reaney, similarly, indicates the retention of
documentary traces in *Sticks and Stones* when he addresses this statement to his audience in its introduction: 'When you immerse yourself
in this play, you may find that your experience matches my own when
I immersed myself some eight years ago in documents which had lain
for years and years in the attics of two local courthouses: after a while
I couldn't stop thinking about them' (*The Donnellys* 11). The legal
setting of Reaney's research activity is significant, since his plays
appeal a conventional verdict, or 'true saying,' on the Donnelly story
as presented, for example, in contemporary newspaper reports or
Thomas Kelley's apparently documentary work *The Black Donnellys*,
which Richard Stingle calls a 'gothic novel' (11). Like *The Collected
Works of Billy the Kid*, *Sticks and Stones* re-tries its evidence by re-contextualizing it in the discursive setting of the literary text. Each uses
a version of 'dramatic' techniques; in *Sticks and Stones*, documentary
citation becomes an explicitly theatrical gesture. Viewing the play is
therefore an extension of the research activity that involves the audience in a dramatic re-searching – a literal rereading – of historical
materials: as Derek Paget puts it, 'Encountering the document in a
theatrical setting defamiliarises the document – it becomes necessary
for the audience to adopt an attitude to the documentary material itself
in order to "read" the drama' (15). The representation of history is not
simply a theme in *Sticks and Stones*; historical documentation is also an
integral element of the play's structure, as well as its verbal, kinesic,
and scenographic codes.[2]

Sticks and Stones thus participates in and extends theoretically
elements of the European and North American tradition of documentary theatre. Gregory Mason defines documentary theatre simply as
drama that 'presents and re-enacts records from history' (263). 'Unlike
traditional drama,' he continues, 'it is not founded on a freely imag-

ined plot' (263). While Mason's description is at first glance broad enough to include most historically inspired dramatic narratives, he goes on to make it clear that the documentary play may be linked, not simply to the events, but also to the records of history. For example, he traces the European roots of documentary theatre to Irwin Piscator's production of *Trotz Alleden* in 1925, a play in which the author's insistence on thoroughly authenticating his historical plot results in a dramatic montage of documentary materials (ibid.). Alan Filewod credits Piscator with establishing the documentary theatre as 'a genre of performance that presents actuality on the stage and in the process authenticates that actuality' (16). Somewhat paradoxically, Piscator's plays often present documentary materials to authenticate a represented reality and, by that very strategy, eschew the conventions of dramatic illusionism. This, significantly, is one way Piscator attempts to further a 'theatre of involvement through documents' (Mason 267). Derek Paget identifies the quotation of printed documentary sources via slide projection, placards, or speeches as one aspect of the 'collision montage' technique of the Piscatorian tradition (61).

The American Federal Theatre Project 'Living Newspaper' productions of the 1930s also envisaged the drama as an authenticating agent, capable of representing and thus affirming what the instruments of mainstream journalism might avoid: the local, the anecdotal, the populist. Although their dramatization of current historical problems often used typical rather than strictly factual representations, their loudspeaker interruption of dramatic action with historical and current documentary information and questions posed directly to the audience (Mason 265) is in sympathy with Piscator's anti-illusionism, and anticipates later attempts – among them the Donnelly plays – to disengage audience members from coherent narrative in order to encourage them to consider their position in relation to both historical and stage representation.

Mason asserts that the demise of the Federal Theatre Project in 1939 ended documentary drama as a concerted movement until the 1960s, when a strong resurgence – and a significant shift in attitude – took place (265). The documentary drama becomes, in the 1960s, not just a method of authenticating a certain reality, but of questioning supposed realities and the ways they are constructed. Mason notes in particular plays in which 'documentary information is presented in a deliberately obtrusive manner, calling attention to the documents themselves as much as to the information they convey ... The *matter* of the documents here serves to confirm certain facts, but the *manner* in which they are presented sharply challenges the notion of documentary objectivity' (270). The document, in other words, no longer necessarily functions merely as invisible background material, or as evidence of events accepted as real, but may be foregrounded and placed at issue. This kind of documentary play does not just attack the notion of 'art' as a region sealed off from history (Zilliacus 225), but calls into doubt 'both the fictional nature of drama and the factual nature of information' (Paget 15). In doing so, it also challenges the notion of historical representation as sealed off from internal conflicts.[3] As Mason suggests, focus on the documents themselves in the drama often functions to interrogate the way we receive reality through its representations (274-5).

Interrogation is a key term, since one of the central elements of the documentary drama of the 1960s and 1970s is the popularity of the 'tribunal play,' centred on the trial of a suspect and the questioning of witnesses. Dorothy Knowles links this development with what she calls (translating Jean Vilar's *pièce-document*) the 'document-play,' which presents a dramatized version of real trial transcripts (79). 'In these limiting cases [Vilar's *Le Dossier Oppenheimer* and Peter Weiss's *The Investigation*],' she writes, '"document" and "play" are identical with each other, because the exact record of the event (in both cases a hearing) is in itself dramatic' (79). To say that the record of the event is inherently dramatic is potentially to say *both* that the record is loosely dramatic in structure (since witnesses give evidence, and the final outcome is delayed) and subject (since the case is usually a controversial one), but also – and here, most important – that the document can dramatize the potential for multivoiced elements within the recording of history itself.

Knowles's examples, *Le Dossier Oppenheimer* (1964) and *The Investigation* (1965), are prime instances of the tribunal/document-play. It is worth mentioning here that Weiss used two terms for *The Investigation* that will be appropriate to this discussion of Reaney's work: he called the play a 'dialectical *collage*' and, significantly mixing generic standards, a 'poem/trial report' (cited in Knowles 84). Plays like Heinar Kipphardt's *In the Manner of J. Robert Oppenheimer* (1964), Michael Hastings's *Lee Harvey Oswald* (1966), Donald Freed's *Inquest* (1970), and, in Canada, John Coulter's *The Trial of Louis Riel* (1968) and Toronto Workshop Productions's *Chicago '70* all employ, to one extent or another, the trial as subject and formal structure. They also use excerpts from trial transcripts to deal with a historical problem or a problematized history.

Sticks and Stones is perhaps not, strictly speaking, a tribunal play, but it borrows from the latter its focus on the presentation and testing of evidence, and, as James Stewart Reaney observes, it draws on the formal structure of the trial in its inclusion of perspectival testimony: 'The language of the play, with its numerous quotations and vigorous replies, reflects a society which has turned everyone into witnesses. All the characters must clear their names somehow, and repeat the truth as they know it' (71). This approach might be associated with Mikhail Bakhtin's characterization of the methods of the Socratic dialogue, in particular the devices of syncrisis, 'the juxtaposing of various discourse-opinions on an object,' and anacrisis, 'a means for eliciting and provoking the words of one's interlocutor, forcing him to express his opinion and express it thoroughly' (*Problems* 110). According to Bakhtin, 'Syncrisis and anacrisis dialogize thought, they carry it into the open, turn it into a rejoinder, attach it to dialogic intercourse among people' (ibid. 111).

While Bakhtin himself argues that the theatre is resistant to dialogism (ibid. 188), Graham Pechey's article 'On the Borders of Bakhtin: Dialogization, Decolonization' demonstrates the extent to which Bakhtin's own theories of dialogism 'rescue' certain approaches to drama (Brecht's in particular) from the 'containing margins and parentheses of Bakhtin's writing' (76). Such approaches, Pechey argues, extend the dialogism of spoken signification to theatrical production, and especially to elements of gesture (76). *Sticks and Stones* accomplishes precisely this effect. In it, the juxtaposition of 'discourse-opinions' approaches the visual-arts model of collage, evoking written texts, and turning their apparently monologic thought into both a dramatic scene and a scene of drama.[4]

The simultaneously speculative and spectacular presentation of perspectives is most obviously thematized in *Sticks and Stones* when Thomas Cassleigh is asked about those who witnessed the murder of the Englishman Brimmacombe. Cassleigh's reply involves a dramatic 'see-sawing' structure of perspectival exchange: 'They saw him. They saw him seeing them seeing him and they saw me seeing him seeing them seeing them seeing him' (35). Reaney's play does not use a simple theatrical distinction between witness and event, subject and object; no perspective can be expressed without 'telling on' itself and others.

The audience, by extension, is also a witness implicated in what transpires on-stage. Spatially, it is included in a playing space that violates the traditional 'box-set-with-lighting' concept of the stage

(Anthony 156) and surrounds the audience with its events (Reaney, 'A Letter' 3). Like Cassleigh, the audience is capable not only of seeing events, but of seeing events being seen and, potentially, of seeing themselves in their positions as spectators, as situated witnesses to, and participants in, the (re)presentation of the events in the play. Not only has the audience, at the point of Cassleigh's speech, heard various descriptions of the murder (32–5); it has also witnessed a dramatic re-enactment of the crime in which the actor playing Brimmacombe has drawn attention, not just to the audience's position as observer, but to a position of responsibility: the stage directions indicate that the question that opens the scene, Brimmacombe's 'What have I done to you, man?' is addressed *directly to us* (32). Self-conscious *re*-enactment, rather than illusionist 'acting,' is a frequent device in *Sticks and Stones*. It establishes a sense of interpretive repetition or embedded mediation of events.

This particular 'return to the scene of the crime' (with an emphasis on *scene/seen* as both theatrical presentation and visual reception) is itself verbally situated within a framing 'confessional' structure instigated by the Friar's questioning. It evokes, therefore, potential judgments, both legal and religious. Another comment by Cassleigh indicates the importance of *written* evidence in the decision-making process. It also refers to the way the strategic suppression of the latter can delay – if not actually alter – a verdict. Questioned by the Friar on the fact that no one has been brought to justice for the murder of Brimmacombe, Cassleigh replies that 'they've been and tried me for it, but I've got a friend who stole the witness papers from the courthouse and I believe they can't try me again till they get them all sworn and copied out again' (35). In a sense, Reaney's retrieval in *Sticks and Stones* of elements of the Donnelly story – in particular his contextualized quotation or 'recopying' of documentation – returns certain suppressed evidence to the courthouse by way of the playhouse, so that the trial of the historical story, if not the historical trial itself, may resume.

In his book *Collective Encounters*, Alan Filewod locates the development of Canadian documentary theatre at the intersection of a tradition of Canadian didactic historical drama, the nationalist alternative theatre of the 1970s, and the international tradition of documentary theatre originating in Europe in the 1920s (5). Filewod examines plays by Theatre Passe Muraille, Toronto Workshop Productions, Regina's Globe Theatre, Saskatoon's 25th St. Theatre, the Mummers Troupe of

Newfoundland, and Edmonton's Catalyst Theatre. He concludes that the most important common features of Canadian manifestations of the documentary drama are their emphasis on collective creation (group collaboration involving the contribution of actors to researching and writing the play as a whole, and especially their own roles) and the transformation of historical or local community experience into drama (185).

Filewod sees collective creation as 'a critique of the traditional role of the dramatic author' (x); his second characteristic may be seen in a similar light, since the contributions of historical research and community experience to some extent undermine the dramatist's traditional position as originating, imaginative subject, just as Kroetsch's sense of 'complicity' with his family in 'their poem of the ledger' did in *The Ledger*. Filewod sees collective creation in the larger context of an international movement to question hierarchies of theatrical production (22). Derek Paget's discussion of the English Theatre Workshop's production of *Oh what a lovely war* affirms this movement, and sets it off against what Foucault calls 'the privileged moment of *individualization*' that constitutes the emergence of the idea of the 'author' (Foucault cited in Paget 67).

The Donnelly trilogy employs and alters elements of collective creation. Certainly its use of a collage technique incorporating 'outside' writings like census records, maps, newspaper headlines, and legal records extends the role of contributing 'author' to agents distant from the plays' twentieth-century composition. In a more conventional sense of the term, the trilogy was developed to some extent by collective creation in a workshop situation by a group of actors and members of the community in Halifax in 1973. Patricia Ludwick, an actor-participant, describes the process as a curious mixture of chaos and authoritative writer-directed activity that takes place in a region where the distinctions between 'stage' and 'life' get blurred:

> From ten to noon, a sort of super-kindergarten convenes: toddlers, teenagers, cousins, neighbours, mothers, and brothers, even a small gang of twelve-year-old lads who can break into any building in the area, and we bleary-eyed actors, led by a self-professed madman, a poet, a scholar, a decidedly ungentle man named Reaney ... This is will-ye, nil-ye ensemble acting; we are part of a pattern that our muscles remember before our minds catch up. It is tribal ritual ... Afternoons, it's the older family members. Anyone who turns up gets cast,

and everyone in the room is onstage. We are following the
words on closely-typed pages of purple ditto ink, Reaney in
the midst of it, choreographing horse-races, logging bees ...
Don't think; Reaney has done all the thinking for you: take a
deep breath and leave your worries behind. (131–2)

Perhaps equally significant, the 1975 national tour of the trilogy by the
NDWT company conducted at each of its stops theatre workshops for
adults and children, meant to develop a sense of theatre's local, everyday origins and a feeling that participation both as audience and actors
is a creative experience accessible to all (see 14 Barrels from Sea to Sea).
These 'hit-and-run' workshops, according to Ludwick, give the actors
'an immediate connection with each particular community' and 'allow
the local participants to expand their understanding of their surroundings and of theatre' (136). This approach puts both local participation
and 'ready-made' materials that evoke a community at the service of
collective creation, in much the same way The Ledger offers its readers
local materials and encourages them to participate as collaborators in
the poem's account. A teaching kit that included a chronology of the
Donnelly story, transcriptions of legal documents, and directions for
making cat's cradles and spinning tops, was distributed to public
schools on the play's tour route (Reaney, 14 Barrels 35–6), and the
'workshop routines' produced by actors and playwright were designed
'to show you how you can write poetry out of found material' (ibid.
37).

   This approach to 'collective creation,' therefore, while it does not
conform exactly to Filewod's demands, has the advantage of including
the audience/community in its scope. Reaney is drawing the attention
of his audiences to their own abilities as readers of the dramatic
potential of the 'found,' as he does in the introduction to Names and
Nicknames, where he suggests to children 'plays they could make up
from gum cards, telephone directories, even arithmetic books!' (5). In
so doing Reaney is indicating that the tradition of the found poem –
the 'strong' poetic re-reading of ostensibly prosaic materials – may be
translated into an overtly theatrical context.

   Perhaps most important to Filewod's argument regarding collective
creation is his assertion that this compositional technique rewrites – or
rather un-writes – the 'literary' view of the theatre, making the documentary play into an 'atextual' (x) 'genre of performance' (185). According to Filewod, 'literary drama' is antithetical to documentary theatre
(viii). Sticks and Stones, however, demonstrates that Filewod's opposi-

tion of 'literary drama' with a documentary drama of 'production' at the very least overstates the case. In an interview with Jean McKay, Keith Turnbull was asked to comment on what differentiated the NDWT from the 25th St. Theatre or Theatre Passe Muraille. He answered: 'I've done a number of shows that are collective creations. But even so, the writing process is much more important to us ... I guess it's that we believe in language. Actually, one of the things that we discussed when we were starting the company was not defining our mandate as Canadian, but defining our mandate as plays of language' (J. McKay 152). Turnbull has violated two of Filewod's central defining characteristics for the documentary drama: he asserts the primacy, not just of the playscript, but of scripted language in general, and he does so at the expense of the primacy of the geographically local subject. As Diane Bessai's article 'Documentary into Drama: Reaney's Donnelly Trilogy' demonstrates, however, the plays do belong in the context of Canadian documentary theatre; they are an example of 'the way in which the documentary trend and its related theatricality also moves in serious literary directions' (186). In fact, the plays tend to erode simple oppositions between literature and document, and, for that matter, theatre and document. *Written language itself* is localized in the plays, since documents that determine local and historical experience are theatrically performed. In this, Reaney's project is similar to Kroetsch's in *The Ledger*. Reaney himself responds to 'those critics who yell about my being too literary' with, 'if it's just a long over-rich poem how come the words breed all these foot and body movements?' ('A Letter' 6). As Reaney implies, the written text is a 'performance' text too; in his drama of documentary-collage, theatricality and textuality are intimately connected.

In *The Donnellys*, theatre becomes a space of intersecting texts. This is literally true of the stage surface, on which historical voices are self-consciously 'scripted.' A review of the NDWT production noted that 'the back and sides of the stage are covered with a brown canvas upon which legends, dates and other graffiti have been written with what appears to be white chalk,'[5] and Reaney recalls 'chalking scores of names on the sets ... not only Roman line names, but also things that historical people had actually said, or that the old people interviewed in the area had actually told me of their memories about the Donnellys' (*14 Barrels* 23). The language of history is 'staged'; it becomes an element of the play's theatrical setting and action.

Sticks and Stones is, moreover, concerned with the processes involved in representing theatrical and geographical space. The epigraph to its playscript, for example, is taken from a speech by Mrs Donnelly: 'Now I've reached the borders of Biddulph' (12). This statement draws attention to the way the play evokes a local setting: as *Sticks and Stones* begins, its audience is, in one sense, transported in place and time into Biddulph Township in the nineteenth century. The epigraph also points to the likelihood that such classic realist 'transportation' may not be possible, since the borders of Biddulph are self-consciously drawn and redrawn by this play of texts. Borders are the places where fictional divisions are represented, and often violated. Like *The Ledger*, *Sticks and Stones* elaborately sets its scene by using the map as both a literal document and a representation of the inscription of social and historical space. In so doing, it challenges the borders between cartographic, historical, and theatrical representation.

The map becomes a kind of found document, set in the larger 'poetic' context of the play. As Stephen Bann comments, 'Perhaps it is essentially within a poetic tradition, that the map is capable of display-ing a richness of significance over and beyond its status as sign, when it becomes (so to speak) a vehicle for contemplation' (508). While *Sticks and Stones* provides a context for the map, the map itself becomes the historical, geographical, and *graphic* setting for the play. For example, when the young Will Donnelly asks his mother about the names that have followed the family across the ocean from Ireland to Canada, a silhouette map of Ireland appears on the back stage wall, *'as if made of forest branches and leaves'* (15, stage direction). 'Nature' itself becomes part of documentary processes of representation. The map functions as a backdrop that provides a geographical context for a re-enacted incident set in Ireland, the burning of the Sheas' house. The act of violence is motivated, Mrs Donnelly tells us in her narration, by the Sheas' refusal to join the Whitefoot society in its persecution of Protes-tant landlords. Gerald Parker comments of this sequence that 'original document and theatrical image ... combine to enforce upon us both the particularities of time, place and event, and, more importantly, the human drama within the assortment of "facts" which results from the determined shaping of documentary material, and its *re*-discovery and transformation through the art-act' ('History' 158). In this sequence, dramatic incident and document become one: the fire makes the shadows of the arsonists *'grow into the branch map of Ireland'* (16, stage direction). Political violence is represented as part of the (represented) landscape of Ireland.

And the (represented) landscape of Ireland becomes part of the Canadian setting of the play, a visual layering that anticipates the re-staging of Irish political conflicts in Biddulph. Because it looks like branches and leaves, the map is also integrated into the forest setting of Will and Mrs Donnelly's conversation, a conversation about the retention of Irish names and politics in the new world. The shadow map later *'shows Ireland drifting away'* (19, stage direction), and is replaced by silhouettes of *'the coasts of Iceland, Greenland, Newfoundland, the River, Lake Ontario, Hamilton, the province of Upper Canada where it comes to rest'* (21, stage direction). Later still, an early map of Biddulph itself appears high on the back stage wall, a map on which is shown *'the net of concessions, roads, farms with owners' names on them and a feeling that we have come from Ireland to a closer look at what is happening'* (23, stage direction).

That 'closer' look, however, is also a 'farther' one, since 'what is happening' bears the traces of the Irish text, the dual perspective effected by the back stage wall / on-stage interaction. The farmers' names that appear on the Catholic Roman Line of the map of Biddulph recall ancient religious conflicts. On-stage, the players physically re-present the line on the map, creating a simultaneously political and formal alignment. Map-making becomes a corporate physical gesture that defines social as well as geographical space. The characters chant their names in a manner the stage directions indicate evokes a kind of double-saying: they speak their names *'with a crouch, and a secret meaning, since most of them are Protestant misunderstandings for Gaelic names'* (28, stage direction). A reinscription of the Irish historical landscape in Canada is represented by this doubled vocal 'labelling' of the stage-map.

Such reinscription is, as G.N.G. Clarke describes the map, 'a verbal pattern through which culture speaks itself *onto* the land; renaming as it wipes clean one history and rewrites, as it renames, its own history onto the surface of the map (and land)' (456). Mapping involves, therefore, not simply the naming of a nameless landscape, but the silencing of previous voices. In *Sticks and Stones* the double-lined opposition between Protestants and Catholics on the stage and map of Biddulph, for example, at one point breaks down to reveal the trace of just such a past that has been written over, or obliterated. The chorus contains one black man, who after the recitation of the names of the region's Irish 'pioneers' asks about the area's previous inhabitants:

What about the Mescoes	& the Washingtons
Taylors	Runcimans
Delkeys	& the Bells. (26)

A re-enacted episode then describes the violent expulsion of black
settlers, to make way for a railway line ... and the Irish (26). This
incident parallels the 'arrivals and departures' section of Kroetsch's
The Ledger, in which the debit-credit census-taking of the poem acknowledges the imposition of European culture on both 'the pristine
forest' and 'Indians if any.'

In *Sticks and Stones*, George Stub and his supporters, whom the play
has portrayed in the act of burning the Negro barns, recite the attor-
ney-general's proclamation regarding the crime, a document that concludes, 'And whereas there is reason to believe that the said fire was
not caused by accident, but was the act of Incendiaries at present
unknown' (26). This reading allows the emergence of an ironic double
voice that both demonstrates Protestant Stub's traditional position as
a historically and legally authoritative speaker, and allows the audience to reassess the authorized version of history Stub and his gang
offer. The landscape, we learn, is a *stratigraphy* of historical stories.

Mapping may seem to articulate the immigrant's myth of arrival in
a 'new' world, but the map not only shapes history; it is determined
by it. William Boelhower writes that the culture of the map is
America's precognition: 'the map needed to have already interpreted
in order to be able to interpret the new continent. At the centre of the
map is not geography *in se* but the eye of the cartographer' (479). The
interaction between stage action (including dialogue), and the mapped
voyage from Ireland to the 'new world' in *Sticks and Stones* underscores this premise. Another incident reiterates it. Mrs Donnelly asserts
the newness of the new world in this speech, addressed to Will: 'We're
where *you* were born – not an old country, but a new country these
Canadas' (20). A choric response, however, undermines her speech.
When Mrs Donnelly affirms her determination to remain in the new
world – 'Here we stay' – the chorus contrapuntally completes her
statement with 'In Ireland,' drawing attention to the discursive 'setting,' and thus blurring the strictly geographical distinction between
'here' and 'there' (21). Later, the chorus repeats 'Ireland' (21) forming,
according to the stage directions, a vocal undercurrent *'just barely there,
but there'* (21). As Diane Bessai puts it, 'psychically, Ireland is never
very far away' (199).

Boelhower encourages us 'to study the map not so much as a representation of space but as a space of representation' (479). Reaney extends this premise by making theatrical space a space of representation, a locus self-consciously constructed through discursive/geographical mapping. Examining a posted notice, Mrs Donnelly warns her husband that their landlord is planning to declare them squatters and to sell their land. As he reads the document, her own colloquial, Irish-accented voice is, significantly, 'trespassed on' by its legal language: 'Oh, did you know this now, Mr Donnelly. There are now again many people going about the country in search of Improved Lands, occupied by Squatters with the intention of' (24). The chorus again completes her speech with 'Purchasing over their heads,' and Mr Donnelly responds, 'Over my head is under my feet' (24). Behind Mr Donnelly, literally over his head, is the land-grant map of Biddulph.[6] His speech, therefore, may be seen as pointing to such parallel dialectics of figure and ground as those between abstract document and the Donnellys' concrete existence, Biddulph map and theatrically represented landscape, backdrop and stage space. When another document, the summons ejecting Donnelly from half of his property, is later read, a line of stones represents its enforcement by redefining the playing area, which, from that point on, is cut in half (43, stage direction). In a statement that relates documentation to the broader mythical folkloric context of the Barley Corn Ballad, Mr Donnelly remarks that his wheat 'was harvested by a piece of paper' (43).

Sticks and Stones re-enacts the geographical survey of the township that lays down the boundaries of the Donnelly farm prior to their arrival. This incident is historical in relation to the main action of the play; it also makes the playing space a space of historical inscription, literally laying the groundwork for future conflicts. The incident further emphasizes the map's role as 'a text of *possession*' (G.N.G. Clarke 455), and attributes a human executor to the historically embedded *process* of representation, whose product then appears in the form of the map of Biddulph (22–3). Ironically, the re-enacted surveyor episode is itself a re-enactment of the very kind of measurement and standardization accomplished by the English Ordnance Survey of Ireland authorized in 1824, a survey that was a central contributor to the political situation that probably led the Donnellys to leave Ireland in the first place (see Hamer).

When the surveyor's assistant asks about the future inhabitants of the lot he and the surveyor have defined, the latter anticipates the 'lot' or fate of the region as a whole: 'Oh, Paddy will fight the coloured folks and drive them out if he can. Then he'll fight his Paddy neigh-

bours and then he'll fight himself and then he'll move on somewhere
else and repeat the process' (22). The surveyor attributes the disputes
he has just described in part to his own actions. Asked what the Irish
will fight about, he replies: 'Well, to begin with the way this lot is laid
out, there's a small creek enters it from the next farm, crosses it and
then flows into the next farm. Farm that is to be. It'll be the subject of
a lawsuit, quarrels about water rights, flooding – they'll love that little
creek' (22). The surveying process is one both of representation and
regulation, a process of abstraction that alters the political lay of the
land. Again, the surveyor comments on this process and situates it in
a larger epistemic context. He is not permitted to alter the shape of the
farm because 'the laws of geometry are the laws of geometry. No,
people must make do with what right angles and Euclid and we
surveyors and measurers provide for them' (22). The landscape is seen
as a kind of Cartesian/cartographic plane on which historical events
are 'plotted.'

The struggles of the Donnelly family are, in part, portrayed as
'making do' with the 'prescriptions' laid down by the surveyors and
the forces they represent. In an essay on the Southwestern Ontario
locale of the Donnelly trilogy, George Bowering makes a general
statement about 'Reaney's region' that could well be applied to the
interaction between the physical, scenic, and textual in *Sticks and
Stones*'s definition of space. 'The peculiar style of a people's gestures,'
Bowering writes, 'is as much environment as the configurations of the
ground they till or pave over. They reside on a map whose scale is
1:1' ('Reaney's Region' 5). In *Sticks and Stones*, physical gestures literally become part of an environmental sign system whose model is the
map.

In fact, the presentation of the Donnellys on stage often shows them
in three-dimensional interaction with props associated with two-
dimensional maps and mapping. For example, as the names of the
roads of Biddulph are chanted a series of ladders is raised at the back
of the stage: '*Stage-right ladder is the tallest, then they get smaller to quite
a stubby one – their shadows and patterns matching the map of Biddulph
which is a triangle*' (24–5, stage direction). Mr Donnelly then climbs
over other ladders, and his speech to the audience provides a commentary on this device: 'Yes, those are the roads of Biddulph ... you're
right to see them as ladders, yes, ladders that we crawled up and
down on and up other ladders – up to Goderich for justice, down to
London to pay our rent ... Why are the roads here rather than here?
Why do I live here rather than here? Wild lands cut by surveyors into
people – with your chain you decided that it would be here, my farm

– that people say I squatted on Concession Six Lot Eighteen – and you decided –' (25). The speech is interrupted by an altered re-staging of the earlier surveyor episode 'intercut' with Mr Donnelly's contemporary comments:

> BOY   So what's this lot, dad?
> MR DONNELLY   That's Mulowney's. At his five-acre slashing
> I should kill Farl and there
> SURVEYOR   Concession Six Lot Fifteen
> MR DONNELLY   I should be caught. Caught in the lines and
> the roads and the farms they made and the quarrels about
> fences and ditches ... (25)

In this chronologically disrupted sequence, the surveyor returns to haunt Mr Donnelly, with his physical presence in this scene, with the language of the document, and with its traces left everywhere on the land. Mr Donnelly's proleptic statement ('At his five-acre slashing I should kill Farl ...') gestures forward to future effects, and indicates a perspective that can see various temporal situations in relation to one another. Later, the Donnelly home is constructed on ladders and stood in front of the map of Biddulph; it is within the parallel lines of the represented landscape that the Donnellys must make their home. (This gesture is not unlike Kroetsch's 'layering' of the ledger on the township map in *The Ledger*). When Mr Fat attempts to pull down their house in a property dispute, it is with *chains*, the very instruments of property measurement earlier used by the surveyor (43–5).

   Other kinds of documentation are involved in mapping the historical landscape. Reaney's article 'Myths in Some Nineteenth-Century Ontario Newspapers' points to a similarity between the 'roads that meet at right angles which the surveyors' instruments had produced' and the 'triumph of order' imposed by the newspaper and its print (255). The rules of genre – be it land-grant mapping or newspaper reporting/mythmaking – construct rather than simply represent their subjects. William Butt's exhaustive survey of the historical, legendary, and literary treatment of the Donnelly story makes a convincing case for the overlap between elements of the theatre and newspaper reporting of the events surrounding the Donnelly tragedy – the fact that it has come to be seen as a tragedy at all is evidence of a dramatic filter. Newspapers, Butt submits, were 'trying to outdo the theatre by imitating its devices' (414), such as doggerel and burlesque stage Irish (417). The 1880 press, he writes, was 'a highly stylized fiction' based on a literary Gothic model (423).

The traditional historical play offers a fictional interpretation of events taken from non-fiction sources; Reaney's version of the documentary exposes fictional elements *already* at play in those sources. Newspaper reports become part of the structure of *Sticks and Stones*, but their 'objective accounts' are almost always placed in question. The masthead for the *London Inquirer* of 20 September 1844, for example, is recited as an introduction to an *ironic* restatement of its description of the Huron Assizes by Mrs Donnelly (29). The newspaper is most obviously paralleled with theatre in the play-within-a-play structure of the Medicine Show, which presents its own highly coloured version of the Donnelly family history.[7] This sequence, like the re-enacted surveyor / Mr Donnelly sequence, violates chronological as well as logical order by presenting the account of the Donnelly massacre to the Donnellys themselves, who talk back to it, paralleling the play's responsive attitude to given history. *Sticks and Stones* thereby implicates the gothicized portrayal of the Donnelly family in predetermining, and not just describing, their fate. Within a gothic system in which the Donnellys are evil incarnate, in which Mrs Donnelly disowns any son who has not committed murder, the midnight burning of their home may be seen as somehow (generically) appropriate.

The Medicine Show juxtaposes a stage Irish lampoon (47–9), doggerel (47), and newspaper headlines 'gothic,' not in type font (since they are chanted), but in their generic treatment of the subject of the Donnelly family murder:

> Five Persons Murdered by a Mob
> An Entire Household Sacrificed
> Result of a Family Feud
> Forty men engaged in the bloody work
> (47)

The Medicine Show also uses – and parodies – a strategy of visual illustration common to newspaper practice. The Showman asks his audience to view 'a few scenes which I have had painted on canvas for your historical information' (47). His use of the word 'scene' makes the canvases into a kind of epitome of his own dramatic presentation: they are *'a big wallpaper sample book, with nothing drawn on its pages'* (47, stage direction). The gesture of providing documentary 'illustration' of the 'facts,' and the empty but appealing *form* of 'historical information,' is foregrounded in this sequence.

William Butt observes that by applying conventions that were familiar and entertaining to their audience, newspapers made it easy for the reading public 'to consume this story; they make it just another consumer product' (436). Certainly the Showman's dual marketing of his show and East India Tiger Fat draws attention to the 'packaging' of the Donnelly story as consumer goods (47). 'So ...,' says the Showman, '$252.35 cents off these yokels tonight that came to see our little penniless dreadful – "The Black Donnellys." Or the Biddulph Horror' (79). It should be noted that the Medicine Show company enters the playing area, not from a distinct 'offstage' space (since there is really no such place), but from the back of the auditorium, through the theatre audience (46, stage direction), thus implicating them, along with the audience onstage, as potentially passive consumers of the kind of story the Medicine Show markets.

Such consumer packaging is part of a more general commodification of the family itself by historical processes. A poster, for example, puts a price on James Donnelly's head (54). The 'interleaving' of the letter of reprieve for Mr Donnelly, the Sheriff's expense claim for taking Donnelly to Kingston Penitentiary (68–9), and Stubs's bill for building a gallows (64–5) achieves a similar effect (Reaney says the episodes are 'interleaved' in 'A Letter' 3). Stubs, significantly, later appears as the Showman, counting his take (78). His characterization of the Donnelly family's guilt participates in the same enterprise as the Medicine Show, revealing that representations of the Donnelly story are themselves embedded in historical situations. The traditional condemnation of the Donnellys benefits this shopkeeper/politician; it is in his financial/political interest.

The recitation of the census report for 1848, presented immediately after the surveyor sequence, may also be seen as indicative of historical processes of 'enumeration' and 'account taking' that make the Donnellys a quantifiable consumable historical product. The census-taker's questions are presented in a formal structure significantly reminiscent of the catechism; both invoke larger structures of power and conventions of response (23). Mr Donnelly answers the questions posed, apparently speaking for himself and his family, but only according to a set pattern, and within a limited set of possible responses defined by the material concerns of his questioner.

Reaney points to the godlike authority of the nineteenth-century newspaper, and notes the few and feeble contemporary protests against its accounts ('Myths' 253–4). Among the forms of reader-rejection that Reaney cites is the 'type-riot,' for instance the attack that destroyed the files of William Lyon Mackenzie's *Colonial Advocate*

('Myths' 254).[8] The 'Return of Convictions' sequence in *Sticks and Stones* physically and verbally presents a court document, 'in*citing*' its own 'type riot' within it, and dispersing the physical components of the document's construction. The impression here is less one of reader-rejection than one of resistance or reassessment that sees the document as signifying a larger pattern of community conflict composed of multiple perspectives. In the stage direction, Reaney writes, *'I see the whole cast drawn up in three files to say and illustrate the three columns. The company should look like an old document which suddenly bristles with stones that hurt as they come zinging through the air'* (29). The Return of Convictions document becomes the Biddulph Riot episode. As Gerald Parker observes of this sequence, 'the documentary world is not simply echoed in the verbal duel between the two sides, it is scenically represented, and as the sequence evolves, the "old document" both inspires and *is* itself the riot' ('History' 156–7).

Narrative disordering, the multiplication of historical voices, and the use of an astonishing variety of generic conventions, or what Stan Dragland calls 'metamorphic' forms (43),[9] in *Sticks and Stones* may be seen as one way of creating a kind of carnivalistic 'riot' within traditional, monolithic, linear historical discourse. The type-riot incident, for example, carnivalistically em-bodies and dis-members the historical document. Certainly *Sticks and Stones* qualifies as the kind of multi-styled, heterovoiced, stylistically disruptive writing that Bakhtin attributes to the 'novelized genres,' which operate in opposition to an 'epic' version of the past, closed off from change and impossible to revise (*Dialogic Imagination* 17).

While the play exposes previous attempts to commodify the Donnelly story, it also participates in a project that refuses to offer narrative as consumable product. Reaney refers to his dramatic style as producing a 'multiple focus effect,' and calls attention to the influence on him of the three-ring circus, in which what determines the composition of the show involves the choice of its viewer, his focus of attention ('A Letter' 2–3). Parker points to the way the multiple-focus effect arranges the raw materials of narrative to create 'a situation wherein the audience is engaged in scene-making as much as scene watching' ('History' 154). As Derek Paget writes, the documentary play 'invites an audience to orientate itself to mater-real documents within the parameters of that audience's own subjective reality – the audience enters into a relationship with documentary material through a frame (the documentary drama)' (28). The viewer's self-consciousness about the processing of historical documentation and the construction of historical narrative via those documents allows the insertion into the play's action of a sense of dialogic 'contact with unfinished, still-evolving contemporary reality' (Bakhtin *Dialogic Imagination* 7).

Documentary materials, then, do not just interrupt an already-determined 'main narrative.' Since the Donnelly story itself is placed at issue, *Sticks and Stones* persistently resists chronological, logical, (seemingly) unmediated telling. Documents are evidence of the complex textual processes often disguised by unified narratives. If Reaney's theatre is a space of intersecting texts, then, it is clearly also a space of conflict. Mr Donnelly's challenge to the Medicine Show version of 'his' story sets up a 'provocative' model for the truth-seeking activity of the play, an interdiscursive model of dialogue not just between perspectives within the play, but also as part of its reception. It has already been suggested that this method might be compared to the Socratic method of anacrisis. The Socratic dialogue, Bakhtin observes, seeks a truth, which is not 'to be found inside the head of an individual person, [but] is born between people collectively searching for truth, in the process of their dialogic interaction' (*Problems* 110).

Indeed, in view of its dialogic method, *Sticks and Stones* might almost be labelled by the name Will dubs his coach line in *The St. Nicholas Hotel*: the Opposition Stage (102). Conflict in the play takes the form not just of the historical confrontations between the Donnellys and their neighbours, but also of the conflicts between and within differing representations of the Donnelly story's different tellings. In an interview with Geraldine Anthony, Reaney discusses the opposing versions of the tale as told by Thomas Kelley and Orlo Miller, which might be termed Gothic and sociohistorical, respectively. 'Aha,' he concludes, 'a double point of view! A mystery!' (154). Elsewhere Reaney remarks on the way he 'kept seeing all the Donnelly events in terms of two viewpoints that cross – *some tell it this way / some tell it this way*: the Donnellys were at heart decent people who were persecuted / the Donnellys were mad dogs who *had* to be destroyed. This resulted in stage movement, scene settings, speeches that form St. Patrick's Xs' ('Ten Years' 78). Kinesic, scenic, and verbal codes, in other words, literally represent a pattern of conflict: the cross. That cross may be seen as a sign of the kind of colloquial 'cross referencing' Reaney finds in nineteenth-century newspaper files in which 'people saw things, but other people saw what they saw and commented on it' ('An ABC' 4).

James Stewart Reaney expands on the pattern of the cross in the Tarragon Theatre presentation of the Donnelly plays. He writes: 'The dominant motif of the Tarragon production was the intersection of huge diagonals across the stage from the corner, back through the middle, and down the opposite corner. This symbolic movement recurs in the form of Mr. Donnelly's mark, his signature and claim to his land; as the hint of the unexpected confines of Biddulph ... and ultimately, as the St. Patrick's cross, the sign of Ireland, which the characters, in their efforts to escape or reform, only find themselves retracing and repeating' (70). As James Stewart Reaney notes, one central instance of the 'X' is Mr Donnelly's mark. That 'signature' appeared in the NDWT program (reproduced in *14 Barrels*). It also appears as one of the final images of *Sticks and Stones*, created in part through sound.[10] The 'X' is inscribed onstage when Mr Donnelly purchases a new piece of land: '*As Mr. Donnelly is holding the pen, the company makes a big sound with sticks on the floor – the sound of his pen scratching*' (88, stage direction). In this scene, Mr Donnelly stakes a *claim*, both to geographical property and discursive space. The stage, at this point, and throughout the play, may be defined as a contract, both a written document and, more generally, a locus where various points of view are brought together. Mr Donnelly's mark, however, does not certify any single perspective, nor does it by any means settle this account. Instead, it defines the documentary theatre as a place of contradictory 'signing' or signification in which the historical text plays a defining role.

CHAPTER FIVE

Log Entries:
Exploring Discursive Space
in Kearns's *Convergences*

... this is the place
you reach
    to name
remember and recite

Eli Mandel, *Out of Place*

In his Introduction to *The Writing Life*, Frank Davey asserts that one cannot fully understand the movement surrounding the Vancouver poetry magazine *Tish* during the 1960s without understanding its sense of community as a 'placing' of the individual within the cosmos, physical geography, social fabric, and language (19). When Davey elsewhere assesses Lionel Kearns's writing of the 1960s, it is Kearns's sense of involvement in the particular '"circumstantial" scene'[1] in his poems that for Davey connects him with the *Tish* group and its interest in the Black Mountain school's 'field theory' ('Lionel Kearns' 148).[2] Kearns's long poem *Convergences* reprises this early interest in place and placing, using the explorer journal as a means of rediscovering a geographical, historical, and linguistic landscape. In *Convergences*, Kearns retheorizes the Black Mountain / *Tish* emphasis on 'stance' and locality as an interactive 'communal' process of *reading* that, as Barbara Johnson puts it of another work, transforms 'the plane geometry of physical space [and, it should be added here, the Cartesian 'plotting' of historical time] into the complex transactions of discursive exchange' (279).

In Black Mountain poetics, Charles Olson's concept 'proprioception' is opposed to the straightforward notion of perception. As Warren Tallman sets forth the distinction, 'The perceptive writer sees himself in the midst of the surrounding world as object,' while 'the proprioceptive writer sees the surrounding world in the midst of himself as subject,' as, for example, did Olson, when he 'subjected himself' to Gloucester, Massachusetts, in *The Maximus Poems*, so that 'he might *incorporate* place into himself and thus become Gloucester' (Tallman 31–2). Expanding on the term 'proprioception,' Olson himself muses that 'the advantage is to "place" the thing, instead of wallowing around sort of outside ... *proprious*-ception / "one's own"-ception / the "body" itself as, by movement of its own tissues, giving the data of, depth' (*Proprioception* 1–2). This may be seen as one version of Olson's insistence on 'getting rid of the lyrical interference of the individual as ego' as part of his 'projective' poetics ('Projective Verse' 59). Frank Davey characterizes this process in Olson's poetics as an assimilation of the scientific ethos of ecology, in which 'the poet's self becomes document; his current being – his articulations, breathing, enthusiasms – a barometer of immediate process' ('Recontextualization' 126).[3]

The Tish writers' similar concern with the poet's relation to his surroundings, C.H. Gervais suggests (194), provides an accidental explanation for Dorothy Livesay's characterization of Canadian documentary poems, which, she writes, 'are subtly used to cast light on the landscape, the topography, the flora and fauna as well as on the social structure of the country' ('The Documentary Poem' 269). Gervais states that the relationship of the poet to place in Tish poetics 'is of such a nature that it allows the poet to participate and extend himself into that "place" whether it be geographical or historical' (206).

Convergences, a work Davey calls 'the most rigorously "documentary" of recent Canadian long poems, containing more than 300 lines of quotations from various records of Cook's voyage to Nootka Sound' ('Recontextualization' 130), situates itself within the *problematic* dynamics of this encounter.[4] In it, the status of distinctions between subject and object, self and other, past and present is placed at issue. Like Kroetsch's *The Ledger* and Reaney's *Sticks and Stones*, Kearns's poem points to the changing, contextual nature of place and/as discursive positioning. 'Consider that word, *circumstance*,' a self-conscious narrating voice in the poem urges readers, 'the circle in which we stand. But we never stand still' (34).[5] *Convergences* formulates its tentative approach to the 'documentary' through the use of what might here be called 'circumstantial evidence': the presentation of provisional, contextualized perspectives, including citations from written records, illustrations, historical narrative, and the contemporary narrator quoted above, who confesses to the difficulties of reading and relaying 'documentary' information and who, notably, eschews the authoritative perspective of the dis-embodied 'objective' historian as documentary 'voice-over' narrator.

The various texts that compose *Convergences* are seen as *in*scribing, rather than simply describing, places/positions in the world. 'Objective fact' is thus problematized by the various discourses that compose it. Historical and geographical place, in this scheme, is always already *dis*-placed; it is situated within a field of often conflicting, literally prescribed systems of meaning. *Convergences*, like Kogawa's *Obasan* and Marlatt's *Ana Historic*, uses the methods of the documentary-collage to advance what Marlatt would call a '"telling" telling' ('Theorizing Fiction Theory' 10), which attempts to re(ad)dress gaps in the historical record by engaging the documents that compose that record in a process of dialogue, one that implicates the 'evidence' itself in the construction of historical significance. In other words, in these poems history itself is presented as embedded in historical, cultural, and gendered ideological predispositions.

David Carroll uses the significant trope of 'grounding' to describe a kind of interrogative approach to history: 'Rather than establishing a *ground*, a critical return to history will inevitably be forced to confront not an abyss, total absence or pure groundlessness ... but the conflictual interpenetration of various series, contexts and grounds constituting any ground or process of grounding' (66). The very title of *Convergences* situates it at just such points of interpenetration. Its front-cover illustration is a reproduction of one of John Webber's 'documentary' engravings of James Cook's 1778 voyage. It sets the poem at a spatial/temporal point of convergence where two cultures intersect: the shoreline meeting of Cook's men with the Mooachaht Indians at Nootka Sound. The perspective of the etching may be identified with European explorers about to arrive on 'the scene.' In fact, a Mooachaht Indian in the lower right-hand corner of the cover appears to be visually addressing the viewer. As Lianne Moyes observes, while Webber's etchings might be used in a conventional history 'to document "how the West Coast Indians live," *Convergences* uses them to emphasize "how European history depicts how the native people live"' ('Dialogizing the Monologue' 27). The presentation of this historical event is not, therefore, simply a detached observation, but one clearly grounded in a particular historical/cultural perspective – a perspective in which the viewer of the volume's cover is implicated. The poem's description of the Mooachaht's initial recognition of the European ships on the horizon as a kind of portable landscape, 'an island moving on the sea' (10), reinforces this sense of grounding at the same time as it implies a coincident 'figurative' perception arising from another spatial/cultural position, a position literally and figuratively represented as marginal to Webber's etching: the 'looking' Mooachaht is spatially de-emphasized on the cover, and his viewpoint is not figured by it, or by the explorer's account it illustrates. The cover illustration is also the point of convergence of the etching as document and the contemporary author/reader Kearns, who re-titles ('Convergences') and re-signs ('Lionel Kearns') the etching, marking his own appropriative re-reading, a reading that attempts, if not to *fill* significant gaps in the historical narrative (a potentially presumptive act that might constitute another version of imperialism), at least to take those gaps into (its) account.

Cited illustrations are later used to reveal cultural convergence as a site of *mutual* interpretation. On opposing pages that contain the narrative description of the first European-Mooachaht contact, there are two drawings: one Webber's rendering of a Mooachaht canoe (an extension of the etching that appears on the front cover), the other presumably a Mooachaht rendering of a European ship (10–11). Cultural difference is inscribed here as both a difference in perspective, and as a disparity in the stylistic conventions of representation. Later in the poem, the contemporary narrator draws attention to the 'realism' and 'authenticity' of Webber's illustrations as an 'accurate visual representation,' not because they objectively present the truth, but because they 'give me a sense of the visual experience of the men on those ships' (36). Webber's drawings are contrasted to Mooachaht art, which 'was more sophisticated in approach, more serious in intent, though the Europeans, their appreciation numbed by their judgement, found it primitive, barbarous, crude' (36). This observation may well turn readers back to their own earlier reaction to the Mooachaht drawing in order to see that assessment as embedded in a European tradition of aesthetic judgment.

The contemporary speaker in *Convergences*, similarly, expresses an awareness of his own historicized responses to the situation he attempts to articulate. Just as the explorers' view of the coastline is determined by their European perspective, the contemporary narrator comments of his historiographic encounter, 'And I too find myself here at the edge of the continent, an expression of genes that have drifted westward through generations. I am the newcomer encountering those others who have been here all the time or have come in the other direction' (13). Subjectivity itself is both textualized and historically embedded. It is, in fact, literally 'relativized,' since, as in *The Ledger* and as we will see in Daphne Marlatt's *Ana Historic*, the individual's subjection to historical and cultural pretexts is imaged in terms of the genealogical inheritance of genetic codes. As described on the first page of *Convergences*, the 'new' arrivals at Nootka Sound are involved in a process of coding that is determined by the past, and that in turn generates the subjectivity of those who follow: 'Their genes move into positions on old chromosomal chains, composing and encoding characteristic details of following generations' (1).

Later, the genetic process is invoked again. This time it is formally associated with the inheritance of a European 'empirical' tradition, that propagates a geographical empire, founded (empirically) on its own 'knowable' experience. On one page, the left-hand column begins, 'Science and empire inspire this expedition. They chart the unknown seas and coastlines, claim in the name of the British Crown whatever they find, and gather information' (19). Language, as it is described here, is significantly empirical; in representing the environment, the explorers assert ownership. The right-hand column draws attention to the contemporary narrator's parallel attempt to interpret history, an attempt situated both geographically, and within a genealogical process of inheritance and reinscription of historical codes, which finally gestures towards future 'generations' of readers: 'The patterns persist. Moving, shifting, the repeated genotypes converge and combine in endless variety to express the unique and individual forms of the actual: persons, situations, events, institutions, cultures, states of mind. I sit on the porch listening to the sound of the creek in the evening stillness, dogs barking in the distance, and beyond that the monotonous murmur of city. As these words fall into the formal patterns of my given language ... I wonder what is happening around you as you read these words' (19). *Convergences*'s use of quoted documents stresses the importance both of 'given' codes and their 'embedded' or contextualized reception: this is an important effect of the documentary-collage. As Martha Rosler perceives, the formal gesture of citation may point to our inheritance of 'a received system of meaning, a defining practice' (80). *Convergences* both acknowledges its indebted stance in relation to inherited accounts, and undermines readings that would allow them to function simply as authoritative, empirical evidence of historical events. By fragmenting and recontextualizing documents, in effect, the poem alters its own heredity, creating recombinant genetic codes. It also displaces the 'given environment' by undermining the document's cognitive 'ownership' of the landscape. Further, it violates the boundaries of textual property, in its appropriation of the historical text, in much the same way crewman John Ledyard 'cribbed whole sections' from a fellow-traveller's journal 'and elaborated on these with his own personal testimony' (66). The volume's cover, for example, as we have seen, is not simply a representation, but the poetic 're-citation' of a representation, whose meaning is dependent both on the interplay of its internal perspectives, and on the context of its reception: it functions quite differently in its role as an element of Kearns's poem than it does as one of the illustrations to Cook's 'authorized version of the voyage' (37).

The self-conscious act of quotation, Rosler asserts, 'can be understood as confessional, betraying an anxiety about meaning in the face of the living world, a faltered confidence in straightforward expression' (80). The contemporary narrator in *Convergences*, located spatially at a desk covered in papers and temporally at a point in an as-yet-undetermined history – both places circumscribed by historical texts – explicitly confesses his discomfort with these texts: 'My desk is covered with papers that I do not want to see. What will I do with them? What will I do with all this information?' (1). When the Mooachahts are confronted with the foreign European presence, 'no one knows which voices to listen to. No one knows which rules apply in a case like this' (11). The contemporary narrator – and the reader of *Convergences* – is similarly confronted with the various voices and sign-systems represented in the poem, and a choice of which conventions or rules of reading through which to interpret them. He may therefore engage in a kind of conversation with the past, a conversation that stands in marked contrast to conventional history's 'monological idea of a unified authorial voice providing an ideally exhaustive and definitive (total) account of a fully mastered object of knowledge' (LaCapra, *History & Criticism* 36).

Citation, as Rosler remarks, 'can reveal the thoroughly social nature of our lives' (80). *Convergences*, then, does not just depict a place of social interaction – the shore at Nootka Sound – it *is* a place of social interaction. Poem and land are seen as parallel loci whose very identities are dependent on verbal relations. The name 'Nootka Sound' might itself be seen as an emblem of this parallel. 'Nootka,' readers learn, is a name marked by the process of transmission and reception;

its naming is historicized in the poem. In an inaccurate translation, a displacement of language between cultures, 'the English hear the Mooachahts repeating *nu-tka-sshi'a, nu-tka-sshi'a*, meaning, *Come around the point into the cove.* They hear the sequence of syllables and think it is the name of this place' (16). When the explorers record the name on their charts, they perpetuate their misapprehension.

'Sound' is a geographical term meaning a passage of water connecting two seas. It is also an utterance, or the production of an utterance. The first page of the poem describes the arrival of 'newcomers' by asserting that 'their talking and groaning and shouting augment the *volume of sound* echoing and fading here in this place' (1, emphasis added). While presence and place are clearly important to the 'passage' (both as quoted text and as geographical space), precisely who is arriving and where remains remarkably indeterminate. As Lianne Moyes points out, in *Convergences*, 'temporal and spatial indicators such as 'here,' 'in this place,' and 'now' are vague and shifting; their point of reference lies in the ever-changing context of enunciation' ('Dialogizing the Monologue' 22). Such ambivalent indicators or 'shifters' play an important role in equivocally situating the legendary subject of *The Collected Works of Billy the Kid*. The passage from *Convergences* quoted above is similarly equivocal: it could conceivably be read as describing the European arrival at Nootka Sound, the European sighting of the Mooachahts, each reader's arrival in the contextual space of the poem as history, and perhaps most appropriately for this argument, all three (or more) together, in which case, context itself is placed at issue.

If 'here,' 'in this place' is potentially the present reading of *Convergences*, where the word is defined by the context of its enunciation, then the poem may well be labelled 'a volume of sound' – both because it is a book that 'contains' a geographical place (Nootka Sound), and because it is a polyphonous point of convergence of historical utterances that the reader may augment, and in which, as Moyes puts it, 'the permanence and authority of the written word are threatened by the fact that meaning cannot be pinned down' ('Dialogizing the Monologue' 23).[6]

The performative processes of transmission and interpretation of even written texts are literally en-acted in Reaney's play, *Sticks and Stones*, through dialogue, gesture, and scenic devices. In *Convergences*, these processes are thematized in the recurring image of 'sound waves,' a motif that incorporates geographical, acoustic, and gestural resonances. For example, a passage by the contemporary narrator is

placed in apposition with a citation from crewman Ledyard's journal
that likens the Mooachahts' physical appearance to the more familiar
eastern Amerindians, and their dress to that of the Chinese. Ledyard
literally 'orients' his understanding of an alien presence with known
points of reference. The narrator describes his own similar 'translation'
of the cited passage itself into the familiar 'scientific' terminology of
the academic, and places that discourse in question: 'Extending outward in space and time, these *wave patterns* induce in my mind ab-
breviated images of their own condition, which I dissect and analyze,
smudge and slur into general concepts, and so speak of geography,
history, culture, heredity – the counters of convenient classroom
drudgery' (21, emphasis added). Reading is seen here as a 'civilizing'
process that filters perception through familiar texts. Civilization, we
are later told, involves 'people behaving in pleasingly *predictable* ways'
(38, emphasis added). That is, it is a conformity to a certain set of
already articulated linguistic conventions.

Later, the speaker again uses the imagery of waves when he comments that the physical convergence at Nootka Sound will 'be followed by a scattering, and other mergings and scatterings of material
and personality, the segments of a rhythm, a pulse, *generating and
broadcasting waves* in every direction, to *interfere* and merge in patterns
beyond our present focus, just as these lines will interfere with the
words and images already in your mind, to emerge as shapes and
shadows and sounds that I will never perceive or imagine' (63, emphasis added). Interpretation is presented as a social process that transpires through time, and involves the 'interference' of various signals.
Meaning might, in fact, be defined both historically and socially as a
moment of intertextual/intersubjective convergence: 'If these words of
mine become words in your head and so connect our lives for a
moment, this will be meaning' (30). 'This' meaning, of course, is
another shifter whose significance is generated at the site of 'interference' of its production and reception, a point of convergence.

Such convergence is represented in explicitly spatial terms on the
first page of the poem: 'At this moment, I know only that I am here
and that others have been here before and have left something for me,
as I leave something for you. Time is ritual exchange, though the gifts
move in a single direction' (1). Location itself (the contextually ambiguous 'here') is marked by the traces of previous presences. This
passage also uses the image of the 'present' text as gift, perhaps even
suggesting the potlatch (a celebration notably foreign to imperial-

ist/capitalist ideas of property ownership), in which the giver distrib-
utes his material goods 'in a single direction.'

Dominick LaCapra encourages a 'rhetorical' reading of past writings
that includes the notion of gift-giving. Such a reading would attend to
the ways documents rhetorically rework rather than simply represent
'reality.' LaCapra likens rhetoric to a 'performative' verbal display,
which 'may be seen as the discursive analogue of the process of gift-
giving as analyzed by anthropologists such as Marcel Mauss. Like the
gift, rhetorical usage has the quality of being both deeply gratifying
and threatening or anxiety-producing, notably with reference to scientific criteria of meaning (such as univocal definition of terms). It also
provides a larger setting for the role of tropes as turns of language
that manifest a playful and sometimes uncanny potential' (*History &
Criticism* 39). The members of the scientific expedition led by Cook are
unable to identify the function of a 'curious' object that appears in a
Mooachaht longhouse in one of Webber's etchings: 'Webber forgot to
ask about the various things he was sketching, and no one was
subsequently able to identify the object in front of the carved figure
beside the people seated on the bench' (54). Given its signifying role
as a spectacular object of symbolic exchange, and Webber's lack of
participation in discursive exchange with the Mooachahts, the European anxiety about the object's meaning is understandable: it is a
trophy/trope (55).

As we have seen, 'Nootka Sound' is both a geographical setting and
a kind of poetic gift that provides a setting for linguistic play. Barbara
Herrnstein Smith observes that when we reread a verbal structure as
something other than what it was given as, we have, in effect, 'regiven
it to ourselves' (50). By re-citing quotations from the journals of Cook
and his men in the format and context of poetry, the documentary-
collage 'gifts' them to its readers, encouraging a self-conscious rhetorical reading of texts that might not ordinarily be seen as rhetorically
impressive. 'Poetry,' the contemporary narrator of *Convergences* notes,
'is language focused on its own form, yet our focus here is upon the
facts as I try to include them all before it is too late. The challenge is
to disguise this unpoetic material in such a way that you will
approach it as poetry, a task which is almost impossible because the
content of this language is more compelling than any formal flourish
I can generate' (51). Cited texts are 'ambivalent words,' caught
between empirical and poetic sign-systems (see Kristeva, 'Word, Dialogue, and Novel' 73). They demand a dual focus, both a 'factual'

reading and a rhetorical rereading. For example, in a cited journal
entry, Ledyard describes the Mooachaht tools for fishing:

> *They have near a dozen different kinds of fish-hooks*
>   *all made of wood,*   `
>   *but was a European to see any one of them*
>   *without previous information*
>   *of their design,*
> *he would as soon conclude they were*
>   *intended to catch men as fish.* (50)

The narrator's commentary – as well as the journal excerpt's formal
presentation and placement in the volume of poetry – draws out the
metaphorical potential of Ledyard's simple description, at the same
time as Ledyard's description reflects on the contemporary notation,
turning the idea of fishing for men on the coast/line into a kind of
double hook that links the two passages, and thus suspends linear
chronology. The commentary, arranged as prose, reads: 'On this coastline two waves are beginning to converge. Two worlds are about to
move together to produce the eventual ambiguous contingencies of my
life. I walk the beach at evening, attentive to the sound of the sea
breaking on the rocks out past the point, watching the sand-laden
rivulets of seawater trickling back down the slope of the shore
between each slap and rush of water. At this moment I do not know
which way the sea is running. Fishing is good at the turning of the
tide' (50). A reading of the cited explorer's log that exceeds its
denotative 'content' might well be said to be 'attentive to the sound ...
out past the point.' The rhetorical reading of either passage does not
eliminate the denotative qualities of its language, but it does relativize
them by introducing other possible contexts beyond the 'objectively'
grounded setting: for instance, the context of cultural convergence as
reading, in which Ledyard struggles to interpret and record the life-
signs of an alien people; the contemporary narrator's parallel interpretive encounter with Ledyard's journal in which he is 'fishing' for an
understanding of past men using a poetic line (of enquiry); and the
ambivalent convergence of 'figurative' and 'denotative' language in the
physical/discursive space of the page that produces *contingent* settings
– neither objectively grounded 'on shore' nor subjectively 'at sea' – for
both the contemporary and historical speaker.

In *Convergences*, the 'log' is both a descriptive device used by the
explorers, and a poetic play on 'word(s)' (Greek, *logos*) in which an

authoritative naming of place and time is undermined in favour of attention to the 'ambiguous contingencies' of rhetorical exchange. The log functions in *Convergences* much as the ledger does in *The Ledger*, as a structure of re-verse-ible metonymic displacement: the log becomes a kind of poem and the poem becomes a kind of log. Each stands in for the other. The contemporary narrator's comments may be seen as 'log entries' in that they are an account of a reading of historical documents. They are simultaneously the record of a 'poetic' explora-tion of the historical text and/as linguistic landscape, and an 'entering in' and undermining of authoritative positions.

Frank Davey has drawn attention to the fact that exploration fre-quently functions in Western Canadian aesthetics as a metaphor for the writer, 'often both in terms of exploring experience and exploring language' ('The Explorer' 147). As *Convergences* demonstrates, explor-ing experience *is* exploring language. The poem allows readers to see both historical explorers and explorers of history as engaged not just in discovering a landscape, but in the rhetorical project of discursively (re)constructing that landscape, and situating themselves within it. As Leslie Monkman comments, exploration narratives are frequently seen by contemporary writers like Kearns as expressions of a European vision: 'the language of the narratives becomes the focus for exami-nation of a whole range of tensions from the meeting of a European discourse of conquest – whether eighteenth-century or twentieth-century – with the North American continent and its peoples' (80–1).

The European explorers claim a position of authority associated with open representational space, literally a *'carte blanche'*: in Second Lieu-tenant John Rickman's words, the ships *'have reached that void space in our maps / which is marked as / country unknown'* (14). In a parallel column, the contemporary narrator reminds the reader of a connection between geographical and cognitive space[7] when he taunts him for attempting to silence the 'nattering voices' in his brain: 'The right hemisphere always gave you problems, didn't it? God, those dreams! So much interference up there in the corpus callosum. But we are considering Cook and his crew as they approach the North West Coast of America. They had other hemispheres to worry about, though they were otherwise much like you' (15). Cook and his crew are like the reader addressed here, *'other/wise'* that is, in their attempt to establish a position of *knowledge* in relation to *others.* Just as this reader uses alcohol to silence the dissension within himself (the voices of his creative right hemisphere) in order to make sense of his life, the explorers must suppress 'other' alter-*native* voices that constitute the

Western hemisphere (America), because they 'interfere' with a monological model of knowledge. This parallel reinforces Dominick LaCapra's assertion that 'alterity ... is not simply "out there" in the past but in "us" as well' (*History & Criticism* 140). *Convergences* suggests a negotiation between 'others' both outside and inside ourselves in its self-conscious questioning of the authority of historical writings and/as historical readings.

In conventional readings of history, map and mapmaker are authority figures; in *Convergences* they are also revealed as *figures* of authority – emblems of privilege in the rhetorical production of historical knowledge. Webber's cited etching of Cook significantly has him holding a map; the passage placed next to it describes the captain as a powerful and enduring signifier of the voyage itself: 'Cook is commander, father, old man, whose life and role and name all identify and characterize the expedition officially, then as now' (6).

The 'character' of the expedition is produced within texts and their consumption: 'Cook *belongs* to his public image, to the portraits and newspapers and history books' (6, emphasis added). It is almost as if Cook is the (historical) word made flesh. If this is the case, his demise enacts a kind of 'poetic justice,' since it is seen as an ironic communion, a violent 'festivity,' in which 'his flesh [is] eaten by those he most impressed' (6). *Convergences* enacts its own textual 'poetic justice' that counteracts the empirical authority of Cook's historical words. By poetically re-citing historical accounts, it effects what Bakhtin would call an anti-authoritarian strategy of textual 'dismemberment' that counteracts institutional history (*Dialogic Imagination* 24). To borrow from the vocabulary of anthropologist Claude Levi-Strauss, the poem does not present the 'Cooked' comprehensive narrative of the voyage. Instead, it self-consciously *re*presents the dis-ordered 'raw' materials of 'historical fiction.'

Convergences places Cook in context. The explorer's recording of his passages through space and time may be seen as 'accurate,' but only within a culturally Eurocentric, ideologically empirical frame of reference. Cook's literal and figurative 'attitude' is oriented towards an imperial point of (temporal/geographical/ideological) reference that determines his viewpoint: 'With his new Harrison chronometer set on Royal Greenwich Observatory time Cook calculates his geographic positions and navigates with an accuracy never before attained' (4). This is a mapping of history that installs powerful new fictions. The European mapmakers 'compose an intricate shoreline on paper' (47) in much the same way the log 'plots' its empirical observations on a narrative line. 'They' – explorers and/as historians – 'bring pen and paper, instruments to confer permanence on the momentary act of reflection. They come with the power to make history and they begin to make it' (46).

For those who engage in such a project, the contemporary narrator comments, writing determines the structure of historical chronology: 'time becomes a line' (17). Just as the unity of the coast/line is disrupted by the poem's contextual representation of space, so too is the simple linearity of historical narrative disrupted by the multiplication, fragmentation, and disordering of documentary accounts, and the 'present' reader's dialogic encounter with them in *Convergences*. Similar strategies of narrative disruption in Kogawa's *Obasan* will be discussed at length in the next chapter. Kearns's poem allows its readers to see any 'given' narrative in the context of other possible readings. 'But do not fasten on that line,' the narrator warns readers. 'The fascination lies in the living' (17). One interpretation of this appropriately multivalent passage might be that a spellbound attachment (fasten-ation) to a prescribed time-line *lies* – is both a fiction and a tie (*lier*, Fr. 'to fasten') that binds us to experience.

While writing makes time a line, then, the reader is warned not to let it string him or her along. *Convergences* suggests the dangers of an unreflective acceptance of the 'official story.' An excerpt from the journal of Charles Clerke, whose name stresses his role as recorder, tells readers of – and reinforces – irreconcilable differences in taste (both as a sense and as Taste, a criterion of judgment) between the explorers and the Mooachahts. The explorers turn down the 'hospitable offers' of the natives, because, in Clerke's words, their

> ... *idea of what is good and palatable*
> *would not permit us to avail ourselves*
>   *of this part of their kindness.*
>   *However, we were very social.* (30)

The historical narrative adds ironically that Clerke was indeed 'sociable,' 'having left behind him in the house of his hosts a deposit of tuberculosis bacilli, an invisible but telling memento of this first wave of European culture on this coast' (30). Clerke's (dis)Tasteful, detached cultural perspective as a 'cultured' member of the scientific expedition contrasts with his literal contamination of the Mooachahts through a deadly bacterial form of 'culture.'

His objective rhetorical stance is similarly contradicted. The infection of the Mooachahts by tuberculosis is potentially paralleled with another *'invisible* but *telling* memento' left by the Europeans: historical writing itself. 'History,' we are reminded in the poem, 'covers its tracks' (53). It is discourse that suppresses the marks of its discursivity. Asserting authority by concealing its own contingencies, and the textual/cultural impressions it *makes*, it appears only to objectively record impressions. Such 'invisible' writing and its strategies are made tangible by the citational method of *Convergences* that reinserts historical writings into a discursive setting.

The poem draws attention to the continuing textual/geographical displacement of the Mooachahts to the margins of contemporary 'Canadian' society: 'The Mooachahts still live on the coast ... But the land, more polluted, less productive, though in many ways the same, is no longer their land. They live only on the fringes, licking Canadian stamps for their occasional letters ... There have been no wars of conquest, no treaties; only waves of people coming and staying and occupying this space and taking control' (56). The European colonizing of geographical space (now represented as non–Native Canadian) is a corollary of its occupation of 'this' discursive space: 'waves of people' replace sound waves.

The stamps the Mooachahts lick in the passage quoted above might be seen as stamps of (the) authority that relegate(s) them to a position on the fringe of contemporary society by regulating the circulation of signs. The stamp that *Convergences* reproduces (courtesy of the *Post-Master General of Canada* [iv]), reinscribes Webber's etching of a Mooachaht longhouse into the contemporary world without any attempt to historicize it. *Convergences*, by contrast, might be seen as a kind of 'occasional letter' (complete with, but subversive of, its stamp), since it clearly calls for an aesthetics of reader-response or 'correspondence,' and since it draws attention to the 'occasional' context of linguistic production and reception. Its recirculation of authoritative signifiers like the stamp places their authority in context, allowing ironies to emerge. For example, although the narrator notes that the Muchalahts and the Ehatisahts and the Nuchatlahts and the Kyuquahts and the Ahts also live there, the stamp claims to be a depiction of the generalized 'Indians of the Pacific Coast' (56). This title effaces cultural differences *between* Native groups, making all West Coast Indians a generalized 'other.' The stamp also sets them in diminished relation to the national and financial considerations signified by the large-print 'Canada 8' on the stamp.

Convergences encourages its readers to accept their continuing implication in historical discourse, and to re-explore that position with a self-consciously 'uncivilized,' challenging attitude. The narrator comments, 'Civilization is fully knowing a situation. It is always the others who are savages. Come here my little savage' (38). The reader of *Convergences* may be, as Eli Mandel once put it, a 'savage' reader (see 'The Function of Criticism' 69–70),[8] an 'other' who stands both within and outside the social process of making sense. This is an unstable position indeed, but is also an ideal place from which to question that process. If, as Martha Rosler asserts, quotation is 'alienated sensibility' (81), the literally 'documentary' quotations in *Convergences* are a key element in the poem's general strategy of 'deliberate alienation' (Mandel 'Imagining Natives' 36). In re-citing the explorers' accounts, *Convergences* also 're-sites' the landscape they describe, displacing the very discursive/geographical ground on which explorers – and the contemporary speaker and reader as their heirs – stand. In a continuing process of establishing its 'setting,' the poem refuses access to history or geography as an extradiscursive product, thus unsettling its readers' conventional position of comfort in 'their' 'home and native land.'

CHAPTER SIX

The Avenues of Speech and Silence: Telling Difference in Kogawa's *Obasan*

... (those who fail to reread are obliged to read the same story everywhere) ...

Roland Barthes, *S/Z*

In one of the closing chapters of Joy Kogawa's *Obasan*, its narrator, Naomi, questions, as she has throughout the novel, her origins in both personal history and the communal history of Japanese-Canadians: 'Where do we come from Obasan?' she asks her aunt. Naomi's own answer, 'We come from cemeteries full of skeletons with wild roses in their grinning teeth. We come from our untold tales that wait for their telling' (226), makes it clear that the telling of tales is in *Obasan* no insignificant act. It is, rather, a strategic act of signification that conditions both individual and collective history and subjectivity. Narrative, in other words, is 'where we come from.' *Obasan*'s use of the juxtapositional methods of the documentary-collage puts into play a 'telling difference' that both dialogically readdresses the narrative of history, and provokes a narrative redress of the record's partial construction of 'historical fact.' The novel, indeed, both tells the story of the efforts of a certain group of people to make the case for redress of injustices committed against Japanese-Canadians by the Government of Canada during and after the Second World War, and provides a fictional forum for the 'hearing' of silenced historical voices.

As Robin Potter perceives, beginning with its prefatory statement, 'Although this novel is based on historical events, and many of the persons named are real, most of the characters are fictional' (v), the novel signals a blurring of borders between fiction and reality, manifest in 'the rhetorical/stylistic strategies chosen by the author and displayed through references to actual government documents, newspaper clippings, letters, journal entries, and, of course, historical events' (124–5). *Obasan*, indeed, provides a particularly compelling example of the intersection of 'political' and 'literary' discourses: on 22 September 1988, the date on which a comprehensive settlement was achieved with members of the Japanese-Canadian community on terms of redress, Ed Broadbent (then leader of the New Democratic Party) read a passage from the novel in the Canadian House of Commons, engaging in a political performance of the literary text, a performance all the more poignant (and, perhaps, ironic) in light of *Obasan*'s 'trial' of the legislative process itself.[1]

Strategies of telling have long been the concern of contemporary narrative theory. Narratology, the collective title for theories of narrative elaborated in the last twenty years, grew out of the structuralist concern with developing a generalized descriptive model applicable to all narrative fictions that would allow the critic to see any individual work in terms of a structure based on the Saussurian linguistic model. Gérard Genette, for example, established a system founded on the distinction between three basic elements: story (*histoire*), 'the signified or narrative content'; narrative (*récit*), 'the signifier, statement, discourse or narrative text itself'; and narrating (*narration*), 'the producing narrative action and, by extension, the whole of the real or fictional situation in which that action takes place' (27). Genette's choice of the explanatory terms 'signifier' and 'signified' is an obvious indication of the debt to Saussurian linguistics. In the Conclusion to her *Narrative Fiction: Contemporary Poetics*, however, Schlomith Rimmon-Kenan points to the possibility of a poststructuralist narratology that would place in question such absolute distinctions. She perceives two interrelated elements of her own fairly typical structuralist approach that a poststructuralist narratology would challenge: first, the fundamental narratological distinction between 'story' as a structure abstracted from any given verbal system, and 'text' (Genette's 'narrative'), the verbal system itself; and second, the easy separation of 'fictive' discourses from those we conventionally consider 'non-fiction,' such as history, philosophy, and theory (130–1).

Marilyn Russell Rose would likely argue that such a poststructuralist approach would be inappropriate to *Obasan*. She contends that Kogawa's novel is predicated on the standards of what Catherine

Belsey calls 'expressive realism,' 'the theory that literature reflects the reality of experience as it is perceived by one ... individual, who expresses it in a discourse which enables other individuals to recognize it as true' (Belsey 3–10, cited in Rose 225, note 1). I would argue, on the contrary, that it is possible to read *Obasan* as interrogating just such expressive realist assumptions, demonstrating how individual experience itself is socially constituted, and revealing how realist presuppositions have worked to marginalize a culture within Canadian history and society, and to justify a politics of racial prejudice. One of the main points of Belsey's discussion in *Critical Practice* is that realism performs the work of ideology, *constructing* and not simply presenting the 'real' or 'true' story (67).

The documentary-collage interrupts the classic or expressive realist illusion of complete, coherent reality in its presentation of documentation in its 'raw' form. As Derek Paget writes of theatre and television, 'Documents are so potentially dangerous to a hegemony that access to them is carefully controlled. Even documents embedded within a drama pose a potential threat to a hegemony, unless a means for control can be found. That means has been readily available in naturalism, the hegemony's preferred dramatic practice' (25). *Obasan* is a novel that both evokes and resists the appeal of naturalism or realism and problematizes the received story via the methods of documentary-collage. In so doing, it addresses precisely the issues Rimmon-Kenan raises. As Linda Hutcheon puts it of what she calls 'historiographic metafiction' – a label that might well be applied to the documentary-collage – a 'theoretical self-awareness of history and fiction as human constructs (historio*graphic* *meta*fiction) is made the grounds for its rethinking and reworking of the forms and contents of the past' (*Poetics* 5). Kogawa's novel radically revises both the concept of a documentary history, which claims to reconstruct once-and-for-all the contents of the past, based on the authority of a body of written evidence, and the formal model of historical realism. The novel does so by focusing on the material documentation of history and story, refusing to see either as simply 'pre-textual' events unconditioned by specific, contextualized 'tellings.'

Roland Barthes calls early formalist analyses of narrative 'the indifferent science,' because they attempt to see all accounts as mere versions of a single immutable structure (*S/Z* 3). Implicit in the notion of both story and history as structures abstracted from their encodings are tactical – one might say *telling* – indifferences (evasions of difference) associated with the kind of empirical operation Barthes condemns. Hayden White asserts that the historian acts like a (realist) novelist in the 'emplotment' of incidents (47). The narrative form to which he assigns events familiarizes them, 'because [the reader] has been shown how the data conform to an icon of a comprehensible finished process, a plot-structure with which he is familiar as part of his cultural endowment' (White 50). The historian, then, whether he acknowledges it or not, acts both as fiction writer and narrative analyst. But what is not taken into (his) account is precisely that which cannot be assimilated to the culture-specific iconic story form, and which is therefore relegated to the marginal realm of the incomprehensible, the foreign, the unfinished, the fundamentally unfamiliar. Both different tellings (accounts that do not conform to the conventions of historical discourse) and tellings of difference (for instance, accounts of what Hutcheon calls 'ex-centrics' of race, gender, class, sexual orientation, and ethnicity [see *Poetics* chapter 4]) – which, it is no accident, often coincide – are placed on the periphery of the historical record, whose conventional reading also suppresses contradictions, inconsistencies, and elisions in the record itself.

Robert Scholes points to postmodern writing's formal and political problematizing of traditional narrative structures, which, he writes, 'are perceived as part of a system of psycho-social dependencies that inhibit both individual human growth and significant social change. To challenge and lay bare these structures is thus a necessary prelude to any improvement in the human situation' (208). In a sense, *Obasan* 'tells on' official history by revealing its guilty construction/suppression of events in Canada during the Second World War, and by giving a version of history alternate in both form and content that draws attention to the inscription of opposition and the suppression of difference.

Régine Robin remarks that, in order to bring about a critical questioning of the historian's discourse, 'one ought to take *Nebbenbwegge*, lateral or oblique paths, detours, to operate displacements, to produce the confusion of genres, of writings, and of disciplines to penetrate surreptitiously into the utmost gaps and interstices of the dominant discourse. To introduce a dialogical process within the heart of a formalized monosemia' (234). *Obasan* represents precisely the kind of 'oblique discourse' Robin encourages. As P. Merivale perceives, Kogawa's collage of documents 'juxtaposes voices in a kind of dialogism' (76). *Obasan* responds to the sort of narrative regime that David Carroll characterizes as 'terroristic or totalitarian,' which 'demands that all alternative narrative possibilities be repressed or subsumed into it' (74). In *Obasan*, institutional history is dismantled – fragmented and disordered – and dis-mantled: the narrative processes that produce *any* 'story' from the 'text' of events are unveiled and questioned.

'Negotiations' between 'story' and 'text' are thus both events *in Obasan*, and acts constitutive of its reading. For both the novel's narrator and its reader, these must be highly self-conscious, equivocal acts of interpretation. Like Kearns's *Convergences*, *Obasan* employs a narrator in the act of reading historical documents, and in theorizing the problematic nature of that reading. Indeed, A. Lynne Magnusson sees these acts of interpretation as the novel's central narrative operation: 'The action of *Obasan* is Naomi's rewriting of her past' (66). The novel's 'main narrative' is composed of Naomi's literal reading of the past. On the eve of her uncle's funeral, schoolteacher Naomi, a Sansei (third-generation Canadian of Japanese origin), is presented with a package of papers compiled by her Aunt Emily, a woman to whom Naomi refers as 'a word warrior': 'She's a crusader, a little old grey-haired Mighty Mouse, a Bachelor of Advanced Activists and General Practitioner of Just Causes' (32). The file is part of Emily's quest for general recognition of a moment in Canadian history whose political dynamics have until recently been strategically neutralized: the persecution, internment, and forced dispersal of Japanese-Canadians by the Canadian government during and after the Second World War. B.A. St Andrews describes Emily's package as 'a box of facts': 'newspaper clippings, editorials, letters from exiled Nisei, headlines from World War II on the domestic front. [Naomi] finds this Pandora's box filled with hatred and historical woes which offers, paradoxically, her only hope. This inclusion of precise documents and speeches ... underscores how completely the stone of silence has covered those victimized by racial misunderstandings. Kogawa presents the fictional Kato-Nakane family to stand nobly against the official, often malicious social memory: history' (31). In response to her reading of the documents, Naomi reluctantly engages in the recollection of her own childhood experiences of the period. These recollections coincide with a re-collection and re-situation of the materials of history within the multivalent narrative of the novel.

Genette's term for what we might think of as the narration of past events in this instance is 'analepsis': 'any evocation after the fact of an event that took place earlier than the point in the story where we are at any given moment' (40). Naomi's recollection of the past, however, is not simply 'after the fact.' It is itself implicated in the process of recollecting and re-contextualizing 'present' documentary evidence. The novel embeds archival material in the fictional narrative, blurring the fiction/history border that so often allows the reader a complacent position 'outside' the narrative, and requiring a literal re-reading of the documents of the past both by Naomi as reader *and* by the reader of the novel. Paradoxically, the acts of re-collection, re-contextualization, and re-reading (Genette's 'producing narrative action') (re)produce the narrative that produces them, or precedes them, as their 'history.' This is a process that might be denoted by a phrase used by psychoanalytic critic Jane Gallop: it is an 'intrication of anticipation and retroaction' (81). 'Where we are at any given moment' is equivocally located in a play of textual 'sources,' none of which it is possible, strictly speaking, to call the 'original.' 'Life is so short,' muses Naomi, unwilling to become mired in memory, 'the past is so long. Shouldn't we turn the page and move on?' (42). As Emily's response implies, however, the grammatical distinction among tenses disguises their intrication, and the linear process of reading conceals the complex of re-readings that composes it: '"The past is the future," Aunt Emily shot back' (42). For the reader of *Obasan*, particularly the Canadian reader, the continuing reconstruction (and thematizing) of both personal and national identity strategically disrupts the experience of classic realist identification and self-effacement, making *Obasan* an 'interrogative text' in Belsey's terms: 'if the interrogative text is illusionist it also tends to employ devices to undermine the illusion, to draw attention to its own textuality. The reader is distanced, at least from time to time, rather than wholly interpolated into the fictional world' (92).

If narrative is 'where we come from,' then, it provides a reliable 'home base' neither for Naomi nor for the reader of *Obasan*. In fact, the novel's recurrent use of the image of the 'family home' treats it as a shifting interpretive space in the reading of narrative, an unstable textual 'house of relations.' The house, for instance, is at several points described in terms of papers or vocal utterances. During Naomi's childhood, her mother repeatedly tells her the reassuring Japanese fairy tale of Momotaro, offering 'the whole telling before she rolls up the tale once more, round and complete as an unopened peach ready for a fresh tasting' (55). In that story, Momotaro lives with his family in a 'whispery rice-paper house' (55). In contrast, Naomi's family, displaced from their beautiful, secure home in Vancouver to an internment camp in Slocan, is displaced into a fictional children's story that suggests stereotypical white European perceptions of people of Japanese origin as both 'diminutive' and hard working: the family lives,

Naomi recalls, in a house that reminds her 'of the house of the seven dwarves' (121), a house that in the fairy tale is taken over by the virtuous Snow White.² Naomi's family's position of exile in Slocan is both literally and figuratively papered over by documentary construction materials that contrast with the soft-spoken ('whispery') Asian rice-paper construction of Momotaro's house: 'The newspapers lining the walls bend and curl showing rough wood beneath' (121).

Naomi's telling of her personal history is in itself both a home-coming and an exile. Most strikingly, her reading of Emily's diary (an extended narrative embedded in the text) is seen, within *Obasan*'s narrative structure, not merely as a return 'home' to past events, but as a transgressory act that trespasses on the 'already known': 'I feel like a burglar as I read,' she comments, 'breaking into a private house only to discover it's my childhood house filled with corners and rooms I've never seen' (79). The metaphor is elaborated when Naomi spends the night after her uncle's death with his wife, Obasan ('aunt'), in Obasan's house. During the night, Obasan rises and explores the attic, finding her husband's identity card from the war, a document that imposed 'alien' identity on him – that is, it marked him as alien in his own country. A generalized description follows: 'All our ordinary stories are changed in time, altered as much by the present as the present is shaped by the past. Potent and pervasive as a prairie dust storm, memories and dreams seep and mingle through cracks, settling on furniture and into upholstery. Our attics and living-rooms encroach on each other, deep into their invisible places' (25). In the dream Naomi has that night, the house image quite literally becomes a textual construct in the process of disintegration: 'a house of cards silently collapses' (29). That collapse signals a breakdown of 'relations.' It both draws attention to and undermines the ways narratives 'relate': they tell a story; they construct fictional connections and differences; they play off against one another. In examining a photograph of her mother and herself as a child, Naomi stresses the reticence of the figures in the picture, a reticence seen in terms of Naomi's position with reference to the past, to her mother, and to her self. When the photograph is turned over 'to see if there is any *identification* on the back,' none is found (46, emphasis added). Naomi is dis-located, metaphorically placed in the rubble of a disintegrated narrative/family home: 'Only fragments relate me to them now, to this young woman, my mother, and me, her infant daughter. Fragments of fragments. Parts of a house. Segments of stories' (53).

When Naomi is on a date with the widower father of one of her pupils – and *dates*, of course, are important to narrative ordering – he asks her a key question that assumes her foreignness to Canada: 'Where do you come from?' (7). Her companion is so inquisitive that Naomi mentally writes an imaginary 'identity card' for herself, listing her personal statistics and finally asking, 'What else would anyone want to know? Personality: Tense. Is that past tense or present tense? It's perpetual tense' (7). While the identity card is not itself an embedded document, it thematizes Naomi's position as subject in relation to documents, her 'identity' (card) within the fragile tension maintained by the text (as fragmentary house of cards).

Japanese-Canadians are placed in a similar position. In a breakdown of what was then perceived as *racial* relations, they are literally dislocated from their family homes in the panic and paranoia that follows the Japanese attack on Pearl Harbor, when their property is confiscated and they are forced to move from coastal British Columbia to internment camps in the interior. Moreover, Japanese-Canadians are dislocated (as Naomi was by her date's question) from their very positions as Canadians, both because they are not recognized as such – 'over here they say "Once a Jap always a Jap," and that means us,' Emily writes in her diary (83) – and, concomitantly, because their civil rights as citizens are flagrantly suspended. 'Once a Jap, always a Jap' is a phrase used by member of parliament A.W. Neill: 'Whatever the opinion of the Prime Minister or of the government here,' he said in a House of Commons debate in 1941, 'we in British Columbia are firmly convinced that once a Jap always a Jap' (cited in Adachi 195). Emily's ironic re-enunciation of Neill's infamous expression is both a form of renunciation and an acknowledgement of the extent to which it and statements like it determined what 'us' meant for Japanese-Canadians of the time.

The concept of a 'Japanese race,' epitomized in the image of the 'Yellow Peril,' becomes what Henry Louis Gates would call a 'dangerous trope' (4), 'a pernicious act of language' that seems to describe 'natural' attributes, but actually *in*scribes an 'ultimate, irreducible difference between cultures, linguistic groups, or adherents of specific belief systems' (5). Emily tells Naomi, 'None of us ... escaped the naming. We were defined and identified by the way we were seen' (118). Racism becomes a way of coalescing and reinforcing wartime nationalism, but the latter reveals racism *already* at work as a contradiction within the supposed Canadian ideal of the very democratic, mutually tolerant society for which the war was supposedly being fought. This contradiction is stated outright in the Memorandum by the Co-operat-

ive Committee on Japanese Canadians, which is cited at the end of the
novel: it calls certain tactics of the government 'an adoption of the
methods of Naziism' itself (250). When Naomi's brother Stephen is
taunted at school for being a 'Jap,' his father tells him simply, 'We're
Canadian,' but Stephen later points to the historically determined
conflict his father's response ignores when he tells Naomi, 'It is a
riddle ... We are both the enemy and not the enemy' (70).

Jacques Derrida observes that 'racism always betrays the perversion
of a man, the "talking animal." It institutes, declares, writes, inscribes,
prescribes' ('Racism's Last Word' 292). The self-conscious citation of
documents, not just as evidence of racism, but as the linguistic
materials that construct it, emphasizes the point. Derrida's article on
South African apartheid sees that system in terms of language, of
racist *relations*. Racism is, he writes, 'a system of marks [that] outlines
space in order to assign forced residence or to close off borders. It
does not discern, it discriminates' (ibid.). The visually 'marked' position of the Japanese-Canadians and the oppositional structure into
which it is inscribed is imaged in *Obasan* by a game given to Stephen
for Christmas: 'The Yellow Peril is a Somerville Game, Made in
Canada' (152). This war/game charts oppositional relationships, asking
its players to close off geographical/racial borders. On the box, a map
of Japan is superimposed with the words:

> *The game that shows how*
> *a few brave defenders*
> *can withstand a very*
> *great number of enemies.* (152)

The representation of people in this game literally reduces them to a
binary set of markers, with the side signifying 'Japanese' as devalued
'pawns': 'There are fifty small yellow pawns inside and three big blue
checker kings. To be yellow in the Yellow Peril game is to be weak
and small' (152). The game also, inevitably, forces Stephen to take
sides against himself; he ultimately chooses a 'Canadian' identity that
entirely excludes – indeed, opposes itself to – the Japanese culture that
is his heritage.

Racist language is used to construct, enforce, and 'naturalize' apparently essential differences, denying or preventing the possibility of
multiplicity within divisions. In Emily's package, Naomi finds (among
many similar others) a document that makes exactly such use of

language, a 'form letter,' surely the most indifferent of writings: 'While it is not necessary that this title be available in order to complete the sale it is preferred that it be surrendered to the Registrar of Land Titles. Will you be good enough therefore ...' (36). Naomi describes this document as one of many letters 'sent to all of us back in the forties asking us to hand over the titles to our properties but advising us that, whether we did or not, our houses would be taken from us' (36).[3] Emily's comment on the letter extends the significance of the government's *linguistic* regulation of Japanese-Canadian (land) titles and position: 'The power of print ... The power of government, Naomi' (36). Much later in the novel Naomi relates this process of enforcing government order(s) through documentation to the literal and figurative/figural dislocation of Japanese-Canadians: 'The Government makes paper airplanes out of our lives and files us out the windows' (242).

Another 'toneless form letter' the novel includes tersely advises Emily that her mother's home has been confiscated by the authorities (37). Naomi, in reading the letter (which is embedded in the text), imagines that Emily had written to ask for a specific accounting, a localized telling of the fate of her family home, and not just a formulaic, in-different response: 'Tell me what happened to my mother's tiny house – the house where my sister was born, with the rock garden in front and the waterfall and goldfish. Tell me what has happened' (37). Naomi's construction of the subtext of the government official's reply constitutes an ironic reading of the document that draws out the power politics of the form letter: the language of the letter does not neutrally inform, but rather imposes conformity on its addressees. The imagined answer uses both patriarchal terms and the language of displaced filial ties, which are denoted as 'illegal,' or outlawed, and therefore unable to (cor)respond. It also incorporates – and therefore implicates – the lyrics of the Canadian national anthem, and the signatory of the letter, the impersonal 'B.Good,' whose very name becomes an imperative: 'Be good, my undesirable, my illegitimate children, be obedient, be servile, above all don't send me any letters of enquiry about your homes, while I stand on guard (over your property) in the true north strong, though you are not free. B.Good' (37). Emily herself evokes a kind of prison-house of (indifferent) documentary language when she comments on the way the detention of Japanese-Canadians under brutal, inhumane conditions is neutralized by familiar terms: 'You know those prisons they sent us to? The government called them "Interior Housing Projects"! With language

like that you can disguise any crime' (34). *Obasan*, employing legal
devices and tropes similar to those used by Ondaatje, Reaney, and
Marlatt, turns the 'legislative' system against itself, testifying to its
injustice. The novel, for example, juxtaposes these two conflicting
newspaper headlines from Emily's scrapbook: '"Bar Japs from B.C."
/ "Claim Deportation of Japs Violates International Law"' (41).

Obasan's discussion of the internment camps is both the filling in of
untold stories and a comment on the way they have been suppressed
within the documents of history. It also foregrounds the recurring
house image. An entry in Emily's journal, for example, describes an
incident in which the floorboards of an internment residence are pried
up to expose a fetid bed of manure and maggots (99). Just as the
floorboards are pulled apart to reveal their unpalatable foundation, so
Obasan's form disorders traditional historical structures that are
founded on suppressed elements. In so doing it reveals the unsavoury
matters that compose the substratum of those structures.

A comment Emily makes when she and her family return many
years after the war to the 'ghost town' where they were interned
connects the scene beneath the residence with the government's
attempt to eliminate through dispersal the Japanese-Canadian presence
in coastal British Columbia: 'It was an evacuation all right ... Just
plopped here in the wilderness. Flushed out of Vancouver. Like dung
drops. Maggot bait' (118). The family, in fact, cannot find the location
of their internment, just as it is constructed as an absented site within
documentation. They find, instead, the site of an erasure, a significant
absence: 'Where on the map or on the road was there any sign? Not
a mark was left. All our huts had been removed long before and the
forest had returned to take over the clearings ... What a hole!' (117–18).
The exclamation recalls an article in *The New Canadian*, 'an independent weekly for Canadians of Japanese origin' (23 May 1942), which
describes a group of evacuees who stepped off a train into a ghost
town and cried, 'O God, what a hole! What a hole, O God!' (cited in
Adachi 256).

Obasan's 'return' to the sites/citations of history through the quotation of historical documents is instrumental in the narrative revision
that exposes such gaps in the record. Like Naomi, these documents are
caught up in a 'tense' network: their citation is by no means a simple
return to the 'bare bones' of a historical story. As Jacques Derrida
indicates, the *récit* (story) is always already involved in a textual
process of repetition or re-citation ('The Law of Genre' 54). The documentary-collage draws attention to this process by accentuating the

document's equivocal contextual positions in narrative. In *Obasan*, the resituating of Emily's writing within Naomi's discourse, for example, is obliquely evoked in Naomi's comment, 'A package from Aunt Emily, *I note*,' when she first catches sight of the box (30, emphasis added). The package of letters is quite literally addressed (to Emily) and readdressed (to Naomi, and subsequently to the reader of the novel), each new enunciation involving a shift in the 'producing narrative action' (Genette 27) and a recontexualization of meaning. For instance, Emily's diary might be considered a composite document cited in the text of the novel, since it is composed almost entirely of quotations from Muriel Kitagawa's writings, an archival source Kogawa acknowledges in a prefatory note (v).[4] The diary might also, however, be seen as an embedded epistolary narrative narrated by Emily in 1942 and addressed to Naomi's mother, or an embedded narrative narrated by Emily and readdressed to Naomi in 1972, or an embedded narrative read by Naomi to herself. Genette's concept of the narrating situation in such a case must be somewhat revised. In fact, it might be more appropriate to talk about the narrating *cit*uation, in order to play, simultaneously, as *Obasan* does, on associations with location, quotation as contexualization, and the Latin root *citare*, to set in motion.

Obasan cites, for example, what might seem to be an objective historical document describing the forced 'repatriation' of a group of Japanese-Canadians to Japan after the war: '"'Indifferent' Jap Repats Start Homeward Trek" was the headline of a report dated June 1, 1946' (185). The article's place in *Obasan*'s revisionist narrative, however, allows it to be read as the site of irony: while the newspaper's use of the word 'Jap' indicates that those described are being sent 'Homeward,' they are, we know, being *de*-patriated, alienated, and deprived of their Canadian 'home and native land.' The newspaper's description, which seems to be a factual account that journalistically tells things just as they are, is itself, the citation makes clear, a contemporary *reading* of events, embedded in a historical situation, that passes itself off as historically 'true.' The account inscribes its biases on what it seems to describe, ascribing its own indifference to the culturally determined reticence of its subjects: 'Solemnness *was written* in their faces; only *indifference* they showed' (185, emphasis added).

Dominick La Capra comments that 'often the dimensions of the document that make it a text of a certain sort with its own historicity and its relations to sociopolitical processes (for example, relations of power) are filtered out when it is used purely and simply as a quarry for facts in the reconstruction of the past' (*Rethinking Intellectual History* 31). This extraction of 'fact' is analogous to the narratological extraction of the 'essentials' of the text to produce a definitive story. It is also a primary method for producing the chronological, authoritative 'reconstruction' we call history. It is just such an essentializing process that *Obasan* dialogically en-counters. Emily's package contains an index card labelled 'Facts about evacuees in Alberta,' which Naomi finds and reads (193). The newspaper clipping filed along with it includes a photograph of a smiling family, captioned 'Grinning and Happy,' and the article itself, quoted in the text, describes 'Jap Evacuees' as the most efficient workers in the Alberta sugarbeet fields, supporting its case with abundant statistical evidence (193). The faces of Japanese-Canadians are again authoritatively de-scribed or written off by documentary writing. Naomi's reading of the clipping, by comparison, places it in contrast with her own harsh experience as a fieldworker, which she cannot simply put behind her: 'Facts about evacuees in Alberta? The fact is I never got used to it and I cannot, I cannot bear the memory. There are some nightmares from which there is no waking, only deeper and deeper sleep' (194). The apparently 'objective truth' of the record conceals its biases. In this context, the document is provocative: Naomi rereads it by relating the counter-story of her own experiences (194–7), and concludes by *interrogatively* re-citing the caption: '"Grinning and happy" and all smiles standing around a pile of beets? That is one telling. It's not how it was' (197).

Another way *Obasan* draws attention to the contextually engaged nature of documentary evidence is its use of the redirected letters included in the package Emily sends Naomi. These are orders from the government instructing Naomi's father and uncle that they must move from their homes. In the practical sense that they are 'orders,' the letters make compulsory a movement eastward; they force the literal (re)orientation of a people. They also enforce a certain kind of social order, orienting Canadian citizens in terms of their nationality, and defining them only in terms of absolute difference: Japanese-Canadians are seen as Japanese in race, in allegiance, and in a position as degraded 'others' in Canadian society. As subjects of the letters, Naomi's father and uncle are subjected to their specific imperative, to the letter of the law they enforce – the Order in Council – and, most generally of all, to an oppressive conception of language that operates on a theory of direct and immutable 'correspondence' between signifier and signified.

Obasan transgresses such laws in its use of the letters. In fact, using the sense of the word made current by Jacques Lacan, it is a 'purloining' of them: it diverts the letters from their path; it prolongs their course (the etymology of 'purloin' involves this sense of extension); it holds up the course of their delivery (59). In the strict chronological sequence of story, the letters are solely analeptic: they refer to past events. In *Obasan*'s narrative, however, the letters speak out of order: 'The orders,' Naomi narrates, 'given to Uncle and Father in 1945, reach me via Aunt Emily's package in 1972, twenty-seven years later. The delivery service is slow these days. Understanding is even slower. I still do not see the Canadian face of the author of those words' (172–3). The letters never 'arrive' in the sense that their meaning is fully determined. They become a 'broken record,' but not in the sense that they are involved in a process that *merely* repeats itself. Because repetition always involves difference, authoritative story order(s) is/are fragmented, 'his master's voice' re(pro)nounced.[5]

Obasan's use of what might be called the 'narrative pun' works towards a similar disorderly end, emphasizing the role of context in determining meaning and extending to the general narration the equivocality more obviously at work in the embedded documents. This is, in effect, the narrative equivalent of the use of equivocal shifters in *The Collected Works of Billy the Kid* or *Convergences*. Conventionally, contextual cues in a narrative passage make clear its place in terms of a chronological story-order. In the case of the narrative pun, however, all contextual cues are ambiguous or absent. For example, after the final entry in Emily's wartime journal, Naomi once again explicitly takes over as narrator and concludes the chapter: 'This is the last word in the journal. The following day, May 22, 1942, Stephen, Aya Obasan, and I are on a train for Slocan. It is twelve years before we see Aunt Emily again' (110). The following chapter begins with this passage: 'I am sometimes not certain whether it is a cluttered attic in which I sit, a waiting room, a tunnel, a train. There is no beginning and no end to the forest, or the dust storm, no end from which to know where the clearing begins. Here, in this familiar density, beneath this cloak, within this carapace, is the longing within the darkness' (111). The paragraph is followed by the date '1942,' isolated on a line, but the orientation of the pronominal 'I' and shifter 'here,' and even the paragraph's tense with reference to story are equivocal.[6] If 'I' is the child Naomi of 1942, confused by her train trip from Vancouver to Slocan, then this is a continuous temporal 'passage' from the previous chapter. Alternatively, the date '1942' may function as a contextual tag for the *following* paragraph, making the chapter's opening a metaphorical – indeed meta-narrative – statement. The very problematic the narrative pun implies, that of establishing the linear continuity, the chronological, causal structure of story, is both evoked and enacted by the passage. And, as Régine Robin remarks, such a problematizing 'ought to raise doubts about the clarity of the most self-confident syntaxes. The polyphony, the proliferation of unmastered signs, breaks through precisely where the historian assembles and joins. *It is a work of unlinking'* (235). 'Narrative meaning' is repeatedly suspended, and can at best be only provisionally decided by reading passages in terms of their temporally embedded enunciations.

Peter Brooks's conception of the role of desire as a 'dynamic of signification' (37) in narrative discourse is by no means unconnected to our hesitation over such passages and to Naomi's 'longing within the darkness.' Brooks sees a desire for meaning 'not only as the motor force of plot but as the very motive of narrative' (48). He draws a connection between that motive and Lacan's concept of a 'chain of signifiers' that metonymically displaces meaning to an 'elsewhere' in an endless process of deferral (Brooks 55). Robin invokes just such a process when she notes that the voice of the historical subject 'cannot be revived, represented, or restored; it can only be displaced, re-produced, by narration, by fiction' (234). *Obasan*'s fictional critique of authoritative history is based on the latter's claim to transcend or circumvent the kind of textual processes Brooks and Robin describe, its claim to offer a 'final accounting,' a closed meaning.

The novel thematizes and puts into play the narrative impulse both to search for a particular story and to search for an alternative, potentially redemptive form of telling that resists narrative closure, that both speaks out of historical silences and takes them into its account. Such a telling would be a provisional, reflexive search grounded in historical/textual re-search. Naomi comments ironically at one point that she and Emily 'should hire ourselves out for a research study' (8) because they are, anomalously, two single women in a small family: 'Must be something in the blood,' Naomi muses wryly, 'A crone-prone syndrome' (8). In light of their 'tense' position within the processes of researching the interactive workings of past and present tellings, Naomi and her aunt represent a *chrone*-prone syndrome too.

Obasan's research project may be seen in much the same way that Barbara Godard characterizes Margaret Laurence's *The Diviners*, as a radical re*writing* of the heroic quest narrative in which 'the narrative of quest becomes the quest of narrative. There are two stories unfolding, a horizontal narrative of events, of succession, of contiguity and a vertical narrative of the pursuit of knowledge, of embedding, of substitution ... The text contains its own gloss' ('*The Diviners* as

Supplement' 35). In fact, succession and substitution, text and gloss are, in *Obasan* and more generally in the documentary-collage, essentially indistinguishable. The novel attests most pointedly to its quest of narrative by repeatedly directing our attention to a particular personal story that is not told, and that is excluded from historical documentation, the story of Naomi's mother after she 'disappears' on a trip to Japan during the crucial time when that country joined the war. This 'disappearance,' clearly, has parallels with the suppression of the Japanese-Canadian victimization in/by Canadian history, since the letter explaining it is delayed, and then withheld from Naomi by her family. The Japanese phrase 'Kodomo no tame' repeatedly alludes, without being able to refer, to information about 'Nesan' (Naomi's mother and Emily's sister) that is suppressed: 'The memories were drowned in a whirlpool of protective silence. Everywhere I could hear the adults whispering, "Kodomo no tame. For the sake of the children ..."' (21). Similarly, a mysterious grey *file folder* in Emily's package and the pieces of blue paper it contains acquire increased importance precisely because their meaning is undisclosed: the file/*fil* or thread of telling is not unfolded. The suspension of sense encountered here is, as Barthes points out, structured 'according to the expectation and desire for its solution' (*S/Z* 75). Barthes calls such reticences 'enigmas,' elements of a hermeneutic code that 'must set up *delays* ... in the flow of discourse' (75). The enigma is not merely a 'gap' in data. It is a metonymy that draws attention to its metonymic status, to the fact that it 'stands in for' what is not present, and in so doing conceals an absence. For both reader and narrator, 'kodomo no tame' and the letter on blue paper written in Japanese are 'pure signifiers,' mere markers. They foreground the fact that the concealment is accomplished by language.

Barthes sees the enigma as a figure within narrative, but it may also be read as a figure for the strategy of the narrative text itself, for, while the apparent unfolding of the narrative seems and seeks to recover a story, it too re-covers an absence with text and is, finally, the mark of that absence. Brooks writes that 'narrative is hence condemned to *saying* other than what it *would mean*, spinning out its movement toward a meaning that would be the end of its movement' (56). Naomi's separation from her mother is, in this context, not merely an event in the narrative; it is an event *of* narrative. Lacanian psychoanalysis teaches that the entry into language divides the child from the mother's body. It makes articulation a profoundly ambivalent act, whose precondition is 'that is not what it represents ... Hence to enter into a world of relationships mediated by language is to enter into a world of endless yearning, where words and substitute objects always register a lack' (Magnusson 62).[7]

Obasan's narrative act may be seen as motivated by the desire for a kind of reunion with a lost past, as a way of attempting to relate mother to daughter, to return 'home.' This past is significantly feminine, an alternate, (m)other telling that exists in differential relation to the implicitly or explicitly patriarchal documents of institutional history. It is a form of telling that the novel presents as an act of love: Naomi tells readers that one of the two Japanese ideographs that signify 'love,' 'was formed of "heart," "to tell," and "a long thread"' (228). The act the ideograph denotes is reminiscent of the *'fort-da'* game described by Freud in *Beyond the Pleasure Principle*: in a re-enactment of the disappearance and return of the mother, the child first throws a toy away, and then, using a string, joyfully draws it back (8–11). Antoine Compagnon, significantly, sees the cut-and-paste of collage as the model of this child's game where, in the symbolic alternation of presence and absence, Freud perceived the origin of the sign (16). In *Obasan*, the documentary-collage both offers evidence of alienation and gestures towards reconciliation.

The idea that 'story line' might unambivalently enact a re-presentation of or reunion with the past is persistently placed in question by *Obasan's* disjunctive collage composition and its accompanying thematic concerns, but it also suggests the possibility of telling as a relational bond. Naomi re-enacts her mother's departure from her in a dream: 'She is here. She is not here ... She is a maypole woman to whose apron-string streamers I cling and around whose skirts I dance. She is a ship leaving the harbour, tied to me by coloured paper streamers that break and fall into a swirling wake. The wake is a thin black pencil-line that deepens and widens and fills with a greyness that reaches out with tentacles to embrace me. I leap and wake' (167). 'Waking' is an entry into morning/mourning, both daybreak with its renewed consciousness and regret over a loss. We learn early in the novel that the Japanese word for 'lost' also means 'dead' (24). Further, a wake is a trace, what is left behind when something (usually a ship) has 'passed away.' In the dream, the paper streamers that connect Naomi with her mother/ship disintegrate into a wake, and the wake is itself a representation, 'a thin black pencil-line,' the trace of a trace. *Obasan* both attests to a desire to form a recuperative representational 'bridge' with the past, and indicates the problems – and dangers – involved in doing so definitively. Erika Gottlieb observes that *Obasan* 'takes shape as a mourner's meditation during a wake' (36). Indeed, as both the evidence of a historical and personal loss and a provisional compensation for it, the novel *is* a kind of wake.

While the mysterious blue letter written by Naomi's maternal grand-mother is finally read, its full meaning remains enveloped in silence – a silence of horror, grief, and cultural reticence that the novel struggles to respect. The letter describes the bombing of Nagasaki, another historical event that reflects guilt on the 'winners' of the war. It forces the reader to face an image that has in *Obasan* come to stand for repressed guilt: '"In the heat of the August sun," Grandma writes, "however much the effort to forget, there is no forgetfulness. As in a dream, I can still see the maggots crawling in the sockets of my niece's eyes"' (234). Naomi narrates the scene in which Grandma Kato is reunited with Nesan after they are separated by the holocaust: 'One evening ... she sat down beside a naked woman she'd seen earlier who was aimlessly chipping wood to make a pyre on which to cremate a dead baby. The woman was *utterly disfigured*. Her nose and one cheek were almost gone. Great wounds and pustules covered her entire face and body. She was completely bald. She sat in a cloud of flies and maggots wriggled among her wounds. As Grandma watched her, the woman gave her a *vacant* gaze, then let out a cry. It was my mother' (239, emphasis added). Naomi's mother is literally dis*figured*. She is, as horrible as it may sound, de-faced, her flesh is eaten away. She has also been dis-figured, displaced from figuration, from signification, because her story, like the story of the Japanese-Canadians, has been suppressed; it is in excess of the recuperative structures of monologic historical narrative. Even this climactic telling, however, is itself an enigmatic displacement that resists finality. Nesan's face is accessible only as type-face. Emily's diary, similarly, a key personal telling that counters official historical narrative, is meant as a Christmas present for Nesan, but it does not make her present. While the documents included in Emily's package may be 'symbols of communion, the materials of communication, white paper bread for the mind's meal' (182), they do not 'transubstantiate' into flesh.

Naomi's aunt Aya Obasan, like Naomi's mother, and unlike the insistently 'Canadian' Emily (33, 39), is in excess of nationalist struc-tures devised to regulate and neutralize cultural multiplicity: Naomi jokingly calls her 'Our Lady of the Left-Overs' (45), and comments that 'she does not dance to the multi-cultural piper's tune or respond to the racist's slur. She remains in a silent territory, defined by her serving hands' (226). Aunt Emily's project, by contrast, as her quotation from the book of Habakkuk indicates, is to 'write the vision and make it plain,' to replace a flawed authoritative history with another, even more authoritative, corrected one (31). As A. Lynne Magnusson notes, however, 'Emily's naive claims that words can render the truth about the past are always attended by the writer's irony and Naomi's scepticism' (62). 'Write the vision and make it plain?' Naomi echoes, 'For her, the vision is the truth as she lives it. When she is called like Habakkuk to the witness stand, her testimony is to the light that shines in the lives of the Nisei, in their desperation to prove themselves Canadian, in their tough and gentle spirit. The truth for me is more murky, shadowy and grey' (32).

Naomi's truth-testing project takes in Emily's 'testimony,' but it also struggles with the representational problems posed by Emily's truth-telling goals. Unwilling to make the leap of faith necessary to make the story Emily constructs fully meaningful, Naomi finds herself arrested at the level of the signifier: 'All of Aunt Emily's words, all her papers, the telegrams and petitions, are like scratchings in the barnyard, the evidence of much activity, scaly claws hard at work. But what good they do, I do not know – those little black typewritten words – rain words, cloud droppings ... The words are not made flesh. Trains do not carry us home' (189). Trains literally do not carry the Nakane family home; they do not return to their Vancouver residence. 'Trains,' perhaps, also 'do not carry us home' because trains, like unilinear narratives, are destination-bound vehicles that travel a track that allows for no digressions, no deviations from form. Emily's diary mentions that those who would not travel to internment camps were put on 'a *wanted* list of over a hundred Nisei who refuse to *entrain*' (97, emphasis added). The 'motor force' of her documentary project is to 'entrain' those who have been left out of the historical story.

Obasan's alterna(rra)tive project, the project of the documentary-collage, in effect redefines the 'train' itself in terms of textuality: like a fabric train, which is drawn along *behind*, *Obasan*'s narrative train is a self-consciously material wake. 'The dance ceremony of the dead,' Naomi tells us, 'was a slow courtly telling, the heart declaring a long thread knotted to Obasan's twine, knotted to Aunt Emily's package' (228). *Obasan*'s telling, similarly, both involves Aunt Emily's realist documentary impulse, literally citing the documents from her file, and acknowledges Aya Obasan's silent language of grief (14), whose 'answers are always oblique and the full story never emerges in a direct line' (18). The novel, in other words, both includes historical documentation and opens it up to the gaps it both encodes and conceals. The book's title alludes to such a double project: 'Obasan' in Japanese means 'aunt,' and refers equivocally to Emily and Aya Obasan.

This ambivalent, double project is caught up in the 'inside-outside position' of being Japanese-Canadian (Hutcheon, *Poetics* 72), and of being able to respond dialogically from various positions. In *Obasan*, readers are asked to see those positions as positions of difference, and not simple opposition.[8] It presents historical telling as an unfinished process, open to responsive reading. It is appropriate, therefore, that the novel is itself open-ended: it concludes with a document, an excerpt from the memorandum sent by the Co-operative Committee on Japanese Canadians to the House and the Senate of Canada, April 1946. This text occupies a position outside Naomi's narration, which concludes on the previous page. While this document is certainly 'evidence for optimism' (199), acknowledging that the Orders in Council for the deportation of Canadians of Japanese origin are 'based upon racial discrimination' (249), it must be noted that it subtly re-encodes that racial fear, maintaining, for example, the removal of Japanese-Candians from the West Coast 'was referrable to the emergency,' and that since many Japanese-Canadians have settled away from British Columbia and do not wish to return, 'there is ... no need for fear of concentration on the Pacific Coast as in the past' (249) – leaving open the possibility that the original fear was justified. Such ambivalences in the text insist on attentiveness, response, and political decisions on the part of the reader. They require an *ongoing* interrogative relationship with the reading of history that extends beyond the borders of the book.

CHAPTER SEVEN

'I quote myself' or,
A Map of Mrs Reading:
Re-siting 'Woman's Place'
in *Ana Historic*

This is a vast commonplace of literature: the Woman copies the Book. In other words, every body is a citation: of the 'already written.' The origin of desire is the statue, the painting, the book ...

Roland Barthes, *S/Z*

'Citing Resistance' pivots on the multiple sonoral play of the law (cite), of space and place (site); and of vision and the senses (sight). The verb 'to cite' means both 'to set in motion, to call,' and 'to quote implying authority.' The contradiction between the unsettling disturbance of the former meaning and the legal authority of the latter suggests how women writers negotiate their inscription in language.

Janice Williamson, *Citing Resistance*

In the course of conducting historical research for her history-professing husband, Annie, the (anti-)heroine of Daphne Marlatt's (anti-)novel *Ana Historic: a novel*, finds herself reflecting on – and reflecting – significant gaps within the language of history, the story it tells, and the stake it claims to 'truth.' The literally subversive alternate text she furtively scribbles, half-hiding it beneath the documentary records of her husband's project (78), like the novel itself, both incorporates and overturns the disembodied, 'neutral' language of those records, countering them with a gendered reading and writing that exceeds the authoritative, monologic historical economy within which they traditionally circulate. This strategic act within – *and of* – the novel puts

into play intertextual relationships that constitute what Evelyn Voldeng calls a cultural misappropriation or overturning [*détournement*]
that may be seen as engaging a political subversion (524).

Ana Historic embeds not just historical, but medical, philosophical,
and economic discourses within it, revealing the degree to which each
is implicated in the others and is always (rhetorically) embedded in
relationships of power. It places documents associated with these
institutional practices in relation to the stories of three women: the
contemporary narrator Annie's autobiographical story, her recollections
of her mother Ina, and her imaginary reconstruction of the life of their
historical foremother Mrs Richards, whom Annie encounters during
the research she conducts for her husband. Pamela Banting writes that
in *Ana Historic*, 'Marlatt takes on the problem of how to write a book
about an historical woman, a contemporary woman, and the relationships among women, when the traces of women's history have been
obliterated, and the official version, that is, men's history, is a narrative of subjection, exploitation and domination' (123). Banting continues, 'When both speech and writing are coded as masculine then,
how does the woman writer write a novel?' (124). The relational,
citational approach Marlatt takes to this problem both constitutes and
provokes a re-reading of the institutional writings she cites, from
positions of difference and resistance that are, in a sense, made possible by the dis-location of authority through documentary citation.

As Glen Lowry points out, in a male economy of language, 'it is
"wrong" to read factual documents outside of their proper field of
discourse' (93). Marlatt's work, as a documentary-collage, literally
moves documents out of their proper field of discourse into the realm
of fiction/theory. The transgressory or 'wrong' reading of documents
also takes place as an event within the narratives of the novel. For
example, Annie's imaginary enactment of husband Richard's reading
of her work-in/of-process has him questioning her method because it
does not logically and linearly work a problem through to its conclusion, because it does not follow proper citational convention and
respect the integrity of the texts to which it refers, and because it
violates the teacher-student model of authority that governs both their
husband-wife relationship, and, implicitly, the relationship of 'respect'
between text and reader on which Richard insists: 'but what are you
doing? i can imagine Richard saying, looking up from the pages with
that expression with which he must confront his students over their
papers: this doesn't go anywhere, you're just circling around the same
idea – and all these bits and pieces thrown in – that's not how to use

quotations' (81). The citational method of *Ana Historic*, with all its 'bits and pieces thrown in,' is similarly transgressive. Marlatt, its female author, deliberately adopts the traditionally feminine role of the researcher who copies out extracts from historical texts, which are, traditionally, consolidated by someone else (the authority) into a 'definitive study,' just as Annie contributes to what her daughter Ange calls Richard's 'Big Book, in which it is written: "and to my wife without whose patient assistance this book would never have been completed"' (79). *Ana Historic* is, however, no such definitive Big Book; its author's assumption of the subordinate (non-authoritative) role of copyist is a subversive gesture that interrupts the various discourses she transcribes – the very discourses that underwrite her own subjectivity – allowing an interrogative rereading of them. This interrogative rereading works to 'unfix' the female subject in/of history. In *Convergences*, the narrator's rereading of historical documentation unsettles the very position of stability from which he speaks as a white male of European origin, playing out, as Lianne Moyes puts it, the contradictions 'which both lyric and history suppress in order to constitute themselves as complete and authentic sources of meaning' ('Dialogizing the Monologue' 19). Annie's reading of historical materials in *Ana Historic*, conversely, disturbs the conventions that *prevent* her from speaking, the constructs that situate 'woman's place' in history as a fixed and unchangeable position of silence. P. Merivale calls Kogawa's similar, although more culturally directed, interrogations 'an oblique feminism of marginality, of a silence finding a voice' (74).

As Douglas Barbour has recently remarked more generally of Marlatt and Betsy Warland, they 'engage what they perceive as a masculinist misuse of monological discourse from a feminist perspective that insists on heteroglossia' ('Transformations' 40–1). In so doing, they are able to resist falling into the trap of mirroring the 'singular discourse' of what has come to be known as 'phallocentric' writing, and merely reproducing 'a new and opposing monological speech' (ibid. 40). Or rather, in the very act of self-consciously reproducing monologic speech, *Ana Historic* draws that speech into a dialogic economy. This re-creative gesture of transgression through transcription suggests the parodic act of mimicry described by Luce Irigaray, in which a woman's 'playing with mimesis' may be an attempt 'to recover the place of her exploitation by discourse, without allowing herself to be simply reduced to it' (76). A woman may thus, according to Irigaray, 'resubmit herself' to ideas developed within 'masculine logic,' 'but so as to make "visible," *by an effect of playful repetition*, what was supposed to remain invisible: the cover-up of a possible operation of the feminine in language' (76, emphasis added). Thus, *Ana Historic* gives (documentary) evidence of the repression of the feminine in history and in so doing it reactivates historical conflicts, and as Dennis Cooley emphasizes, bases its struggle within language itself (see 'Recursions'). In this novel, Marlatt plays with the 'merely reproductive' feminine position of historical researcher *and* with the mimetic function of historical writing itself, in which 'woman's place' is inscribed within the 'real.'

Ana Historic is structured as the site of a number of interrelated dialogues that tend to unsettle the historical 'given.' Annie, for example, like Naomi in *Obasan*, and the contemporary speaker in *Convergences*, engages in an ongoing discursive exchange with the historical research project in which she is involved, and the particular texts that endeavour requires that she read. Her responses to those texts might be seen as counterproductive to what E.L. Doctorow would call traditional history's prescriptive 'power of the regime' (216): they include, for example, Annie's informal musings on the language of history and the history of language, as well as the fictional account that both arises out of and provokes those musings, the story of Mrs Richards, an inhabitant of early Vancouver who is acknowledged (that is constructed *as* knowledge) in the historical record in a passing reference to her in the history book *Vancouver: From Milltown to Metropolis* as a 'young and pretty widow' (*Ana Historic* 48 / Morley 48) and who is known to history, significantly, only by her husband's name. *Ana Historic* becomes a kind of 'hyst(o)rionic' stage for what Brenda Carr calls 'the drama of a writing woman reading and writing another woman's life/text,' who engages in an ongoing dialogue with readers of her life (as) writing (4). Stan Dragland draws attention to the way this reading/writing takes in the author of *Ana Historic*: 'One has a pleasant, mildly vertiginous feeling, imagining Marlattwriting-AnniewritingAnawriting...' ('Out of the Blank' 179).

Annie's re-naming of Mrs Richards, as 'Ana Richards' alerts the novel's readers to connections between the historical figure and Annie, the contemporary writer-researcher: because the latter also appears in print within her husband's writing, under his name, she is, as Linda Hutcheon observes, at least partly 'Richard's Annie' ('telling accounts' 17). The name also points to the necessity of 'rereading' both Ana and Annie as heterogeneous subjects composed of multiple discourses that break down the boundaries between the 'historical' and 'extra-historical,' since 'ana–' as a prefix means 'back' or 'again' (see *Ana Historic*

43), and as a noun (or suffix) refers to a collection of anecdotes or literary gossip about a person. Like Kroetsch's *The Ledger*, then, *Ana Historic* engages in a kind of colloquial historical 'back talk.' Mrs Richards, a schoolteacher, is described in Annie's account as carrying the materials of her trade, 'the recitation book from which she must choose a passage, the test papers which must be marked' (41). *Ana Historic* may be seen – by ana-logy – as a kind of re-citation book in which 'memory work' – the revisionist project of historical research – involves more than simple repetition: in choosing 'passages' of/through historical writings, and using the 'truth-testing' methods of the documentary-collage, the novel is able to re-mark (on) the past.

Annie's research also elicits recollections of her own unresolved family history, provoking imagined exchanges between Annie and her dead mother, Ina, whose name – An(n)i(e) pronounced backwards – points once again to the role of a 'retroactive' rereading or re-enunci-ation of personal history in *Ana Historic*'s more general reconstitution of historical subjectivity. Ina's 'hysterical' behaviour during Annie's youth is diagnosed by medical authorities as a mental illness and treated, finally, with electric shock therapy. This scientifically sanc-tioned 'cure' effectively silences Ina by cancelling her relation to the past: 'they erased whole parts of you, shocked them out, overloaded the circuits so you couldn't bear to remember' (148–9). As one piece of cited medical evidence shows, the shocks, to put it mildly, would make Ina 'absent-minded': '*The stronger the amnesia, the more severe the underlying brain cell damage must be*' (146 / cited in Frank 58).[1] Freud writes that 'the hysteric suffers mostly from reminiscence' (cited in Wills 141); electro-shock therapy eliminates this symptom. The imag-ined mother-daughter conversations in *Ana Historic* take shape as Annie is coming to terms with the terms of a history that represses both the feminine and the personal or 'subjective.' These conversations become, like the 'therapeutic' act of assembling documents in *Obasan* (see Willis 242), literally, a talking cure for that other cure, fictionally refiguring Ina's voice, and, in effect, regenerating elements of Annie's (absented) heredity.

Ana Historic is punctuated at several points with quotations from psychiatric sources that situate Ina's 'illness.' The acknowledgments at the end of the text indicate that Marlatt found these citations in Leonard Roy Frank's book *The History of Shock Treatment*. This work might itself be considered a fascinating example of the documentary-collage. Frank is an ex-psychiatric patient who lost two years of memory through electro-shock treatment. His book pieces together conflicting perspectives on shock treatment from a variety of sources and discourses covering a wide span of years. It includes, for example, excerpts from psychiatric journals (both defending and attacking shock therapy), cartoons, the personal accounts of psychiatric patients, correspondence, and newspaper articles and advertisements for medical products: it is, in other words, a therapeutic text on/of (the treatment of) 'madness.'

Ana Historic recopies an excerpt from one such advertisement that promotes electro-shock treatment by minimizing the onset of its immediate effects through the appealing musical term 'Glissando' (144 / cited in Frank 48), as well as a psychiatric text that identifies the mental patient's behaviour as pathological and thus 'treats' the family by absolving them of any accountability for her condition, or perhaps for the consequences of its treatment: *'The patient is clearly identified as the "sick" member of the family and the family is reassured they don't need to feel guilty or in any way responsible'* (145 / cited in Frank 91). The novel also cites a female patient's description of the consequence of shock treatment: *'It was something like science fiction. I was alive. I could feel. I felt as if I could think. But the fuel of thinking wasn't there. And it didn't come back'* (149 / cited in Frank 95).[2] These non-fiction citations work to implicate medical authorities in constructing the fictions of science, the apparatuses that frame both physical and social norms, while appearing simply to describe medical histories. The novel similarly cites a number of newspaper articles from the Vancouver area during the nineteenth century, among them a gossipy column called 'FALSEHOODS OF THE HOUR' (69–70, 114, 116, 121), a title whose citation in *Ana Historic* points to the newspaper's complicity in erecting the fictions of history.

The fragmentation and juxtaposition of public, institutional discourses with unofficial, private testimony, both in the instance cited above and elsewhere in *Ana Historic*, itself may be seen as enacting a kind of 'hysterical' disposition. Clair Wills sees an analogy between this sort of disruptive gesture in women's texts and the Bakhtinian carnivalesque's upsetting of official public norms, both of which are linked to the persistent representation of the past within the present:[3] '[the hysteric's] cyclical return to the past mirrors the relation to the past Bakhtin takes as the mark of carnival: in opposition to "official" time, which presents a linear and hierarchical teleology of events, carnivalesque time is aware of "timeliness" and crisis in the version of history which it represents' (130–1). In her discussion of hysteria and Bakhtinian theory, Mary Russo expands on the significance of 'hysterical' representation and the representation of hysteria: 'hysterics and madwomen generally,' she writes, 'have ended up in the attic or in the asylum, their gestures of pain and defiance having served only to put them out of circulation. As a figure of representation, however, hysteria may be less recuperable' (222). *Ana Historic*'s carnivalesque *re*circulation of official and unofficial discourses of the past both violates what Russo calls 'the political economy of the sign as it is produced in dominant discourse' (222) by exceeding the 'original' 'denotative' – or 'recuperable' – significance of the texts it includes, and in so doing resists the 'recuperative' discursive project that seeks to 'cure' those who do not conform to its codes by silencing them.

The process involved in such silencing is indicated obliquely when Annie looks up in the dictionary the apparently dismissive word Ina uses for women's writing – 'scribbling' – only to find that it means 'writing': 'why do we think it so much less? because a child's scribble is unreadable? (she hasn't learned the codes, the quotes yet.) scribe is from the same root, *skeri*, to cut (the ties that bind us to something recognizable – the "facts")' (81). This passage draws attention to the authority of the verbal given, or the inheritance of 'quotes' in defining and enforcing what it is to be normal. Its etymological 'excavation' of the verbal site/cite – in this case a single word – reads historically (both in terms of etymological history and personal history), rerouting/rooting significance, and exposing the value judgments at work in simple 'factual' definition that may, like the psychiatrist's quoted assurances to the mental patient's relations, cut 'the ties that bind,' making the feminine somehow un-familiar. In a system where norms are male, the feminine must be a kind of '*skeri*/scary monster.' The term is not a frivolous one. Later in the novel the monster 'Frankenstein' is pointedly feminized. Readers are reminded that, like Mrs Richards, the monster is, correspondingly, situated as monstrous within a certain circum*scribed* gendered definition of the normal: 'now we call the monster by his name. a man's name for a man's fear of the wild, the uncontrolled. that's where *she* lives' (142).[4]

In her essay 'musing with mothertongue,' Marlatt describes how etymology can *re*familiarize readers with a network of verbal signification: 'in etymology we discover a history of verbal relations (*a family tree, if you will*) that has preceded us & given us the world we live in' (172, emphasis added). As Dennis Cooley perceives, etymology in Marlatt's work announces an engagement with the textual world ('Recursions' 99). It also acknowledges historical determinants at work in textuality. The dictionary, Cooley argues, presides over both

Marlatt's interest in origins and in reflexive writing within a system (ibid.). These two concerns, I would argue, are indistinguishable in *Ana Historic*.[5] The dictionary helps Annie redefine the 'real' as a discursive product; it helps to open up the authority of the written documentary past: it 'saves me when the words stop, when the names stick' (17). Indeed, it 'unsticks' truth itself, offering an alternative definition that demonstrates the extent to which, far from being an absolute, 'truth' depends on assimilation to a 'recognizable' predetermined system of signification. The novel offers this alternative definition: 'true: exactly conforming to a rule, standard, or pattern; trying to sing true' (18).

Lola Lemire Tostevin pursues the correspondence Marlatt suggests between the history of verbal and that of family relations. She objects, however, to a perceived essentialist 'originary' bias in Marlatt's recent work that links these two concerns: 'This genealogy, the *filiation* of a direct line leading back to a fundamental original signification, parallels the search for the lost mother on which traditional Western philosophy and literature are based and contradicts the open-endedness and new beginnings of *l'écriture féminine* which attempts to displace and exceed authority, truth, and the illusionary essence of origins' (35). Lianne Moyes responds to Tostevin, however, that Marlatt's use of etymological connections multiplies and disperses origins, displacing authority in a manner perfectly consonant with the practices of *l'écriture féminine*: 'Root words are ... a site for word-play, a way of disturbing the historical and institutional privileging of certain forms and meanings' ('Writing' 209).

In *Ana Historic*, etymology does, in fact, 'parallel the search for the lost mother' (Ina is Annie's 'Lost Girl' [11]), but not in the essentialist sense to which Tostevin takes exception. Rather, as in *Obasan*, the search is associated with a 'radical' opening up of language to heterogeneous, contradictory, disruptive traces of what Julia Kristeva calls the 'semiotic' – forces that predominate before the child's sense of separation from the mother and entry into the Symbolic, and which may continue thereafter to undermine the *definite*, reified, articulate linguistic Law of the Father that represses these forces (see *Revolution in Poetic Language* 48–51).

The mother as subject in *Ana Historic* becomes what Nancy K. Miller refers to in a more general context as a maternal *text* (798). The novel engages this text in an intertextual relationship. As Miller argues, in representing her mother, the daughter who writes, who writes herself, cannot but begin from that which is always already there (797–8). In

Ana Historic, Ina is (like Frankenstein's monster) a composite, contradictory body of (non-original) citations, the verbal matter/mater that
contributes to Annie's inheritance of genetic/gender/linguistic codes.
One strand of Annie's etymological investigation of her mother's use
of the restrictive term 'woman's lot' as 'what you learn to accept, like
bleeding and hysterectomies, like intuition and dizzy spells – all the
ways we don't fit into a man's world' (79), for example, evokes just
such arbitrary 'genetic' codes that determine her (subject) position in
life and are determined, figuratively, by written symbols: 'woman's lot,
lot: an object used in making a determination or choice by chance (X
and Y or XX or XY and all that follows from that chance determination); a number of people or things ... a piece of land ... one's fortune
in life; fate ...' (79). *Ana Historic* 'relativizes' history and subjectivity by
'characterizing' origins as historical/cultural 'pretexts.' Marlatt's novel
reinforces the point by citing the Bible, *the* great 'genetic' code of
Western culture, and one powerful (textual) source of women's subju-
gation. *Ana Historic* quotes this passage from Genesis, in which the
authoritative voice of God the Father designates woman's lot, tying it
to biology: '*To the woman he said: I will greatly multiply your pain in
childbearing; in pain shall you bring forth children*' (Genesis 4:16 / *Ana
Historic* 118).

Annie finds herself repeating (and *finds herself*, repeating) such
inherited codes: 'echoing your words, Ina – another quotation. except
i quote myself (and what if our heads are full of other people's words,
nothing *without* quotation marks?)' (81, first emphasis added). Annie's
very subjectivity is determined by previous texts, 'other people's
words.' As Linda Hutcheon puts it of the female protagonist of
Thomas's *The White Hotel*: 'she is presented as the "read" subject of her
own and others' interpretations and inscriptions of her. She is literally
the female product of readings' (*Poetics* 161). Annie's subjectivity is,
therefore, paradoxically, intricated (in much the same way as the
subjectivity of the narrators of *The Ledger*, *Convergences*, and *Obasan*) in
her own altered reiteration or rereading of those texts in the process
of historical re-search: 'i quote myself.'

This act of reiteration of the various codes of the past involves re-
membering, a rejoining of misplaced branches or limbs of Annie's
family tree, forgotten etymological branches of meaning, and that
which has been cut off from or ignored by the category of the historical. This is, Annie affirms, a creative gesture: 'now i'm remembering.
not dis- but re-membering' (51). The novel's appropriation of one
particular historical text both enacts and thematizes this process,

reconnecting the account's economic concerns with a broader 'political economy of the sign,' and in so doing unsettling that economy. Pamela Banting calls this a process of 'translation' in which 'the language of history breaks down into its components, namely, the language of nominalization, categorization, hierarchization, domination, coloniz- ation, subordination, and control' (125). The cited text describes the important 'productive' role of certain types of trees in the development of British Columbia: '*Douglas fir and red cedar are the principal trees. Of these, the former – named after David Douglas, a well–known botanist – is the staple timber of commerce. Average trees grow about 150 feet high, clear of limbs, with a diameter of 5 to 6 feet. The wood has great strength and is largely used for shipbuilding, bridgework, fencing, railway ties, and furniture. As a pulp-making tree the fir is valuable. Its bark makes a good fuel*' (13–14). This passage locates the tree within both a masculine linguistic econ- omy (it is 'named after David Douglas') and within a utilitarian mon- etary economy in which de-limbing or dis-membering is necessary in order for the tree to be made into a coherent, objectified, and hence valuable commodity; in the logging business it is economical to trim off the excess: 'clear of limbs? of extras, of asides. tree as a straight line, a stick. there for the taking' (14). The novel's next words align the dual linguistic-financial economy of technological dominance with the economy of a monologic historical line of enquiry: 'Mrs Richards, who stood as straight as any tree (o that Victorian sensibility – backbone, Madame, backbone!) wasn't there for the taking' (14). Except in her noteworthy 'post' (14) as schoolteaching widow, in which she does, temporarily, fit into the historical economy, Mrs Richards is in excess of historical commodification. When she takes up the position of schoolteacher, Mrs Richards fills a gap in that economy since the post had been 'suddenly vacated' by the marriage of its previous occupant (21). *Ana Historic* cites A.M. Ross's appropriately titled 'The Romance of Vancouver's Schools,' drawing attention to the processing of single women through the historical economy, and their displacement/re- cuperation into marriage: '*Miss Sweney was shortly succeeded by Mrs. Richards, who soon became Mrs. Ben Springer and cast her lot with the struggling little hamlet, giving place to a Miss Redfern ... great difficulty was experienced in keeping a teacher longer than six months*' (*Ana Historic* 39 / Ross 13). Annie recalls the logging image of trimming back excess, obliquely relating it to both financial privation and familial excom- munication when she wonders about Mrs Richards's relationship with her father at one point, and asks, significantly, 'Did he cut her off, disallow her?' (55).

Ana Historic's extension of the meaning(s) of history, particularly through its recontexualization of documents, responds to the kind of selective 'illiteracy' by which dominant historical discourse may strategically foreclose on or 'cut off' signification, inscribing women within its codes as 'unreadable' or 'unrecognizable.' Ina's own shock-induced amnesia is related to the economical 'cutting back' of 'excesses' of the biological/botanical/significative body. Placed in juxtaposition with the quotation on brain-cell damage and amnesia mentioned above is a response that relates the historical text's concern with the economics of the production of lumber with the male-defined 'economics' that regulate a woman's reproductive body, as well as her position as product in the marriage market: 'taking out the dead wood. pruning back the unproductive. it was all a matter of husbandry, "the careful management of resources." for everybody's good, of course. a matter of course. (by definition)' (146–7).

Ina's amnesia is related to the enforced 'forgetting' of women within the restrictive monologic narrative of official history, a *mute*-ilation connected in *Ana Historic* with the surgical mutilation of women's 'excessive' bodies: 'hystery. the excision of women (who do not act but are acted upon). hysterectomy, the excision of wombs and ovaries by repression, by mechanical compression, by ice, by the knife' (88). Glen Lowry reads 'Ina as a version of "the other" who exists outside the realm of meaning, and who is unable to fit the confines of her body as it is imagined in phallogocentric bourgeois society. She is victim to "women's trouble" ...' (88). A cited passage from James Hillman's *The Myth of Analysis* gives troubling medical evidence of the literal repression of women's bodies, evidence that also testifies to medicine's historical and philosophical grounding: '*Mechanical devices were invented for compressing ovaries or for packing them in ice. In Germany, Hegar (1830–1914) and Friederich (1825–82) were using even more radical methods, including ovarectomy and cauterization of the clitoris. The source of hysteria was still, as in Plato's time, sought in the matrix of the female body, upon which surgical attacks were unleashed*' (*Ana Historic* 89 / Hillman 89). Annie's frustration with history's claim to 'closure' of its narrative line is also phrased in significantly medical terms that stress the teleological linear progression Bakhtin associates with 'official time': 'that fiction, that lie that you can't change the ending! it's already pre-ordained, prescribed – just what the doctor ordered – in the incontrovertible logic of cause and effect' (147). The 'closed' historical narratives that Annie reads as part of her research, ordered by her husband Richard, that scholarly *Doctor* of Philosophy, might be deemed official

'master narratives' in several senses, but their dis-ordered re-inscrip-
tion within the documentary-collage reveals and to some degree
'controverts' or opens up their logic, counteracting their prescriptive
value.

These narratives tell the story of male dominance over the environment of early British Columbia, a 'historical romance' of possession,
construction, and completion, as this exuberant fragment from M.
Allerdale Grainger's *Woodsmen of the West* leaves little doubt:

> Watch Carter when the 'donk' (his donkey!) has got up first steam;
> and when the rigging men (his rigging men!) drag out the wire
> rope to make a great circle through the woods. And when the circle
> is complete ... and when the active rigging slinger (his rigging
> slinger!) has hooked a log on to a point of the wire cable; and when
> the signaller (his signaller!) has pulled the wire telegraph and made
> the donkey toot ... Think what this mastery over huge, heavy logs
> means to a man who has been used to coax them to tiny move-
> ments by patience and a puny jack-screw ... (*Ana Historic* 25 /
> Grainger 74–5)

Ana Historic's re-citation of the passage asks readers to re-'think what
[and how] this mastery ... means to a *man*,' accentuating the extent to
which this account enacts a politics of power, not simply by describing
the domination and commodification of the landscape as a heroic act,
but also by authoritatively asserting the reality of what is provisional
and contingent on the gender-specific codes of history. The passage
uses an ejaculatory language of possession, but it also relies, implicitly,
on a sense of the possession of, and dominance over, language itself
as instrumental. This interpretation is reinforced if readers violate the
declarative 'intention' of the passage and reread it, drawing out the
figurative implications of Carter's 'mastery of logs,' ownership of the
'signaller,' and control of the 'wire telegraph' line's circuit. As is the
case in other examples (and as we shall see for this instance), Marlatt's
own poetic refiguring of language used 'prosaically' in documentary
citations provokes just such a strategic rereading of that language.

It is worth reiterating here that apparent masculine control over
language stands in contrast to an alternative carnivalesque linguistic
model, related to Kristeva's semiotic, which is associated in the novel
with the reinscription of a feminine body (of writing). The novel
quotes a fragment from Simone de Beauvoir's *The Second Sex* on the
repressed 'hysteric' body of women in general, which is *'worn away in*

service to the species, bleeding each month, proliferating passively, it is not for her a pure instrument for getting a grip on the world but an opaque physical presence (*Ana Historic* 133 / de Beauvoir 619). The quotation is retroactively readdressed to Ina, and then reread in terms of women's relation to language: 'perhaps that explains why our writing, which we also live inside of, is different from men's, and not a tool, not a "pure instrument for getting a grip on the world"' (133). In *Ana Historic*, this 'feminine' approach to language counters both specific official discourses and 'the abstracted, disembodied concept of meaning that the Platonic philosophical tradition has favoured' (Glazener 113). Annie's rebellion against Richard's research project happens when her mind will no longer 'come to grips with lot numbers and survey maps' (79). Instead of 'coming to grips' with historical documents – and the place they map out for women – the novel's carnivalesque use of citation materially em-bodies (or re-*members*) their language, allowing it to be seen as 'an opaque physical presence.' The documentary-collage also allows that language to be intertextually infiltrated, engaging it in dialogue and weakening its grip on the 'real.'

For example, while the Grainger citation reproduced above seems to construct the kind of 'joined story' Robert Kroetsch associates with historical claims to 'authenticity' ('For Play' 93), its citation in the novel un-joins it from its narrative context. Further, the remark that follows the citation points to 'mastery' not just as what is described in the passage, but as the rhetorical effect of its narrative: 'history the story, Carter's and all the others, of dominance. mastery. *the bold line of it*' (25, emphasis added). In a passage early in the novel, Annie recalls a forest landscape of her childhood, a landscape from which she is forbidden: 'those woods men worked in, building powerlines and clearing land for subdivision' (12). In its implicit claim to neutrality, to comprehensive referential mastery over the raw materials of history, its appearance of telling *the* story of the past, *Woodsmen of the West* also builds a linguistic/narrative power line that short-circuits the representation of/by women. This 'power line' is connected to the 'overloaded circuits' of electro-shock therapy that stun Annie's mother into oblivion.

In the course of her historical education Annie learns to recognize and question, however parenthetically, this closed 'patrilineal' circuit: 'i learned that history is the real story the city fathers tell of the only important events in the world ... so many claims to fame. so many ordinary men turned into heroes. (where are the city mothers?) the city fathers busy building a town out of so many shacks labelled the

Western Terminus of the Transcontinental, Gateway to the East – all these capital letters to convince themselves of its, of their, significance' (28). Letters themselves are here shown to be powerful producers of the 'real story.' They are conceived as valued property, 'capital' for the historiographic venture. Annie's focus on Mrs Richards's refusal to adopt the role of Proper Lady, 'Lady capitalized,' is one way she pursues a reading of the teacher as rejecting a commodified 'woman's place' as *real estate* within this truth-telling historical economy: 'it is barely sounded,' Annie comments, 'the relationship between proper and property' (32). As Linda Hutcheon observes, 'The brief accounts of such women that do exist in the historical archives place them only as ancillary, as adjuncts to men and their capital. (Hence, perhaps, Annie's reluctance to "capitalize" her first person pronoun "i")' ('telling accounts' 17). In this reluctance to 'capitalize,' Annie attempts to reconstruct by reappraised repetition of the given (capital 'I' becomes small-case 'i') a subjectivity that unsettles the existing patriarchal discursive economy.

The comments on Annie's historical education quoted above are juxtaposed with an excerpt from J.S. Matthews's historical study, *Early Vancouver*, describing the process of making Vancouver a capital(ist) or first-rate city: '*A world event had happened in Vancouver ... On the eve of the Queen's Birthday, 1887, the Canadian Pacific Railway ... closed the last gap in the "All-Red Route," and raised the obscure settlement on the muddy shore of Water Street, sobriquetly termed "Gastown," to the status of a world port.* Major Matthews' (28). Matthews's description of this event gives the local incident the authority of global significance: it is a 'world event.' In *Ana Historic*, the story of the closing of the last gap in the railway may be read meta-historically; it comes to signify narrative closure itself. Reaney's *Sticks and Stones* makes similar use of the railway image: in it, black settlers are 'railroaded' off their land – and out of the historical record – in order to make way for a railway and the Irish. The railway image is also associated with the mastering narrative impulse in *Obasan*, in which Japanese-Canadians who refuse to 'entrain' to work camps are entered on a 'wanted list.' In chapter 6, this image is deconstructed via the fabric train (wake)/railway pun suggested by the novel's narrative strategies.

The railway is first associated with prior masculine control of the processes of signification in *Ana Historic* when, in the disoriented opening passage of the novel, Annie awakens to 'the sound of a train, in some yard where men already up were *working signals*' (9, emphasis added). Formally, *Ana Historic*, like the other works just enumerated,

derails monologic historical narratives using the methods of the documentary-collage, fragmenting and disrupting the impetus of the given
story, and incorporating alternative historical tellings. In *Reading for the
Plot*, Peter Brooks investigates the steam engine in a number of nineteenth-century texts as a figure for narrative desire (see 37ff.). Using
railway imagery, *Ana Historic* refigures this desire, effecting a kind of
'derailment'/*deraillement* ('talking nonsense') of narrative and even
syntactical sense in which the parenthetical becomes primary, and (the)
story gets off track, or, to return to the language of logging, it deviates
from the 'trunk line.' Annie, for example, says she 'can't seem to stay
on track, nor can my sentence, even close its brackets' (17). She cannot,
in other words, conform to established norms of behaviour, which are
elsewhere imaged as a matter of *training*: Richard assures Annie that
if she cannot complete the research project he 'can always *train* one of
my grad students to replace you' (147, emphasis added). An obvious
example of 'off track' historical narrative is Annie's novel-within-the-
novel, which fabricates and revalues the story of the 'insignificant' Mrs
Richards by interpreting the personal journal Annie discovers in the
archives, an account labelled '"inauthentic," fictional possibly' (30) by
archival authorities, for whom it is 'a document, yes, but not history'
(31).[6]

Annie's fictional return to Mrs Richards's private history is an
alternative to Richard's version of documentary history. It is an
attempt, not simply to fill in historical blanks, but to theorize the
construction of the (absent/inauthentic) feminine within the authoritative fiction of history. This aspect of the novel draws on the premises
of 'fiction theory,' writing so called by feminist writers because it, in
Marlatt's terms, allows its readers to identify 'the fiction we've been
conditioned to take for the real, fictions which have not only constructed woman's place in patriarchal society but have constructed the
very "nature" of woman' ('Theorizing Fiction Theory' 10). Fiction
theory, Marlatt continues, both deconstructs such fictions and proffers
an alternative, self-consciously fictional 'angle on the real' (ibid.).

Annie's 'derailment' or deviation from given narrative/syntactical
codes is produced by her perception of incoherences in both historical
accounts and the plot-lines within which she is asked to live. As Annie
says to Ina, 'you didn't teach me about asides, you never told me the
"right track" is full of holes, pot holes of absence' (17). Next to two
conflicting documentary accounts of Mrs Richards's place of residence,
one of which says that she lived in Gastown, the other that she lived
in a cottage with her new husband, the novel 'settles on' neither one

nor the other, but opts for the space of fictional possibility between the two citations: 'for that is where she is. in the gap between two versions' (106). Annie's own 'incoherence' is associated with her inability – and unwillingness – to adopt a stable, coherent subject position from which to speak authoritatively. She is, as she illustrates, the site of contending forces: 'i don't even want to "pull yourself together," as Richard urges' (17). Like Mrs Richards, she is 'subject to self-doubt in a situation without clearly defined territory' (32).

On the other hand, both apparent narrative coherence – the 'right track' – and the coherent, effective subject of historical enunciation are linked with the construction of the main line of the railway. Two first-person historical documents that gain authority via their historically specific numerical and spatial detail (28–9) are followed by this remark: 'I/my laying track with facts rescued against the obscurity of bush' (29). The novel, however, as we have seen, questions the constitution of such facts. In this instance, it formally breaks down the word 'fact' itself: 'what is fact? (f) act. the f stop of act. a still photo in the ongoing cinerama' (31). In this fictional etymology (a parallel to the fictional narrative of Mrs Richards), 'fact' turns out to be an act that brackets the feminine [(f)], making the latter parenthetical to 'the only important events in the world.' The 'obscurity' of that which lies outside the realm of the factual is literally 'dark,' but the 'obscure' is also both that which is 'not clearly expressed' (or incoherent) and what goes 'unnoticed.' These qualities, the novel reveals, are not absolute but are measured by the standards of the instrument of representation itself, in this case, the 'f stop,' literally a photographic gauge for calculating the opening of the lens aperture, which *regulates* the amount of light reaching the film, thus predetermining the 'obscurity' of its subject, just as conventional history prescribes what constitutes the 'significant.' The instrument of representation is here also responsible both for limiting the scope of what it represents, and for 'stopping' or reifying it: it produces a 'still photo' as opposed to the process-oriented wide-screen *motion* pictures of 'cinerama.' Finally, in appearing to be true and objective, fact also 'stops up' gaps that might reveal its provisionality.

As in Ondaatje's *The Collected Works of Billy the Kid*, photographic framing is associated in *Ana Historic* both with the objectifying language of historical narrative, and with a juridical setting in which an individual is convicted through 'framing,' or the construction of an incriminating plot. Framing, in its judicial sense, is often accomplished by the marshalling of damning – but fictional – evidence against the individual charged. In traditional historical narrative, paradoxically, documentary evidence damns women by giving them what amounts to an *alibi*: it testifies to their absence as effective subjects. If that evidence is revealed as a construct, or fiction, however, the alibi can be broken. *Ana Historic* compounds the notion of historical/photo-graphic/legal framing with a gendered scenario in which women are reified by the male gaze, a 'look' Annie is taught to solicit, first inces-tuously from her father, then more generally within patriarchal society. As film theorist Laura Mulvey puts in her well-known essay 'Visual Pleasure and Narrative Cinema,' 'In a world ordered by sexual imbal-ance, pleasure in looking has been split between active/male and passive/female. The determining male gaze projects its phantasy onto the female figure which is styled accordingly' (11). The 'female figure,' one might say, is a rhetorical figure in a male-defined discursive situation. In this passage from *Ana Historic*, Annie relates a concept quite similar to Mulvey's to the notion of truth as styled to historical norms: 'whose truth, Ina? the truth is (your truth, my truth, if you would admit it) incest is always present, it's there in the way we're trained to solicit the look, and first of all the father's, Our Father's. framed by a phrase that judges (virgin/tramp), sized-up in a glance, objectified. that's what history offers, that's its allure, its pretence. "history says of her ..." but when you're so framed, caught in the act, the (f) stop of act, fact – what recourse? step inside the picture and open it up' (56). The novel's re-citative rereading of historical materials is accomplished precisely by a re-course that goes back over the narrative 'tracks' of history with a disruptive, interrogative effect that 'steps inside the picture,' appealing (to) the definitive sentence ('the phrase that judges'), and incriminating the evidence itself. The extended network of significance put into play by intertextual citation thus produces what Laurent Jenny appropriately terms 'a definitive rejection of the full stop which would close the meaning and freeze the form' (60).

Ana Historic's re-contextualized quotation of historical texts also re-sights the masculine eye/I behind the (historical) camera, itself subject to historical determinants. To refigure the sexual trope, the novel sol*icit(e)s* the documents that constitute the male gaze, but suggests the empowering possibilities of returning that gaze through rereading. Annie, looking through photographs of herself and her sisters, reverses the subject-object scenario described above, remembering the historiographic *act* of 'our father invisible behind the camera imaging moments of this female world' (51). Roland Barthes asserts that the objective 'reality effect' (Historical Discourse' 154) of historical writing is 'a particular form of fiction,' linked to the realist novel, and based on the suppression of the 'I' that would make the narrator visible: 'the historian tries to give the impression that the referent is speaking for itself' (ibid. 149). Using the language of documentary-film sound (where voice-over narration is often used), *Ana Historic* refers to that voice as a retrospective, interpretive meta-voice, identified with the reductive male gaze that closes the past off from reinterpretation by seeming to offer a final account: 'history is the historic voice (voice over), elegiac, epithetic. a diminishing glance as the lid is closed firmly and finally shut. that was her. summed up. Ana historic' (48). As Derek Paget observes, the montage strategy disrupts any single context, providing a 'complex seeing' in which 'no one position achiev[es] pre-eminence for long enough to acquire the reassuring tone of the voice-over commentary' (48).

In her writing of Mrs Richards's life, Annie re-stages a 'looking back' on/in history similar to the memory of Annie's own framing by her father's eye behind the camera. In this incident, Mrs Richards becomes aware of the fact that she is being visually framed by invisible observers. Her solitude in her cabin is invaded one night by 'a sudden rapping at her door': 'she opens the door – onto darkness, obscure as black pall in the drumming rain. she hears feet thudding back up the trail, stifled laughter, someone shouts, "Knockie Knockie, Run Awa'"' and sees herself as she must be seen, caught in the doorway in nightclothes' (65). This incident is reminiscent of the self-conscious 'see-sawing' of perspective evoked in Reaney's *Sticks and Stones*. *Ana Historic*'s self-conscious use of documents extends the scenario: the woman reading reads herself as she is read in the texts of history. Unlike Mrs Richards in the particular incident described above, however, the novel offers potential responses to the historical reading. The knocking at Mrs Richards's door recalls the opening of *Ana Historic*: 'Who's there? she was whispering. knock knock. in the dark' (9). As Linda Hutcheon writes, documents are 'signs within already semiotically constructed contexts, themselves dependent upon institutions (if they are official records) or individuals (if they are eye-witness accounts)' (*Poetics* 122). *Ana Historic*'s interrogative 'Who's there?' addresses just such contexts. The novel describes and enacts a kind of responsive knocking back through/as recontextualized readings of documents. Annie, for example, sits at her desk, extending her research by typing a fictional story and (re)defining the limits of 'woman's place' as it is given in the writings she studies: 'she was knocking on paper, not wood, tapping like someone blind along the wall of her solitude' (45).

The question, then, is from the beginning one of positionality and address. Mrs Richards's journal runs out at the same time the record shows that she married Ben Springer. Her silence, like Ina's, 'was all a matter of husbandry' (146): 'Entered as Mrs., she enters his house as his wife. she has no first name. she has no place, *no place on the street*, not if she's a "good woman." her writing stops' (134, emphasis added). As a wife, she has, in other words, no position from which to speak, no appropriate form of *address*. *Ana Historic* adopts the same 'wifely' position, but only as a pose, since its appropriative or inappropriate reading of past writing is itself a form of address that talks back to history by reiterating it: it is, simultaneously, a 'mis-reading' of history, a Mrs (or wife) reading history, and a rereading of Mrs (Annie/Ina/Ana)/misses in history. It offers, in other words, a feminist rereading of the past in which, as Barbara Godard suggests, the ownership of the discursive property that defines 'woman's place' is itself placed in dispute: 'Alerted to the ways in which woman is eternally the object, the absence, the minus in patriarchal discourse, the feminist reader confronts the issue of control. Who owns the meaning of the black marks on the page, the writer or the reader?' ('Becoming My Hero' 144–5).

The appropriation of a series of newspaper excerpts in *Ana Historic* effects one such contestation of ownership. The newspaper account describes a boat race in which, as is traditional, all the boats have feminine names. This cited description asserts the importance of primacy associated with official narratives. The competition takes place on *Dominion* Day, and includes an official who judges the positions of the boats: *'It is, as a general thing, a rule in these cases that the first boat to pass the Judge wins – in fact, the one which comes in first. This was to be the rule, too, in the race on Dominion Day. But as the 'Annie Fraser' came in first, the 'Pearl' could not do more than come in second, and was consequently beaten; while the 'Annie Fraser' came in first, and consequently won. That is really the true solution of the whole matter'* (124). The novel's appropriation and recontextualization of the boat-race passages calls attention to the hierarchical positioning of historical subject-matter, which is, after all, a matter of judgment. The description is interspersed with the novel's fictionalized description of a 'first place' that does not appear as such in the historical record: the site of the first white birthing, a communal, woman-centred event at Hastings Sawmill (intermittently, on 120–7). This place appears in the historical record, but is identified in a photo caption only as 'Hastings Sawmill. First dwelling of R.H. Alexander, afterwards manager. Later occupied by office men as bachelors hall' (120). The fictionalized account, in effect, re-occupies the historical cite/site as a woman's place.

In *Ana Historic* citation is a playfully feminine 'reproductive' gesture that breaks the closed patrilineal circuit in which the documents of history circulate only within a masculine discursive economy. As Janice Williamson seems aware, the question 'Who's there?' at the beginning of *Ana Historic* can be directed to various places, and in fact puts positionality itself in question: 'Is this addressed to another character in the novel? To ana herself who asks it? Or does the question interpellate the reader herself into the text, calling to her, to him, to interrogate her/his own relation to the writing at hand?' (7). As Linda Hutcheon adds, 'None of us/you escapes this address, escapes being written into this woman's history, her story' ('telling accounts' 19).

Annie's writing is a 'looking for the company of another who was also reading – out through the words, through the wall that separated her, an arm, a hand –' (45). It is a form of reading as re-membering a highly provisionalized, carnivalized 'body of knowledge' that, as Williamson and Hutcheon indicate, takes in both the past and the historical present, transgressing the boundaries that separate reader from text. Annie finds a woman reading in her friend (and eventual lover) Zoe, who asks, 'don't you think we read with a different eye?' (107). Or, perhaps, with a different 'i,' a different subject position, or relationship to the text.[7]

When Zoe takes Annie to her home, Annie finds a group of women engaged in informal conversation, at the same time literally addressing letters that disseminate their version of 'woman's place' as a site of dialogue: 'Eunice and Zoe were talking at the kitchen table while they folded and applied stamps to a pile of flyers' (151). Annie joins in this activity, in which she appropriates the historical image of a woman (as she appropriates the figure of Mrs Richards in her writing), but subjects it to a new use: 'hundreds of tiny images of the Queen, passing under my thumb' (151). The activity of these women in sending out 'flyers,' as well as the name of the historical lover Annie imagines for Ana – Birdie – evokes Hélène Cixous's punning play on the French word *voler* as both a transgressory feminine stealing of language, as well as a taking off from the 'solid ground of fact' as it is established in male discourse (*Ana Historic* 111). In a passage that might be used as a general description of *Ana Historic*'s feminist use of the methods of documentary-collage, Cixous elaborates on the significance of the pun:

> Flying is woman's gesture – flying in language and making
> it fly ... We've lived in flight, stealing away. finding, when
> desired, narrow passageways, hidden crossovers, It's no acci-
> dent that *voler* has a double meaning, that it plays on each
> of them and thus throws off the agents of sense. It's no acci-
> dent: women take after birds and robbers just as robbers
> take after women and birds. They [*illes*] go by, fly the coop,
> take pleasure in jumbling the order of space, in disorienting
> it, in changing around the furniture, dislocating things and
> values, breaking them all up, emptying structures, and turn-
> ing propriety upside down. (258)

Ana Historic acknowledges that since it is impossible to forget or completely neutralize the language of history, 'one might as well,' as Laurent Jenny puts it, 'subvert its ideological poles' (59), turning propriety – and linguistic property – upside down. The novel does so, in part, by effecting the kind of radical intertextual return to past writing described by Jenny in which 'the possibility of a new *parole* will open up, growing out of the cracks of the old discourse, rooted in them. In spite of themselves these old discourses will drive all the force they have gained as stereotypes into the *parole* which contradicts them, they will energize it' (59). It is precisely such an energized economy of reading that *Ana Historic* fosters, a 'feminized' economy in which a woman seizes the occasion to speak, and in doing so 'transform[s] directly and indirectly *all* systems of exchange based on masculine thrift' (Cixous 252). Cixous writes, 'As subject for history, woman always occurs simultaneously in several places. Woman un-thinks [*dé-pense*] the unifying, regulating history that homogenizes and channels forces, herding contradictions into a single battlefield' (252). This economy of un-thinking at the expense of the given is neither outside history (a-historic) nor assimilated to it, but ana-historic: it redefines an intertextual space in which the writings that map out 'woman's place' are forced to 'finance their own subversion' (Jenny 59).

Postscript

Finally, that art of difference, of discontinuity – collage – I take to be a quintessential expression of the temper of the time, or of the 'passage' through this century that is now coming to an end.

Bert M.-P. Leefmans

Bert M.-P. Leefmans sees the strategy of collage as advancing two major ideas, two halves of a 'paradoxical (or complementary) whole,' which have come to prominence in the twentieth century. The first is that language, 'while it clearly is used to communicate ideas that are already extant, is also involved in the creation of thought in the first place'; the second is the notion that 'context determines the significance of any given word' (186). The examples of documentary-collage investigated in this study acknowledge, in keeping with the first half of Leefman's formulation, the extent to which our positioning in the world (site-ing), and our vision of it (sighting), also involves an implicit citation of the textually given. In the juxtapositional process of literally re-citing documentary texts, these works put into play the second half of that formulation, opening up the possibility of contextual/interpretive difference and multivoicedness. This may be a playful, re-creative literary gesture, but, as demonstrated by several of the works examined here, it is an important political one as well.

In rereading this study, I note that it is traversed not only by the voices of other texts, but also by several significant metaphoric patterns that, while they do not define the documentary-collage, do offer some useful figures for both the literary form and the critical act it both enacts and provokes. These patterns both suggest the contingencies of the world as it is represented and assert a continuing process of reformulation, revision and response. Mapping, for example, is a recurrent trope that in these works tends to incorporate a sense of historicized *textual* grounding as well as the inscription of a provisional positionality for the subject – several texts overtly raise the issue of Canadian geographical/social space, problematizing or ironically revisioning the idea of a North American 'new world' or a Canadian 'home and native land.' I have been calling the works of documentary-collage examined here 'truth-testing' textual apparatuses. They often work to interrogate the very nature of truth and the institutions that legislate it, and this interrogation is frequently suggested by way of a judicial metaphor. The formal construction of the documentary-collage participates in the trope by offering 'evidence' and 'testimony' from a variety of sources and, implicitly, by placing the reader in a position in which it is necessary both to make judgments of fact and value *and* to place such judgments in question. The multivoiced discursive exchange between positions is also sometimes featured as dramatic or conversational, and the conversation is again one in which the reader must participate. When drama is employed or evoked, the audience is never simply a passive spectator: in the act of reading, the courtroom and theatre overlap. Intersecting concerns of ethical, interpretive, and financial value and its exchange are often foregrounded by means of the language of economics. Lastly, the image of documentary film itself is both raised at several points and problematized, particularly the notion of the authoritative voice-over narration of the documentary film, a narration that supersedes other possibilities, and is therefore in confict with the effect of the documentary-collage, which while it may include the voice of authority, en-counters it dialogically.

The first chapter of this study suggests that the found poem is a kind of 'post-scripting,' since it is both after writing and a writing, after. This book might itself be considered a post-scripting in relation to the literary/critical writings it examines. As Antoine Compagnon puts it of his critical work, *La Seconde Main, ou le travail de la citation*, this study is as much a discourse *of* citation as it is a treatise *on* citation (12). As such, it takes on 'the work of citation,' a work that has no conclusion since it both examines and is the production of a text, a 'working paper' (37). As a reading of the Canadian writing at issue here suggests, the work of citation is critical work indeed.

Notes

Introduction

1 Livesay also discusses at length Isabella Valancy Crawford's 'Malcolm's Katie,' but, as Stephen Scobie comments, 'as fine and important a poem as "Malcolm's Katie" is, it is *not* a documentary, by any stretch of the definition, and one suspects that Livesay was using any excuse to give it some prominence at a time when Crawford was unjustly neglected' ('Amelia' 267). Owing largely to Frye's commentaries, the other poet Livesay considers at length, E.J. Pratt, was already assured a canonical position.

2 Leslie Monkman identifies a more general broadening of interest in what Frye considered beyond the literary pale: 'Despite Northrop Frye's claim that the exploration narratives surveyed in the opening chapters of the *Literary History of Canada* are "as innocent of literary intention as a mating loon," a survey of recent criticism and textbook anthologies reveals the increasingly prominent place of these accounts in the canon of English-Canadian literature' (80). For a summary of these sources, see Monkman's note (95–6).

3 The distinction is also subverted in a volume of found poems discussed in chapter 1, Colombo's *Leonardo's Lists*, which transforms prosaic 'inventories' into 'inventive' poems, thereby drawing attention to the fact that 'invent' comes from a Middle English word meaning 'discover.'

4 Davey also identifies a clash in the meaning of terms in Livesay's article, noting that 'there lurks in Livesay's essay a second dialectic – between the dictionary word "document" and the use she wishes to make of it,

between its insistence on "actual data" and her recognition that the poems she seeks to name are themselves variously "lyrical" (269), "prophetic" (274), and reach for "prophetic truth." This is a dialectic between poetry as scientifically true, as pound and Olson hoped, and poetry as oxymoronically true – as Birney, Ondaatje, and Kroetsch appear to assume' ('Recontextualization' 129).

5 Godard refers to the original title of the article as it appeared in *Open Letter* (6th ser., nos. 2–3 [Summer–Fall 1985]: 33–44), 'Countertextuality in the Long Poem.'

6 One precedent for grounding the 'past identity' of the cited text in reader-recognition is Peter Rabinowitz's categorization of various approaches to 'literary recycling' according to the audience's perception of the 'recycled' text in '"What's Hecuba to Us?" The Audience's Experience of Literary Borrowing.' An advantage of this strategy is, first, that it roots the identity of the text in the reading of the text, a key theoretical move discussed further in chapter 1. Second, it allows us to avoid the very theoretical crux raised by the documentary-collage: that of calling the cited text 'true' or 'real.' It also circumvents the problem of minor textual alterations in the translation of the quoted text from context to context.

7 Kristeva calls 'inferential agents' words that mediate between the author's enunciation and that of others, such as 'if, *as* Vergil says ... ,' 'and *thereupon* Saint Jerome *says*,' etc.: 'These are empty words whose functions are both *junctive* and *translative*. As junctive, they tie together (totalize) two minimal utterances (narrative and citational) within the global, novelistic utterance. They are therefore internuclear. As translative, they transfer an utterance from one textual space (vocal discourse) into another (the book), changing its ideologeme. They are thus intranuclear' ('The Bounded Text' 45–6).

8 All citations of Compagnon are my translation.

Chapter One

1 My translation

2 George Bowering's long poem *George, Vancouver* plays with a similar correspondence of names and place names. See 'Colombo Fails' for another found poem that plays with the fortuitous correspondence of names (*Translations* 67).

3 This poem's advice also bears a marked similarity to Tristan Tzara's instructions in 'How To Make a Dadaist Poem' (39). Colombo re-cites Tzara's manifesto in *Variable Cloudiness* (50).

4 See, for example, Colombo's 'Twin Definitions' (*Translations* 29),
'Canada: Etymologies' (*The Sad Truths* 39–40), 'Interrogation' (*Variable
Cloudiness* 20), 'The Conventional Wisdom' (ibid. 20–1), 'Rhymed Pro-
verbs' (ibid. 22–3), 'Rhymes without Reason' (ibid. 24–6) and 'Proverbial
Ruth' (ibid. 27–8).

Chapter Two

1 Henri Béhar points out that, although it is less known than the visual-
arts movements of the 1920s, there was an identical movement in the
literary world, from Lautréamont's adaptations, to Marcelin Playnet,
Jean-Pierre Faye, Michel Butor, Maurice Roche, and so on ('Débris,
collage et invention poétique' 102–3).
2 Unless otherwise indicated, all references to *The Ledger* are to the 1979
Brick/Nairn edition. This edition is unpaginated.
3 Breunig is discussing the name of the artist or poet. His point is, I think,
equally applicable to other kinds of historical names included in the
text.

Chapter Three

Throughout this chapter, *CWBK* is used as an abbreviation for *The
Collected Works of Billy the Kid*.
1 See *Grierson on Documentary*, especially part 5, 'Education: A New Concept' (191–226).
2 *The Collected Works*'s use of multiple unnarrated perspectives and the
legendary character of its hero have certainly made it conducive to theatrical productions and readings. See Judith's Brady's 'A Bibliography'
in *Spider Blues* for a list of sixteen mountings of the play (A24: 347–8)
and three readings on CBC Radio (B17–19: 350). Most recently, *The
Collected Works of Billy the Kid* was staged at the Tarragon Theatre in
Toronto in the 1989–90 season, directed by Joann McIntyre.
3 Perry Nodleman and T.D. MacLulich, for example, both see the volume
as a kind of photograph album that assembles a series of still images
(Nodleman 68; MacLulich 108), and the latter reads it as 'a warning
against the dehumanizing consequences of photographic voyeurism'
(109). Lorraine York similarly sees the image of the photograph as a
metaphor for Billy's destructive attempt to control and fix his own
world, and for Ondaatje's attempt to fix Billy's character (104, 106),
while Dennis Cooley conducts an analysis of the tension between images

of 'modernist' still photography and 'postmodern' cinematic reference in
the poem ('"I am here"'). Stephen Tatum, finally, sees a parallel between
the poem's 'violent manipulations of time and ideas' and rapid editing
techniques in cinema and television, and comments that this style 'usefully parallel[s] the violence in the outlaw's life (and death)' (152).

4 See Barthes's comments on desire and the blind field in erotic photography (*Camera Lucida* 57–8).

5 Other extracts from Burns include those found in *The Collected Works* on
pages 19 (Burns 194–5), 29 (Burns 196), 30 (Burns 11, 15), 52 (Burns
15–16), 80 (Burns 222), 87 (Burns 16, 17), 89 (Burns 18, 19), and 96 (Burns
183–4).

6 I would like to thank Dominick Grace for showing me the original of
this comic book.

7 The interview is invented by Ondaatje as what Kenneth Rexroth would
call a 'false document' (cited in Doctorow 220).

8 Gilliam's playful generic combination of science and fiction is appropriate to Ondaatje's poetic undermining of empirical proof.

Chapter Four

1 Bowering 'Reaney's Region,' 8

2 These 'code names' are used by Issacharoff (27).

3 In his study *True Stories: Documentary Drama on Radio, Screen and Stage,*
Derek Paget makes the connection between a certain kind of documentary drama and the film tradition of early Soviet 'collision montage'
editing that, unlike Hollywood's concealed or 'invisible edits,' focused
on the jarring juxtaposition of images, insisting on the viewer's ability to
mediate conflict, and to pay attention to the way the seen/scene is constructed: 'There is a healthy (although by no means valorised) tradition
of collision montage in theatre in which "joins" are not concealed at all'
(41). It is surely no coincidence that the film-maker Ondaatje cites on the
subject of the documentary, Jean-Luc Godard, is one of the artists best
known for deliberately disrupting the illusionist or 'continuity' editing
associated with the Hollywood tradition, perhaps most famously
through his use of the 'jump cut.'

4 Reaney, among others, uses the term 'collage' in various senses to
describe the plays. Reaney observes that 'there's a collage of song, choral
speech, a downpour of small scenes, mime, dance, images created by
props, cats cradles, tops spinning &c' ('A Letter' 2), and comments elsewhere that 'my recent plays have been ribbon collages of metaphors
both visual, tactile and auditory; these strips are then threaded through

the projector of audience-cum-actors' ('"Your plays are like movies"' 40). Patricia Ludwick maintains that, in the Donnelly plays, 'we have to open our ears; each word, each bell, each throwing of a stone is a carefully placed effect in a collage of created sound' (133), and notes that the actors' physical idiosyncrasies function as 'pieces of [Reaney's] collage' (136). Gerald Parker calls the variety of verbal and auditory structures used a kind of 'pop collage' ('Melodrama and Tragedy' 167). George Bowering, as my chapter title indicates, calls the Donnelly plays 'the collage in motion' ('Reaney's Region' 8). Susan Sontag, interestingly, refers to the performance-art 'Happenings' of the 1960s as 'animated collages' (270). She observes that Happenings extend the Surrealist 'collage principle' by which counter-meanings are created by means of radical juxtaposition (271). Her statements are certainly applicable to Reaney's dramas.

5 *Montreal Star*, 1 December 1975, cited by Reaney in *14 Barrels* 153. The graffiti are also apparent in Lise Steele's photographs in *Black Moss*.

6 This positioning was confirmed by photographs of a production of *Sticks and Stones* shown to me by Gerald Parker. I am grateful to him for sharing them.

7 As James Noonan and others have observed, the Medicine Show is a satire of Thomas Kelley's work of 'pulpular fiction' (Butt 508), *The Black Donnellys*. The Showman Murphy is a send-up of Kelley himself. The Showman's doggerel recitation is from the song that introduces each chapter of Kelley's book (Noonan 5).

8 This is the same type riot described by Mackenzie in Colombo's found poem 'The Type Riots,' discussed in chapter 1.

9 Dragland catalogues these forms, which include film, the novel, poetry, songs, dances, puppet theatre, mime theatre, detective fiction, the trial scene, and the Roman Catholic liturgy (40).

10 Gerald Parker expands on the importance of sound as thematic and structural device in the Donnelly plays in '"The key word ... is 'listen'": James Reaney's "sonic environment."'

Chapter Five

1 The title of Kearns's first book of poems is *Songs of Circumstance* (1962).

2 Warren Tallman writes that when George Bowering, Frank Davey, David Dawson, Kearns, James Reid, and Fred Wah decided to start *Tish* magazine, Kearns declined to be an editor, but acted as one for all practical purposes (53).

3 In his 'Introduction to Robert Creeley,' Olson notes the possibility of

'what I call DOCUMENT simply to emphasize that the events alone do the work, that the narrator stays OUT, functions as pressure not as interpreting person, illuminates not by argument or "creativity" but by master of force ... the art, to make his meanings clear by how he juxtaposes, correlates, and causes to interact whatever events and persons he chooses to set in motion' (127). The version of documentary offered in Kearns's *Convergences* is based on a model of juxtaposition in which there is no *master* narrator, and in which passages attributed to the poem's contemporary speaker are formally separated from the cited documents. Both these features are in keeping with Olson's comments. However, the poem also implies that 'staying out' of the interpretation of documents/events is an impossibility; their reading is always contextually embedded.

4 Lianne Moyes describes the formal arrangement of the poem: 'The columns of large typeface present a discontinuous, "historical narrative" written in prose with a ragged right-hand margin; the columns of italics are "historical documents," direct quotations from explorers' journals written in prose but transformed into verse with ragged left and right margins; and the columns of small typeface present a self-conscious discourse written in prose with justified margins' ('Dialogizing the Monologue' 16).

5 *Convergences* is strategically unpaginated: the narrator comments, 'You are free to shuffle these pages and browse, but I cannot answer your questions because I am too busy answering my own questions and posing new unanswerable questions.' Since I quote extensively from the poem, for the sake of convenience, I have committed the self-conscious injustice of numbering its pages.

6 George Bowering points out that as early as *Songs of Circumstance*, Kearns 'employed a Saussurian idea of the transcription as transmission between ear and ear' ('Metaphysic in Time' 117). *Convergences* does not seem to valorize the 'originality' of the oral, as Saussure does. Rather, as I will argue, orality becomes a provocative image, stressing the performative quality of language in general.

7 Frederic Jameson uses the term 'cognitive mapping' to indicate the ideological implications of spatial perception.

8 In his article, 'The Function of Criticism at the Present Time,' Eli Mandel proposes, in opposition to the New Critical / New Aristotelian 'civilized' literary critic, a concept of the critic as 'savage.' The 'savage' critic, Mandel argues, challenges established canons. Mandel describes this critic in language that strongly recalls Bakhtin's idea of the carnivalesque in almost every respect: its emphasis on 'misrule,' its associ-

ation with festival, its focus on laughter, the irrational, the grotesque. The savage critic might well be seen as an agent of the carnivalesque: 'He appears as the image of all that is irrational in the human being: revelry and misrule, gluttony and mischief, folly and trickery, cunning and simple-mindedness. And it is precisely this which the civilized and cultivated man is not prepared to admit into his life, unless only in the few holidays he will allow himself, and then only in the most cautious and disguised way. But if there is any sense at all in which art is an expression of irrational urges, the desire of man, it follows that the civilized or cultivated approach to art will invariably either turn it into an illusion or into an intellectual structure. As the language of the body, anarchic, grotesque, ludicrous, art remains an illusion to the intellect and a threat to the ordering powers of man' ('The Function of Criticism' 70).

Chapter Six

1 See *House of Commons Debates* 15 (22 September 1988), 19501. At a press conference on the same date, Gerry Weiner, then minister of state for multiculturalism and citizenship, also read from the novel (Multiculturalism and Citizenship Canada news release, 22 September 1988). I would like to thank Laura Cinkant and Tadeusz Wieclawek, two of my students of Canadian Literature at Carleton University, and Wilma Gray of Multiculturalism and Citizenship Canada for helping to track down these references.

2 Arun Mukherjee describes how non-white writers appropriate fairy tales in order to comment on their experience of racism, using another example from *Obasan*, a 'racialized version' of 'Goldilocks and the Three Bears' (*Obasan* 126). 'In Kogawa's version,' Mukherjee writes, 'the fairy tale becomes a myth about the last five centuries of the history of imperialism. The incarceration of Naomi's family at Slocan can now be read as part of a larger story of racism' (165). This, like the other uses of fairy tales, may be seen as an example of a recontexualized retrospection on childhood stories.

3 The letter is cited in Kitagawa 193. Using Loretta Czernis's work on Canadian unity policy, Robin Potter points to the importance of anonymity in such documents, as demonstrated in *Obasan*: 'The voice of the good becomes universalized because no one author can be isolated, let alone questioned. The Government Document is as such an authorless piece of writing that is nevertheless implemented and reacted to as given' (122). It is no coincidence that the 'voice of history' is just such an

anonymous voice, whose 'objectivity' relies on the suppression of the author's 'I' (see the next chapter, and Barthes's 'Historical Discourse'). Naomi's subjective, particularized responses to documents work to counteract this false objectivity.

4 These writings are often slightly altered by Kogawa to suit the exigencies of her fictional telling. Since the publication of *Obasan*, they have appeared in book form as *This Is My Own: Letters to Wes and Other Writings on Japanese Canadians 1941–1948*.

5 The image of the dog listening to 'His Master's Voice' that appears on record labels is obliquely suggested, and associated with documentary (photographic) records in a description of the Nakane living room: 'Beside the sofa is a large *record*-player with a shiny handle on the left-hand side which I can just reach. Below are thick *wine-coloured* albums with silver rings on the back. Some of the records have flags or *pictures of a dog*, some have only gold or black printed letters. The ones with Japanese writing have green labels' (50, emphasis added). A record-player is later referred to as a 'cameraphone' (125), which is packed among more documents: 'fistfuls of crumpled newspapers' (176). Just before Naomi's family leaves Slocan, during a communion service, Stephen accidentally breaks one of his mother's records: 'He looks up at Father as he brings out Mother's "Silver Threads Among the Gold" record. One small piece is broken off like a bite off a giant cookie' (176). The connection between records and communion (e.g., the wine-coloured album and the cookie/record) and records and fabric texts is developed later in this chapter.

6 The attic is used specifically (Obasan's attic) earlier in the novel, but it also appears in the more general context of a space where the past/documents is/are recollected: 'Everything, I suppose, turns to dust eventually. A man's memories end up in some attic or in a Salvation Army bin. His name becomes a fleeting statistic and his face is lost in fading photographs, the clothing quaint, the anecdotes gone' (25).

7 A. Lynne Magnusson, in her article 'Language and Longing in Joy Kogawa's *Obasan*,' describes other aspects of this Lacanian dynamic in relation to the novel (61–2). For example, she relates it to the novel's treatment of Mr Gower's sexual abuse of the young Naomi, an important aspect of the novel I do not deal with in this discussion.

8 In 'Born Again Asian: The Making of a New Literature,' Anthony B. Chan discusses how 'Joy Kogawa and other East Asian artists peered in as both outsiders and insiders within a distinct Asian tradition in Canada' (67).

Chapter Seven

1 Marlatt's source is Leonard Roy Frank's *The History of Shock Treatment*. Frank cites Manfred J. Sakel, 'Sakel Shock Treatment,' in Arthur M. Sackler et al., eds, *The Great Physiodynamic Therapies in Psychiatry: An Historical Perspective* (New York: Hoeber-Harper 1956), 69.

2 The last three quotations are from an advertisement in *American Journal of Psychiatry* (Oct. 1954); Viscott's *The Making of a Psychiatrist* (Greenwich, Conn.: Fawcett 1972), 364; and Marilyn Rice's 'The Rice Papers,' *The Madness Network News* (April 1975), respectively.

3 Glen Lowry's recent article 'Risking Perversion & Reclaiming Our Hysterical Mother: Reading the Material Body in *Ana Historic* and *Double Standards*' uses Bakhtin's notion of the carnivalesque to posit that the texts of Lola Lemire Tostevin and Marlatt '(re)present a world view that reincorporates the Grotesque body within a dialogic relationship with the atomic individual' (85). Lowry's article also usefully incorporates elements of Allon White's 'Hysteria and the End of Carnival,' which reads Freud's studies of hysteria through Bakhtin's notion of the carnival or the Grotesque body (88–9).

4 See other references to Frankenstein or monstrosity on pages 10, 16, 46, 135, 141, and 152 and in Stan Dragland's article 'Out of the Blank: *Ana Historic*,' which deals with gothic elements in the novel.

5 See Lianne Moyes's article, 'Writing, the Uncanniest of Guests: Daphne Marlatt's *How Hug a Stone*.' Moyes argues that in *How Hug a Stone*, 'origins are marked by the difference of writing, inscribed in the order of the "always already written." The text has a stake in exploring the largely unrepresented and perhaps unrepresentable *material* contingencies of beginnings' (203). She discusses the figure(ing) of the mother in *How Hug a Stone* in a way that is also relevant to *Ana Historic*: 'the mother is not a person as such; she is a subject written, a subject writing. Double within herself, the mother is one of the ghosts of the text' (210). I am indebted to this analysis.

6 As Marlatt comments in an interview, the diary is invented (Bowering, 'On *Ana Historic*' 98).

7 In a conclusion Lola Lemire Tostevin calls 'unexpectedly conventional,' this feminine discourse is aligned with a lesbian relationship between Annie and Zoe, and in Annie's novel between Ana and Birdie, an enterprising bordello owner. Tostevin writes that, 'while the radical rewriting and rereading of dominant forms aspire to displace master narratives, whether they be historical, mythological or literary many women

may find solutions to complex social problems limited if confined to the
sexual sphere' (38). Tostevin's point is well taken, but it would be a mis-
take to underestimate the social and textual significance of Marlatt's
revision of the heterosexual romantic love plot. As George Stambolian
and Elaine Marks point out, 'homosexuality perpetually questions the
social order and is always in question itself' (26). It also becomes, in *Ana
Historic*, the site of an extended economy of erotic/textual exchange
based on difference rather than opposition and dominance: 'we give
place, giving words, giving birth, to / each other – she and me' (152).
Shirley Neuman comments, too (discussing Nicole Brossard's *L'Amer*),
that lesbianism supplements 'the reproductive sexuality of women with
the excess that is female sexual pleasure, sexual difference,' and may
conquer 'the Oedipal incest that theoretically prohibits women's entry
into language unless they are phallicized' ('Importing Difference' 399).
Marlatt ironically titles the final section of *Ana Historic* 'Not a Bad End'
(138), refusing to reinstall, by simply reversing, the conventional hetero-
sexual/homosexual good/bad binary opposition.

Works Cited

Critical Works

Adachi, Ken. *The Enemy That Never Was: A History of Japanese-Canadians*.
 Toronto: McClelland and Stewart 1976
Anthony, Geraldine. Interview with James Reaney. In *Stage Voices: Twelve
 Canadian Playwrights Talk About Their Lives and Work*, 139–64. Toronto:
 Doubleday 1978
Bakhtin, Mikhail. *The Dialogic Imagination: Four Essays*. Ed. Michael Holquist.
 Trans. Caryl Emerson and Michael Holquist. Austin: University of Texas
 Press 1981
– *Problems of Dostoevsky's Poetics*. Ed. and trans. Caryl Emerson.
 Minneapolis: University of Minnesota Press 1984
– *Rabelais and His World*. Trans. Helene Iswolsky. Bloomington: Indiana
 University Press 1985
Baltensperger, Peter. 'Places in Time: Poetry of Historical Roots.' *CVII* 7.3
 (Sept. 1983): 50–2
Bann, Stephen. 'The Truth in Mapping.' *Word & Image* 4.2 (April–June 1988):
 498–509
Banting, Pamela. 'Translation A to Z: Notes on Daphne Marlatt's *Ana
 Historic*.' In *Beyond Tish: New Writing, Interviews, Critical Essays*. Ed.
 Douglas Barbour, 123–9. Edmonton: NeWest 1991
Barber Bruce. 'Appropriation/Expropriation: Convention or Intervention.'
 Open Letter, 5th ser., nos. 5–6 (Summer–Fall 1983): 206–33
Barbour, Douglas. 'John Robert Colombo.' In *The Oxford Companion to*

Canadian Literature, ed. William Toye, 138–40. Toronto: Oxford University Press 1983

- 'Transformations of (the Language of) the Ordinary: Innovation in Recent Canadian Poetry.' *Essays on Canadian Writing* 37 (Spring 1989): 30–64

Barthes, Roland. *Camera Lucida: Reflections on Photography*. Trans. Richard Howard. New York: Hill and Wang 1981

- 'The Death of the Author.' In *Image Music Text*, 142–7. New York: Hill and Wang 1977

- 'From Work to Text.' In *Textual Strategies: Perspectives in Post-Structuralist Criticism*, ed. Josué Harari, 73–81. Ithaca: Cornell University Press 1979.

- 'Historical Discourse.' In *Structuralism: A Reader*, ed. Michael Lane, 145–55. London: Jonathan Cape 1970

- *S/Z*. Trans. Richard Miller. New York: Hill and Wang 1974

Béhar, Henri. 'Le collage ou la pagure de la modernité.' *Cahiers du 20 siècle* 5 (1975): 43–68

- 'Débris, collage et invention poétique.' *Europe* (June 1976): 102–14

Belsey, Catherine. *Critical Practice*. London and New York: Methuen 1980

Benveniste, Émile. 'The Nature of Pronouns.' In *Problems in General Linguistics*, trans. Mary Elizabeth Meek, 219–22. Coral Gables, Fla.: University of Miami Press 1971

Bessai, Diane. 'Documentary into Drama: Reaney's Donnelly Trilogy.' In *Approaches to the Work of James Reaney*, ed. Stan Dragland, 186–208. Downsview, Ont.: ECW Press 1983

Billy the Kid. Carlton Comics 1.2 (May 1969)

Blodgett, E.D. 'After Pierre Berton What? In Search of Canadian Literature.' *Essays on Canadian Writing* 30 (1984–5): 60–80

- 'The Book, Its Discourse, and the Lyric: Notes on Robert Kroetsch's *Field Notes*.' *Open Letter*, 5th ser., nos. 8–9 (Summer–Fall 1984): 195–205

Bloom, Harold. *The Anxiety of Influence: A Theory of Poetry*. New York: Oxford University Press 1973

Boelhower, William. 'Inventing America: A Model of Cartographic Semiosis.' *Word & Image* 4.2 (April–June 1988): 475–97

Bowering, George. 'Metaphysic in Time: The Poetry of Lionel Kearns.' In *The Human Element*, 2nd ser., ed. David Helwig, 113–31. Ottawa: Oberon 1981

- 'On *Ana Historic*: An Interview with Daphne Marlatt.' *Line* 13 (Spring 1989): 96–105

- 'Reaney's Region.' In *Approaches to the Work of James Reaney*, Ed. Stan Dragland, 1–14. Downsview, Ont.: ECW Press 1983

Brady, Judith. 'A Bibliography.' In *Spider Blues: Essays on Michael Ondaatje*, ed. Sam Solecki, 344–65. Montreal: Véhicule 1985.

Breunig, Le Roy C. 'Kolar/Collage.' *New York Literary Forum* 10–11 (1983): 105–19

Brooks, Peter. *Reading for the Plot: Design and Intention in Narrative.* New York: Alfred A. Knopf 1984

Brown, Russell. 'Seeds and Stones: Unhiding in Kroetsch's Poetry.' *Open Letter*, 5th ser., nos. 8–9 (Summer–Fall 1984): 154–75

Buchloh, Benjamin H.D. 'Allegorical Procedures: Appropriation and Montage in Contemporary Art.' *Open Letter*, 5th ser., nos. 5–6 (Summer–Fall 1983): 164–93

Burnham, Jack. *The Structure of Art.* New York: George Braziller 1971

Burns, Walter Noble. *The Saga of Billy the Kid.* Garden City, NY: Doubleday, Page 1926

Butt, William D. 'The Donnellys: History, Legend, Literature.' Unpublished Ph.D. thesis. London: University of Western Ontario 1977

Canada. *House of Commons Debates* 15 (1988)

Carr, Brenda. 'Daphne Marlatt's Salmon Texts ↦ Swimming / Jumping the Margins/Barriers.' Unpublished Ph.D. dissertation. London: University of Western Ontario 1989

Carrard, Philippe. 'Writing the Past: Le Roy Ladurie and the Voice of the New History.' *Studies in Twentieth Century Literature* 10.1 (Fall 1985): 9–30

Carroll, David. 'The Alterity of Discourse: Form, History, and the Question of the Political in M.M. Bakhtin.' *Diacritics* 13.2 (1983): 65–83

Caws, Mary Ann. 'Framing, Centering, and Explicating: Virginia Woolf's Collage.' *New York Literary Forum* 10–11 (1983): 57–78

Chan, Anthony B. 'Born Again Asian: The Making of a New Literature.' *Journal of Ethnic Studies* 11.4 (Winter 1984): 57–73

Cixous, Hélène. 'The Laugh of the Medusa.' In *New French Feminisms: An Anthology*, ed. Elaine Marks and Elizabeth de Courtivron, 245–64. Amherst: University of Massachusetts Press 1980

Clarke, George Elliott. 'Michael Ondaatje and the Production of Myth.' *Studies in Canadian Literature* 16.1 (1991): 1–21

Clarke, G.N.G. 'Taking Possession: The Cartouche as Cultural Text in Eighteenth-century American Maps.' *Word & Image* 4.2 (April–June 1988): 455–74

Colombo, John Robert. 'A Found Introduction.' In *The Avant-Garde Tradition in Literature*, ed. Richard Kostelanetz, 304–9. Buffalo: Prometheus Books 1982. Rpt. from *Open Poetry: Four Anthologies of Expanded Poems*. New York: Simon and Shuster 1973

– 'A Note on the Composition of Some of These Poems.' In *ABRACA-DABRA*. Toronto: McClelland and Stewart 1967

Compagnon, Antoine. *La Seconde Main, ou le travail de la citation*. Paris:
Éditions du Seuil 1979

Cooley, Dennis. '"I am here on the edge": Modern Hero / Postmodern
Poetics in *The Collected Works of Billy the Kid*.' In *Spider Blues: Essays on
Michael Ondaatje*, 211–39. ed. Sam Solecki, Montreal: Véhicule 1985

– 'Recursions Excursions and Incursions: Daphne Marlatt Wrestles with the
Angel Language.' *Line* 13 (Spring 1989): 66–79

Culler, Jonathan. *Structuralist Poetics: Structuralism, Linguistics and the Study
of Literature*. London: Routledge and Kegan Paul 1975

Davey, Frank. 'The Explorer in Western Canadian Literature.' In *Surviving
the Paraphrase: Eleven Essays on Canadian Literature*, 137–49. Winnipeg:
Turnstone 1983

– Introduction. *The Writing Life: Historical and Critical Views of the Tish
Movement*, ed. C.H. Gervais, 15–24. Coatsworth, Ont.: Black Moss 1976

– 'Lionel Kearns.' In *From There to Here: A Guide to English-Canadian
Literature since 1960*, 148–50. Victoria: Press Porcépic 1974

– 'Recontextualization in the Long Poem.' In *Reading Canadian Reading*,
123–36. Winnipeg: Turnstone 1988

de Beauvoir, Simone. *The Second Sex*. Trans. H.M. Parshley. New York:
Alfred A. Knopf 1978

Derrida, Jacques. 'The Law of Genre.' Trans. Avital Ronnell. In *On
Narrative*, ed. W.J.T. Mitchell. Chicago and London: University of Chicago
Press 1981

– 'Racism's Last Word.' Trans. Peggy Kamuf. *Critical Inquiry* 12.1 (Autumn
1985): 290–9

– 'Signature Event Context.' Trans. Samuel Weber and Jeffrey Mehlman. In
Glyph I, 172–97. Baltimore: Johns Hopkins University Press 1977

Dickie, George. *Art and the Aesthetic: An Institutional Analysis*. Ithaca and
London: Cornell University Press 1974

Doctorow, E.L. 'False Documents.' *American Review* 26 (Nov. 1977): 215–32

Dorscht, Susan Rudy. 'The Concept of Agency in Eli Mandel's "The Long
Poem: Journal and Origin."' *Canadian Literature* 131 (Winter 1991): 251–7

Dragland, Stan. 'James Reaney's "Pulsating Dance In and Out of Forms."'
In *The Bees of the Invisible: Essays in Contemporary English Canadian Writing*,
29–46. Toronto: Coach House 1991

– 'Out of the Blank: *Ana Historic*.' In *The Bees of the Invisible*, 172–90

Duchamp, Marcel. 'The Great Trouble with Art in This Century.' In *The
Essential Writings of Marcel Duchamp, Salt Seller*, ed. Michel Sanouillet and
Elmer Peters, 123–6. London: Thames and Hudson 1975. Rpt. from
Bulletin of the Museum of Modern Art 13.4 (1946): 19–21

Dudek, Louis. Introduction to F.R. Scott, *Trouvailles: Poems from Prose*, 1–3.
Montreal: Delta, 1967

Dykes, J.C. *Billy the Kid: The Bibliography of a Legend*. Albuquerque: University of New Mexico Press 1951

Eagleton, Terry. *Literary Theory: An Introduction*. Minneapolis: University of Minnesota Press 1983

Ehrmann, Jacques. 'The Death of Literature.' Trans. A. James Arnold. In *Surfiction: Fiction Now and Tomorrow*, ed. Raymond Federman, 229–53. Athens: Ohio University Press 1975

Ernst, Max. *Ecritures avec cent vingt illustrations extraites de l'oeuvre de l'auteur*. Paris: le point du jour 1970

Filewod, Alan. *Collective Encounters: Documentary Theatre in English Canada*. Toronto: University of Toronto Press 1987

Fish, Stanley. 'How Ordinary Is Ordinary Language?' In *Is There a Text in This Class? The Authority of Interpretive Communities*, 97–111. Cambridge, Mass.: Harvard University Press 1980

– 'How to Recognize a Poem When You See One.' In *Is There a Text in This Class? The Authority of Interpretive Communities*, 322–37. Cambridge, Mass.: Harvard University Press 1980

Foster, Stephen C. 'Dada Criticism, Anti-Criticism and A-Criticism.' In *Dada Spectrum: The Dialectics of Revolt*, ed. Stephen C. Foster and Rudolf E. Kuenzli, 29–49. Madison, Wis.: Coda Press 1979

Foucault, Michel. 'Nietzsche, Genealogy, History.' *The Foucault Reader*, ed. Paul Rabinow, 76–100. New York: Pantheon, 1984

– 'What Is an Author?' *Textual Strategies: Perspectives in Post-Structuralist Criticism*, ed. Josué V. Harari, 141–60. Ithaca: Cornell University Press, 1979

Fowkes, William. 'A Hegelian Critique of Found Art and Conceptual Art.' *Journal of Aesthetics and Art Criticism* 37.2 (Winter 1978): 157–68.

Frank, Leonard Roy, ed. *The History of Shock Treatment*. San Francisco: L.R. Frank, 1978.

Freud, Sigmund. *Beyond the Pleasure Principle*. Trans. James Strachey. New York: Liveright, 1950.

Frye, Northrop. 'Conclusion to a *Literary History of Canada*.' In *The Bush Garden: Essays on the Canadian Imagination*, 213–51. Toronto: Anansi, 1971

– 'The Narrative Tradition in English Canadian Poetry.' In *The Bush Garden*, 145–55

– 'Preface to an Uncollected Anthology.' In *The Bush Garden*, 163–79

Gaillard, Françoise. 'An Unspeakable (hi)story.' *Yale French Studies* 59 (1980): 137–54

Gallop, Jane. *Reading Lacan*. Ithaca and London: Cornell University Press 1985

Gates, Henry Louis, Jr. 'Writing "Race" and the Difference It Makes.'

Critical Inquiry 12.1 (Autumn 1985): 1–20

Genette, Gérard. *Narrative Discourse: An Essay in Method*. Trans. Jane E.
   Lewin. Ithaca: Cornell University Press 1980

Gervais, C.H. 'Tish: A Movement.' In *The Writing Life: Historical and Critical
   Views of the Tish Movement*, ed. C.H. Gervais, 193–207. Coatsworth, Ont.:
   Black Moss 1976

Glazener, Nancy. 'Dialogic Subversion: Bakhtin, the Novel and Gertrude
   Stein.' In *Bakhtin and Cultural Theory*, ed. Ken Hirschkop and David
   Shepherd, 109–29. Manchester and New York: Manchester University
   Press 1989

Godard, Barbara. 'Becoming My Hero, Becoming Myself: Notes Towards a
   Feminist Theory of Reading.' *tessera III/Canadian Fiction Magazine* 57
   (1986): 142–8

– '"Body I": Daphne Marlatt's Feminist Poetics.' *American Review of
   Canadian Studies* 15.4 (1985): 481–96

– '*The Diviners* as Supplement: (M)othering the Text.' *Open Letter*, 7th ser.,
   no. 7 (Spring 1990): 26–73

– 'Epi(pro)logue: In Pursuit of the Long Poem.' *Open Letter*, 6th ser., nos.
   2–3 (Summer–Fall 1985): 301–35

– 'Other Fictions: Robert Kroetsch's Criticism.' *Open Letter*, 5th ser., nos. 8–9
   (Summer–Fall 1984): 5–21

– 'Stretching the Story: The Canadian Story Cycle.' *Open Letter*, 7th ser., no.
   6 (Fall 1989): 27–71

Godeau, Abigail Solomon. 'Winning the Game When the Rules Have Been
   Changed: Art Photography and Postmodernism.' *Screen* 25.6 (1984):
   88–102

Gottlieb, Erika. 'The Riddle of Concentric Worlds in *Obasan*.' *Canadian
   Literature* 109 (Summer 1986): 34–53

Grainger, M. Allerdale. *Woodsmen of the West*. London: Edward Arnold
   1908

Grierson, John. 'The Course of Realism.' In *Grierson on Documentary*, 132–44.
   London: Collins 1946

– 'First Principles of Documentary.' In *Grierson on Documentary*, 84–9

– 'Flaherty's Poetic *Moana*.' In *The Documentary Tradition: From Nanook to
   Woodstock*, ed. Lewis Jacobs. New York: Hopkinson and Blake 1971. Rpt.
   of review in *New York Sun*, 8 February 1926

Hamer, Mary. 'Putting Ireland on the Map.' *Textual Practice* (June 1989):
   184–201

Hansen, Tom. 'Letting Language Do: Some Speculations on Finding Found
   Poems.' *College English* 42 (1979): 271–82

Hillman, James. *The Myth of Analysis: Three Essays in Archetypal Psychology*.
   Evanston: Northwestern University Press 1972

Hofmann, Werner. 'Marcel Duchamp and Emblematic Realism.' In *Marcel Duchamp in Perspective*, ed. J. Mashek, 53–66. Englewood Cliffs, NJ: Prentice Hall 1975

Humble, P.N. 'Duchamp's Readymades: Art and Anti-Art.' *British Journal of Aesthetics* 22.1 (Winter 1982): 52–64

Hutcheon, Linda. *A Poetics of Postmodernism: History, Theory, Fiction*. New York and London: Routledge 1988

– 'The Politics of Representation in Canadian Art and Literature.' Robarts Centre Working Papers. North York, Ont.: York University 1988

– 'The Postmodern Challenge to Boundaries.' In *The Canadian Postmodern: A Study of Contemporary English–Canadian Fiction*, 78–106. Toronto: Oxford University Press 1988

– 'telling accounts: Daphne Marlatt's *Ana Historic: A Novel*.' *Brick* 34 (Fall 1988): 17–19

Illustrated Atlas of the County of Bruce, containing authentic maps of the townships. Toronto: H. Belden 1880. Offset ed., Port Elgin 1970

Irigaray, Luce. 'The Power of Discourse and the Subordination of the Feminine: Interview.' In *This Sex Which Is Not One*, trans. Catherine Porter, 68–85. Ithaca: Cornell University Press 1985

Issacharoff, Michael. *Discourse as Performance*. Stanford: Stanford University Press 1989

Jameson, Frederic. 'Cognitive Mapping.' In *Marxism and the Interpretation of Culture*, 347–57. Urbana and Chicago: University of Illinois Press 1988

Jenny, Laurent. 'The Strategy of Form.' *French Literary Theory Today: A Reader*, ed. Tzvetan Todorov, trans. R. Carter, 34–63. Cambridge: Cambridge University Press 1982

Johnson, Barbara. 'Thresholds of Difference: Structures of Address in Zora Neale Hurston.' *Critical Inquiry* 12.1 (Autumn 1985): 278–89

Kamboureli, Smaro. *On the Edge of Genre: The Contemporary Canadian Long Poem*. Toronto: University of Toronto Press 1991

Kelley, Thomas P. *The Black Donnellys*. Winnipeg: Harlequin 1954

Kitagawa, Muriel. *This Is My Own: Letters to Wes and Other Writings on Japanese Canadians 1941–1948*. Ed. Roy Miki. Vancouver: Talonbooks 1985

Knowles, Dorothy. 'The "Document-Play": Vilar, Kipphardt, Weiss.' *Modern Languages* 52.1 (March 1971): 79–85

Kristeva, Julia. 'The Bounded Text.' In *Desire in Language: A Semiotic Approach to Literature and Art*, ed. Leon S. Roudiez; trans. Thomas Gora, Alice Jardine, and Leon S. Roudiez, 36–63. New York: Columbia University Press 1980

– *Revolution in Poetic Language*. New York: Columbia University Press 1984

- 'Word, Dialogue, and Novel.' In *Desire in Language: A Semiotic Approach to Literature and Art*, 64–91. New York: Columbia University Press 1980
Kroetsch, Robert. 'Beyond Nationalism: A Prologue.' *Open Letter*, 5th ser., no. 4 (Spring 1983): 83–9
- 'The Exploding Porcupine: Violence of Form in English–Canadian Fiction.' *Open Letter*, 5th ser., no. 4 (1983): 57–64
- 'For Play and Entrance: The Contemporary Canadian Long Poem.' *Open Letter*, 5th ser., no. 4 (Spring 1983): 91–110
- 'On Being an Alberta Writer.' *Open Letter*, 5th ser., no. 4 (Spring 1983): 69–80
- Statement by the Poet. In *The Long Poem Anthology*, ed. Michael Ondaatje, 311–12. Toronto: Coach House 1979
Kronigsberg, Ira. *The Complete Film Dictionary*. New York and Scarborough, Ont.: New American Library 1987
Lacan, Jacques. 'The Seminar on "The Purloined Letter."' Trans. Jeffrey Mehlman. *Yale French Studies* 48 (1972): 38–72
La Capra, Dominick. *History & Criticism*. Ithaca and London: Cornell University Press 1985
- *Rethinking Intellectual History: Texts, Contexts, Language*. Ithaca and London: Cornell University Press 1983
Lecker, Robert. *Robert Kroetsch*. Boston: Twayne 1986
Leefmans, Bert M.-P. '*Das Undbild*: A Metaphysics of Collage.' *New York Literary Forum* 10–11 (1983): 183–227
Li, Victor. 'The Rhetoric of Presence: Reading Pound's *Cantos* I to III.' *English Studies in Canada* 14.3 (September 1988): 296–309
Livesay, Dorothy. 'The Canadian Documentary: An Overview.' *Open Letter*, 6th ser., nos. 2–3 (Summer–Fall 1985): 127–30
- 'The Documentary Poem: A Canadian Genre.' In *Contexts of Canadian Criticism*, ed. Eli Mandel, 267–81. Chicago and London: University of Chicago Press 1971
Lowry, Glen. 'Risking Perversion & Reclaiming Our Hysterical Mother: Reading the Material Body in *Ana Historic* and *Double Standards*.' *West Coast Line* 5 (25/2) (Fall 1991): 83–96
Ludwick, Patricia. 'One Actor's Journey with James Reaney.' In *Approaches to the Work of James Reaney*, ed. Stan Dragland, 131–7. Downsview, Ont.: ECW Press 1983
MacFarlane, Susan. 'Picking up the Pieces: *Coming Through Slaughter* as Paragram.' *Open Letter*, 7th ser., no. 6 (Fall 1989): 72–83
McKay, Don. 'At Work and Play in *The Ledger*.' *Open Letter*, 5th ser., nos. 8–9 (Summer–Fall 1984): 146–53
McKay, Jean. 'Interview with Keith Turnbull.' In *Approaches to the Work of*

James Reaney, ed. Stan Dragland, 138–50. Downsview, Ont.: ECW Press 1983

MacLulich, T.D. 'Ondaatje's Mechanical Boy: Portrait of the Artist as Photographer.' *Mosaic* 14.2 (1981): 107–19

Magnusson, A. Lynne. 'Language and Longing in Joy Kogawa's *Obasan*.' *Canadian Literature* 116 (Spring 1988): 58–66

Mallinson, Jean. 'John Robert Colombo: Documentary Poet as Visionary.' *Essays on Canadian Writing* 5 (1975): 67–71

Mandel, Eli. 'The Function of Criticism at the Present Time: The Silent-Speaking Words.' In *Criticism: The Silent-Speaking Words*. Toronto: CBC Publications 1966

– 'Imagining Natives: White Perspectives on Native Peoples.' In *The Native in Literature: Canadian and Comparative Perspectives*, ed. Thomas King, Cheryl Calver, and Helen Hoy, 34–49. Oakville, Ont.: ECW Press 1987

– 'Strange Loops.' In *The Family Romance*, 11–27. Winnipeg: Turnstone 1986

Marlatt, Daphne. 'musing with mothertongue.' In *in the feminine: women and words/les femmes et les mots*, ed. Ann Dybikowski et al., 171–4. Edmonton: Longspoon 1985

Marlatt, Daphne, Barbara Godard, Kathy Mezei, and Gail Scott. 'Theorizing Fiction Theory.' *tessera III/Canadian Fiction Magazine* 57 (1986): 6–12

Mason, Gregory. 'Documentary Drama from the Revue to the Tribunal.' *Modern Drama* 20.3 (Sept. 1977): 263–77

Merivale, P. 'Framed Voices: The Polyphonic Elegies of Hébert and Kogawa.' *Canadian Literature* 116 (Spring 1988): 68–82

Meyer, Herman. *The Poetics of Quotation in the European Novel*. Trans. Theodore and Yetta Ziolowski. Princeton: Princeton University Press 1968

Miller, Nancy K. 'D'une solitude à l'autre: Vers un intertexte féminin.' *French Review* 54.6 (1981): 797–803

Monkman, Leslie. 'Visions and Revisions: Contemporary Writers and Exploration Accounts of Indigenous Peoples.' In *The Native in Literature: Canadian and Comparative Perspectives*, ed. Thomas King, Cheryl Calver, and Helen Hoy, 80–98. Oakville, Ont.: ECW Press 1987

Morawski, Stefan. 'The Basic Functions of Quotation.' In *Sign. Language. Culture*, ed. A.J. Griemas et al., 690–705. The Hague: Mouton 1970

Morley, Alan. *Vancouver: From Milltown to Metropolis*. Vancouver: Mitchell Press 1961

Moyes, Lianne. 'Dialogizing the Monologue of History and Lyric: Lionel Kearns' *Convergences*.' *Open Letter*, 7th ser., no. 5 (Summer 1989): 15–27

– 'Writing, the Uncanniest of Guests: Daphne Marlatt's *How Hug a Stone*.' In *Beyond Tish: New Writing, Interviews, Critical Essays*, ed. Douglas Barbour, 203–21. Edmonton: NeWest Press 1991

Muecke, D.C. *Irony and the Ironic*. London and New York: Methuen 1970

Mukherjee, Arun. 'Ironies of Colour in the Great White North: The Discursive Strategies of Some Hyphenated Canadians.' In *Double Talking: Essays on Verbal and Visual Ironies in Canadian Contemporary Art and Literature*, ed. Linda Hutcheon, 158–71. Toronto: ECW Press 1991

Mulvey, Laura. 'Visual Pleasure and Narrative Cinema.' *Screen* 16.3 (Autumn 1975): 6–18

Nesselroth, Peter. 'Lautréamont's Plagiarisms; or, the Poeticization of Prose Texts.' In *Pretext/Text/Context: Essays on Nineteenth-Century French Literature*, ed. Robert L. Mitchell, 186–95. Columbus: Ohio State University Press 1980

– 'Literary Identity and Contextual Difference.' In *Identity of the Literary Text*, ed. Mario J. Valdés and Owen Miller, 41–53. Toronto: University of Toronto Press 1985

Neuman, Shirley. 'Allow self, portraying self: Autobiography in *Field Notes*.' *Line* 1.2 (Fall 1983): 104–21

– 'Importing Difference.' In *A Mazing Space: Writing Canadian Women Writing*, ed. Shirley Neuman and Smaro Kamboureli, 392–405. Edmonton: Longspoon/NeWest 1986

Neuman, Shirley, and Robert Wilson. *Labyrinths of Voice: Conversations with Robert Kroetsch*. Edmonton: NeWest Press 1982

Nodleman, Perry M. 'The Collected Photographs of Billy the Kid.' *Canadian Literature* 87 (Winter 1980): 68–79

Noonan, James. Foreword to *The Donnellys: Sticks and Stones, The St. Nicholas Hotel, Handcuffs, a Trilogy by James Reaney*, 1–8. Victoria: Press Porcépic 1983

Olson, Charles. 'Introduction to Robert Creeley.' In *Human Universe and Other Essays*, ed. Donald Allen, 127–8. New York: Grove 1967

– 'Projective Verse.' In *Human Universe and Other Essays*, 51–61

– *Proprioception*. San Francisco: Four Seasons Foundation 1965

Ondaatje, Michael. 'What Is in the Pot.' Introduction to *The Long Poem Anthology*, ed. Michael Ondaatje, 11–18. Toronto: Coach House 1979

Owens, Judith. '"I Send You a Picture": Ondaatje's Portrait of Billy the Kid.' *Studies in Canadian Literature* 8.1 (1983): 117–39

Paget, Derek. *True Stories? Documentary Drama on Radio, Screen and Stage*. Manchester and New York: Manchester University Press 1990

Parker, Gerald D. '"History, Story and Story-style": James Reaney's The Donnellys.' *Canadian Drama* 4 (Fall 1978): 150–9

– '"The key word ... is 'listen'": James Reaney's "sonic environment."' *Mosaic* 14.4 (Fall 1981): 1–14

– 'Melodrama and Tragedy in James Reaney's Donnelly Trilogy.' In

Approaches to the Work of James Reaney, ed. Stan Dragland, 165–85. Downsview, Ont.: ECW Press 1983

Pearson, Alan. Review of John Robert Colombo, *ABRACADABRA*. *Canadian Forum* 47 (March 1967): 283–4

Pechey, Graham. 'On the Borders of Bakhtin: Dialogization, Decolonization.' *Oxford Literary Review* 9.1–2 (1987): 59–84

Pignatari, Décio. 'Montage, Collage, Bricolage or: Mixture Is the Spirit.' *Dispositio* 6.17–18 (Summer–Fall 1981): 41–4

Potter, Robin. 'Moral – In Whose Sense? Joy Kogawa's *Obasan* and Julia Kristeva's *Powers of Horror.' Studies in Canadian Literature* 15.1 (1990): 117–39

Rabinowitz, Peter J. '"What's Hecuba to Us?" The Audience's Experience of Literary Borrowing.' In *The Reader in the Text: Essays on Audience and Interpretation*, ed. Susan R. Suleiman and Inge Crosman, 241–63. Princeton: Princeton University Press 1980

Reaney, James. 'An ABC to Ontario Literature and Culture.' *Black Moss*, ser. 2, no. 3 (Spring 1977): 2–6

– Foreword to *The Donnelly Tragedy 1880–1980*, 2. London, Ont.: Phelps Publishing 1980

– *14 Barrels from Sea to Sea*. Erin, Ontario: Press Porcépic, 1977

– Introduction to *Names and Nicknames*, 5–6. Vancouver: Talonbooks 1978

– 'A Letter from James Reaney: Hallowe'en.' *Black Moss*, ser. 2, no. 1 (Spring 1976): 2–10

– 'Myths in Some Nineteenth–Century Ontario Newspapers.' In *Aspects of Nineteenth-Century Ontario*, ed. F.H. Armstrong et al., 253–66. Toronto: University of Toronto Press 1974

– 'Ten Years at Play.' In *Dramatists in Canada: Selected Essays*, ed. William New, 70–8. Vancouver: University of British Columbia 1972

– '"Your plays are like movies – cinemascope ones."' *Canadian Drama* 5 (Spring 1979): 32–40

Reaney, James Stewart. *James Reaney*. Agincourt, Ont.: Gage 1977

Redekop, Magdalene. 'Authority and the Margins of Escape in *Brébeuf and His Brethren.' Open Letter*, 6th ser., nos. 2–3 (Summer–Fall 1985): 45–60

Riddel, Joseph. 'Decentering the Image: The "Project" of "American" Poetics?' In *Textual Strategies: Perspectives in Post–Structuralist Criticism*, ed. Josué V. Harari, 322–58. Ithaca: Cornell University Press 1979

Rimmon-Kenan, Schlomith. *Narrative Fiction: Contemporary Poetics*. London and New York: Methuen 1983

Robin, Régine. 'Toward Fiction as Oblique Discourse.' Trans. Ramie-Rose Logan. *Yale French Studies* 59 (1980): 230–42

Rose, Marilyn Russell. 'Politics into Art: Joy Kogawa's *Obasan* and the
Rhetoric of Fiction.' *Mosaic* 21.2–3 (Spring 1988): 215–26

Rosler, Martha. 'in, around, and afterthoughts (on documentary photography).' In *Martha Rosler, 3 works,* 59–86. Halifax: Press of the Nova Scotia
School of Art and Design 1981

Ross, A.M. 'The Romance of Vancouver's Schools.' In *Schools of Old
Vancouver,* ed. James M. Sandison, 11–25. Vancouver: Vancouver
Historical Society 1971

Russo, Mary. 'Female Grotesques: Carnival and Theory.' In *Feminist
Studies/Critical Studies,* ed. Theresa de Lauretis, 213–29. Bloomington:
Indiana University Press 1986

St Andrews, B.A. 'Reclaiming a Canadian Heritage: Kogawa's *Obasan.'*
International Fiction Review 13.1 (Winter 1986): 29–31

Scholes, Robert. 'Language, Narrative, and Anti-Narrative.' In *On Narrative,*
ed. W.J.T. Mitchell, 200–8. Chicago and London: University of Chicago
Press 1981

Schwartz, Arturo. 'Contributions to a Poetic of the Readymade.' Trans. John
A. Stevens. In *Marcel Duchamp: Ready-mades, etc. (1918–1964),* 13–41. Paris:
le Terrain Vague 1964

Scobie, Stephen. 'Amelia, or: Who Do You Think Yor Are? Documentary
and Identity in Canadian Literature.' *Canadian Literature* 100 (Spring 1984):
264–85

– *Signature Event Cantext: Essays by Stephen Scobie.* Edmonton: NeWest Press
1989

– 'Two Authors in Search of a Character: bp Nichol and Michael Ondaatje.'
In *Spider Blues: Essays on Michael Ondaatje,* ed. Sam Solecki, 185–210.
Montreal: Véhicule 1985

Sekula, Allan. 'Dismantling Modernism, Reinventing Documentary (Notes
on the Politics of Representation).' In *Photography Against the Grain: Essays
and Photoworks 1973–1983,* 53–75. Halifax: Press of the Nova Scotia
College of Art and Design 1984

Smith, Barbara Herrnstein. *On the Margins of Discourse: The Relation of
Literature to Language.* Chicago and London: University of Chicago Press
1978

Smith, Duncan. 'Prose and Found Poetry and Anti-Modernist Aesthetics: A
Modernist Response to Capitalist and Socialistic Aesthetic Neutralization.'
Minnesota Review 15 (1980): 98–111

Solecki, Sam. 'An Interview with Michael Ondaatje (1975).' In *Spider Blues:
Essays on Michael Ondaatje,* ed. Sam Solecki, 13–27. Montreal: Véhicule
1985

Sontag, Susan. 'Happenings: An Art of Radical Juxtaposition.' In *Against
Interpretation and Other Essays,* 265–76. New York: Dell 1969

Stambolian, George, and Elaine Marks. Introduction to *Homosexualities and French Literature: Cultural Contexts/Critical Texts*, ed. George Stambolian and Elaine Marks. Ithaca and London: Cornell University Press 1979

Stanzel, Franz. 'Texts Recycled: "Found" Poems Found in Canada.' In *Gaining Ground: European Critics on Canadian Literature*, ed. Robert Kroetsch and Reingard M. Nischik, 91–106. Edmonton: NeWest Press 1985

Steele, Lise. Photographs of 1975 *Donnelleys* tour. In *Black Moss*, ser. 2, no. 1 (Spring 1976): 10–28

Stingle, Richard. 'The Donnellys: Ritual Victims.' *Alphabet* 6 (June 1963): 11–26

Tallman, Warren. 'Wonder Merchants: Modernist Poetry in Vancouver During the 1960s.' In *The Writing Life: Historical and Critical Views of the Tish Movement*, ed. C.H. Gervais, 27–69. Coatsworth, Ont.: Black Moss 1976

Tatum, Stephen. *Inventing Billy the Kid: Visions of the Outlaw in America, 1881–1981*. Albuquerque: University of New Mexico Press 1982

Thomas, Jean-Jacques. 'Collage/Space/Montage.' *New York Literary Forum* 10–11 (1983): 79–102

Tostevin, Lola Lemire. 'Daphne Marlatt: Writing in the Space That Is Her Mother's Face.' *Line* 13 (Spring 1989): 32–9

Tyler, Parker. 'Documentary Technique in Film Fiction.' In *The Documentary Tradition: From Nanook to Woodstock*, ed. Lewis Jacobs, 251–66. New York: Hopkinson and Blake 1974

Voldeng, Evelyn. 'L'intertextualité dans les écrits féminins d'inspiration féministe.' *Voix et Images* 7 (1982): 523–30

Voloshinov, V.N. *Marxism and the Philosophy of Language*. Trans. Ladislav Matejka and I.R. Titunik. New York and London: Seminar Press 1973

Waring, Wendy. '"Mother(s) of Confusion": End Bracket.' In *Double Talking: Essays on Verbal and Visual Ironies in Canadian Contemporary Art and Literature*, ed. Linda Hutcheon, 145–57. Toronto: ECW Press 1991

Weisgerber, Jean. 'The Use of Quotations in Recent Literature.' *Comparative Literature* 22 (1970): 36–45

White, Hayden. 'The Historical Text as Literary Artifact.' In *The Writing of History: Literary Form and Historical Understanding*, ed. Robert H. Canary and Henry Kozicki, 41–62. Madison: University of Wisconsin Press 1978

Whiteside, Anna. 'The Double Bind: Self-Referring Poetry.' In *On Referring in Literature*, ed. Anna Whiteside and Michael Issacharoff, 14–32. Bloomington and Indianapolis: Indiana University Press 1987

Williamson, Janice. 'Citing Resistance: Vision, Space, Authority and Transgression in Canadian Women's Poetry'. Unpublished Ph.D.

dissertation. Downsview, Ont.: York University 1987

Willis, Gary. 'Speaking the Silence: Joy Kogawa's *Obasan.' Studies in Canadian Literature* 12.2 (1987): 239–49

Wills, Clair. 'Upsetting the Public: Carnival, Hysteria and Women's Texts.' In *Bakhtin and Cultural Theory*, ed. Ken Hirschkop and David Shepherd, 130–51. Manchester and New York: Manchester University Press 1989

Wood, Susan. 'Reinventing the Word: Kroetsch's Poetry.' *Canadian Literature* 77 (Summer 1978): 28–39

Wordsworth, William. *Prose Works*. Ed. W.J.B. Owen and Jane Worthington Smyser. Oxford: Oxford University Press 1974

York, Lorraine M. '"Making and Destroying": The Photographic Image in Michael Ondaatje's Works.' In *'The Other Side of Dailiness': Photography in the Works of Alice Munro, Timothy Findley, Michael Ondaatje, and Margaret Laurence*, 93–120. Downsview, Ont.: ECW Press 1988

Zilliacus, Clas. 'Documentary Drama: Form and Content.' *Comparative Drama* 6 (1972): 223–53

Poetry and Fiction

Bowering, George. *George, Vancouver*. Toronto: Weed Flower Press 1970

Colombo, John Robert. *ABRACADABRA*. Toronto: McClelland and Stewart 1967

– *John Toronto: New Poems by Dr. Strachan Found by John Robert Colombo*. Ottawa: Oberon 1969

– *Leonardo's Lists*. Toronto: Weed Flower Press 1972

– *The Mackenzie Poems*. Toronto: Swan 1966

– *The Sad Truths*. Toronto: Peter Martin 1974

– *Translations from the English: Found Poems*. Toronto: Peter Martin 1974

– *Variable Cloudiness: New Poems by John Robert Colombo*. Toronto: Hounslow 1977

Davey, Frank. *The Clallam*. Vancouver: Talonbooks 1973

Eliot, T.S. 'The Wasteland.' In *Collected Poems: 1909–1962*. London: Faber 1963

Ferns, John. *Henry Hudson, or Discovery*. Windsor: Sesame 1975

Gutteridge, Don. *The Quest for North: Coppermine*. Ottawa: Oberon 1973

– *Riel: A Poem for Voices*. Fredericton: Fiddlehead 1968

– *A True History of Lambton County*. Ottawa: Oberon 1977

Kearns, Lionel. *Convergences*. Toronto: Coach House 1984

Keeshig-Tobias, Lenore. '(a found poem).' In *A Gathering of Spirit: Writing and Art by North American Indian Women*, ed. Beth Brant, 123–4. Toronto: Women's Press 1988

Kogawa, Joy, *Obasan*. Markham, Ont.: Penguin 1983

Kroetsch, Robert. *The Ledger*. London, Ont.: Applegarth Follies 1975;
  Coldstream, Ont.: Brick/Nairn 1979
– *Seed Catalogue*. Winnipeg: Turnstone 1977
McKay, Don. *LePendu*. Ilderton, Ont.: Nairn Coldstream 1978
Mandel, Eli. *Crusoe: Poems Selected and New*. Toronto: Anansi 1973
– *Out of Place*. Erin, Ont.: Press Porcépic 1977
Marlatt, Daphne. *Ana Historic: a novel*. Toronto: Coach House 1988
– *How Hug a Stone*. Winnipeg: Turnstone 1983
– *Steveston*. Vancouver: Talonbooks 1974
Morrissey, Kim. *Batoche*. Regina, Sask.: Coteau Books 1989
Morton, Colin. *The Merzbook: Kurt Schwitters Poems*. Kingston, Ont.: Quarry
  1987
Ondaatje, Michael. *The Collected Works of Billy the Kid: Left-handed Poems*.
  Toronto: Anansi 1970
– *Coming Through Slaughter*. Toronto: Anansi 1976
– *Running in the Family*. Toronto: McClelland and Stewart 1982
Reaney, James. *The Donnellys: Sticks and Stones, The St. Nicholas Hotel,
  Handcuffs, a Trilogy by James Reaney*. Victoria: Press Porcépic 1983
St Maur, Gerald. *Odyssey Northwest: A Trilogy of Poems on the Northwest
  Passage*. Edmonton: Boreal Institute for Northern Studies, Occasional
  Publication no. 18 1983
Saskatchewan. Department of Culture and Youth. *Towards a New Past
  Vol. II: Found Poems of the Métis People*. 1975
Scott, F.R. *Trouvailles: Poems from Prose*. Montreal: Vendôme 1967
Smith, Marion. *Koo-Koo-Sint: David Thompson in Western Canada*. Red Deer,
  Alta.: Red Deer College Press 1976
Sproxton, Birk. *Headframe:* Winnipeg: Turnstone 1985
Tzara, Tristan. *Seven Dadaist Manifestos and Lampisteries*. Trans. Barbara
  Wright. London: John Calder 1977
Whyte, Jon. *Homage, Henry Kelsey*. Winnipeg: Turnstone 1981
Wiebe, Rudy. *The Temptations of Big Bear*. Toronto: McClelland and Stewart
  1973
– 'Where Is the Voice Coming From?' In *Personal Fictions*, ed. Michael
  Ondaatje, 73–81. Toronto: Oxford University Press 1977
Yeats, William Butler, ed. *The Oxford Book of Modern Verse: 1892–1935*.
  Oxford: Clarendon 1936

Index

ABRACADABRA. See Colombo

Adachi, Ken, 127, 130

American Federal Theatre Project, 87

Ana Historic. See Marlatt

Anthony, Geraldine, 103

appropriation: aesthetic, 26; allegory of textual, 60; and authorship, 25, 26, 29, 30, 31, 36, 38, 40, 57, 110, 158; and collage, 52; and definition of 'documentary,' 13; of fairy tales, 169 n.7; and found poetry, 25, 29; of language of authority, 48, 49, 149; from the lexis, 42; of 'non-literary' materials, 7, 29, 75, 110, 148, 158; and subversive reading strategies, 29, 75, 108, 141, 148, 156, 158, 159, 160. *See also* citation

archaeology, 9, 10, 53, 56, 57–8. *See* Foucault

audience: as consumers, 101; distanced from narrative, 87; of Hallowe'en, 17; and literary borrowing, 164 n.6; as participants in production of meaning, 17, 31, 82, 86, 87, 89–90, 92, 96, 101–3, 162, 166 n.3, 167 n.4; responsibility of, 90. *See* reader

authority: and authorship, 33, 69, 75, 91, 142; disruption of, in documentary-collage, 15, 16, 18, 19, 36, 37, 45, 47, 115, 116, 118, 133, 134, 140, 141, 147; documents as, 12, 16, 101, 109, 111, 122, 146; of history, 7, 8, 19, 107, 116, 118, 122, 132, 134, 138, 140, 151, 154; institutional, 16, 47, 48, 75, 77, 115, 116, 118, 144, 145; and reader, 77; and voice, 8, 69, 77, 155, 162

authorship, 11, 15, 29, 30, 33, 36, 38

Bakhtin, Mikhail: on ambivalence in language, 61–2; on carnival, 16, 56, 70, 83, 145, 168 n.8, 171 n.3; on dialogism in language, 16; and folk culture, 17; on the grotesque, 83, 171; on heteroglossia, 14; on